state of world population 2005

**The Promise of Equality**

Gender Equity, Reproductive Health and the Millennium Development Goals

Copyright © UNFPA 2005

United Nations Population Fund
Thoraya Ahmed Obaid, Executive Director

# Contents

## Chapters

**1 Overview** ............ 1

**2 Strategic Investments: The Equality Dividend** ............ 9
  A Poverty of Opportunity and Choices ............ 9
  Critical Investments, Large Payoffs
  *(Education, Reproductive Health, Economic Rights)* ............ 10
  Reconciling Productive and Reproductive Roles ............ 15
  Accountability for Gender Justice ............ 17

**3 The Promise of Human Rights** ............ 21
  Human Rights and Poverty Reduction ............ 22
  The Human Rights of Girls and Women ............ 22
  Human Rights: Essentials for the MDGs ............ 24
  Reproductive Rights in Practice ............ 25
  Rights, Gender and Culture: Seeking Convergence ............ 27
  Support for Disenfranchised Groups ............ 28

**4 Reproductive Health: A Measure of Equity** ............ 33
  Maternal Death and Disability ............ 34
  The Feminization of HIV/AIDS ............ 37
  Reaping the Rewards of Family Planning ............ 41

**5 The Unmapped Journey: Adolescents, Poverty and Gender** ............ 45
  Adolescence: Opportunities and Risks ............ 45
  Reproductive Health in the Lives of Adolescents and Youth ............ 48
  Young People and HIV/AIDS ............ 51
  Child Marriage ............ 53
  Young People and Employment ............ 55

**6 Partnering with Boys and Men** ............ 57
  Men's Roles in Achieving the Millennium Development Goals ............ 57
  The Impact of Gender Roles on Men ............ 58
  Reaching Out to Boys and Men ............ 60
  Reinterpreting Masculinity ............ 60
  The Formative Years ............ 61
  Accelerating Progress ............ 62

**7 Gender-Based Violence: A Price Too High** ............ 65
  The Magnitude and Many Forms of Gender-Based Violence ............ 65
  Violence Against Women and the MDGs ............ 68
  Mobilizing for 'Zero Tolerance' ............ 70
  Men Take a Stand ............ 72

**8 Women and Young People in Humanitarian Crises** ............ 75
  After a Crisis: Opportunities for Equity and Peace ............ 75
  An Evolving Human Rights Framework ............ 76
  Participation of Women and Gender Equality: The Path to Recovery ............ 78
  Empowering Young People in the Aftermath of Crises ............ 78
  Safeguarding Reproductive Health and Rights in Humanitarian Emergencies ............ 80

9 Road Map to the Millennium
Development Goals and Beyond       85
   Women's Empowerment: Lifting Families and
   Nations Out of Poverty            85
   Empowering Young People: The MDGs and Beyond  85
   Universal Reproductive Health: Fulfilling
   Cairo to Reach the MDGs           85
   Rights and Equality: Guiding Poverty
   Reduction Policies                88
   Resources: A Modest Price Tag for
   Human Dignity and Equity          89

## Notes and Indicators          93

## Sources for Quotations        105

## Sources for Boxes             105

## Indicators                    107
Monitoring ICPD Goals: Selected Indicators    107

Demographic, Social and Economic Indicators   111

Selected Indicators for Less-Populous
Countries/Territories            115

Notes for Indicators             117

Technical Notes                  117

## Graphs and Tables

Figure 1
The Global Burden of Sexual and Reproductive
Health Conditions                34

Figure 2
Births Attended by Skilled Personnel Among
the Poorest and Richest Women    36

Figure 3
Contraceptive Use According to Wealth    42

Figure 4
Childbearing Among the Poorest and
Richest Adolescents              50

Figure 5
Women Who Believe Wife Beating is Justified for
at Least One Reason              68

## Photo Captions and Credits    120

## Editorial Team                120

# 1 Overview

*"No new promises are needed—only following through on commitments already made."*
— UN Millennium Project

The world has an unprecedented opportunity to realize the promise of equality and freedom from want. During the next decade, hundreds of millions of people can be released from the stronghold of poverty. The lives of 30 million children and 2 million mothers can be spared.[1] The spread of AIDS can be reversed. Millions of young people can play a larger role in their countries' development and, in turn, create a better world for themselves and generations to come.

Gender equality and reproductive health are indispensable to the realization of this promise.

In the year 2000, leaders from 189 countries met at the United Nations Millennium Summit and forged a unique global compact to reduce poverty. From the Summit's declaration, eight Millennium Development Goals (MDGs) were derived, with 2015 set as the date for their achievement. In 2002, the UN Millennium Project brought together more than 250 leading experts to advise the UN Secretary-General on how to implement the MDGs. Their conclusions are reflected throughout this year's *State of World Population* report.

Gender equality is a human right, one of the Millennium Development Goals and key to achieving the other seven. The UN Millennium Project concluded that reproductive health is essential to achieving the MDGs, including the goal of gender equality. Investments in gender equality and reproductive health offer multiple rewards that can accelerate social and economic progress, with lasting impact on future generations.

**Gender Equality and Equity:** The costs of gender discrimination are highest for low-income countries, and within countries, for the poor. Women constitute a large share of the labour force and play a central role in rural economies and food production. They are also primary guardians of the next generation. Gender discrimination squanders human capital by making inefficient use of individual abilities, thus limiting the contribution of women. It also undermines the effectiveness of development policies.[2]

When discriminatory burdens are removed, the capacity and earning power of women increase. Furthermore, women tend to reinvest these gains in the welfare of their children and families, multiplying their contributions to national development. Empowering women propels countries forward towards the MDGs and improves the lives of all.

**Reproductive Health and Rights:** The considerable, and largely preventable, burden of poor reproductive health falls most heavily on the poorest women and their families, who can least afford its consequences. The ability to make free and informed choices in reproductive life, including those involving childbearing, underpins self-determination in all other areas of women's lives. Because these issues affect women so profoundly, reproductive health cannot be separated from the wider goal of gender equality.

## The Equality Dividend: Strategic Investments, Large Payoffs

Countries will need to invest scarce resources wisely if they are to meet the MDGs by the fast-approaching 2015 deadline. As discussed in **Chapter 2**, experience shows that simultaneous investments in three areas can be particularly effective in spurring progress at the country level: education for girls and women; reproductive health information and services and women's economic rights.[3] Women engaged in the political process, as individuals or members of civil society organizations, can help keep these priority issues high on national agendas, and hold governments and other key actors accountable to commitments made.

**Expanding Education for Girls and Women:** The gender gap in education has left nearly twice as many women as men illiterate. In the poorest regions, more girls than boys are out of school, and the gap widens at the secondary level—even though secondary and higher education for girls is especially significant in reducing poverty. Educational attainment increases women's income-earning potential, reduces maternal and infant mortality and improves reproductive health overall. It is associated with lower rates of HIV. Educated girls are more likely to delay marriage and childbearing, and instead acquire skills to improve economic prospects for themselves and their families. The multiple benefits of girls' education also lead to better health and education for the next generation.

**Improving Reproductive Health:** Reproductive health problems comprise the leading cause of death and disability for women the world over.[4] Most are preventable. Universal access to reproductive health services is an international commitment and a human rights imperative. It is also a powerful investment for countries fighting poverty.

Impoverished women and adolescent girls with limited access to reproductive health care suffer the most. These women and their families are least able to afford the consequences of reproductive health conditions: The costs of health care, the loss of a woman's contributions to family survival and the impact of AIDS can push poor families into destitution. The opportunity to pursue other productive and community activities, and to secure stable employment and higher wages, is compromised when a woman is unable to determine the number, timing and spacing of her children.

The costs to national development and public budgets are considerable. According to some estimates, reproductive health conditions result in 250 million years of productive life lost each year worldwide and reduce the overall productivity of women by as much as 20 per cent.[5] Adolescent pregnancy, the AIDS epidemic, and excess fertility due to lack of family planning services further strain national budgets, slow social and economic development and deepen poverty.

**Providing Economic Opportunities:** Although women have entered the paid workforce in increasing numbers, they confront many forms of discrimination, including restricted choice of occupations and lower wages. Entrepreneurial efforts may be frustrated by laws and customs that combine to prevent women from owning property, acquiring credit or controlling income. In some regions, women cannot inherit, even from deceased husbands. Many end up working in the informal sector, where work is unregulated, poorly paid, insecure and often unsafe.[6]

The labour of rural women accounts for 60 to 80 per cent of food production in developing countries,[7] but many face restrictions on the rights to own, use and inherit land. Research in some sub-Saharan African countries found that output could increase

---

**1 | 2005: MILESTONES IN THE COUNTDOWN TO THE MDGS**

This year begins the 10-year countdown to the 2015 deadline for achieving the Millennium Development Goals. It also offers several milestones by which to measure progress and intensify action to improve the human condition. The year 2005 marks:

- The 10th anniversary of the Fourth World Conference on Women

- The 30th anniversary of the First World Conference on Women

- The 60th anniversary of the 1945 United Nations Charter, which enshrined "the equal rights of men and women" in its Preamble

- The 10-year review of the World Programme of Action for Youth to the Year 2000 and Beyond.

The year 2005 also follows closely after the 10-year anniversary of the 1994 International Conference on Population and Development that reaffirmed gender equality and reproductive health and rights as cornerstones of sustainable development.

by up to 20 per cent if more women had equal access and control over farm income, agricultural services and land.[8] In many of these countries, AIDS further limits the productivity of women, who often struggle with few social supports to both provide for their families and care for the sick.

## The Promise of Human Rights

One of the proudest achievements of the 20th Century was the establishment of an international human rights system affirming the equal rights of all. The MDGs are grounded in respect for human rights—to human dignity, to personal security and to freedom from want, fear and discrimination. Achieving them, as discussed in **Chapter 3**, is not a matter of charity: It is both an ethical obligation and a collective responsibility. Meeting the MDGs and furthering human development requires empowering the poor, especially women, young people and marginalized populations, who are often doubly or triply disenfranchised.

The framework for the human rights of women is well established. International and regional conventions, and national constitutions and laws in many countries enshrine protections for women's rights. Nevertheless, in practice, the denial of the human rights of women remains persistent and widespread. Where laws safeguarding women's rights exist, enforcement is often weak and undermined by limited budgets. Gender biases permeate social institutions charged with upholding women's rights. In many countries, custom and tradition take precedence over official policy. Women and under-age girls are married against their will; violence against girls and women is tolerated; rapists are exonerated; and women are denied their equal rights within the family and marriage to property and inheritance and in other areas as well.

Reproductive rights are central to human rights, especially the human rights of women. They derive from the recognition of the basic right of all individuals and couples to make decisions about reproduction free of discrimination, coercion or violence. They include the right to the highest standard of health and the right to determine the number, timing and spacing of children. They comprise the right to safe childbearing, and the right of all individuals to protect themselves from HIV and other sexually transmitted infections.

Social and cultural contexts present both challenges and opportunities for promoting the human rights of women. Culturally sensitive approaches build on positive values, enlist the support of community leaders and influential individuals, and mobilize broad-based community ownership of initiatives that promote human rights and gender equality.

The rights of marginalized groups merit priority attention. These groups account for a large proportion of the global population, and many live in poverty. Disabled persons make up 10 per cent of the world population (or 600 million).[9] An estimated 370 million indigenous people live in some 70 countries.[10] International migrants number an estimated 175 million people.[11] Gender inequality compounds the multiple forms of discrimination women from these groups already face.

## Reproductive Health: A Measure of Equity

Reproductive health bears directly on three MDGs—reducing child mortality, improving maternal health, and combating HIV/AIDS—and has implications for all of the others, as discussed in **Chapter 4**. No other area of health presents such large disparities between rich and poor, within and among countries.[12] And no other area of health so clearly demonstrates the impact of gender inequality on women's lives.

Virtually all—99 per cent—of maternal deaths occur in developing countries. The lives of most of these women—and those of their newborns—could be saved through emergency care readily available to wealthier women. Every minute a woman dies from the complications of childbirth or pregnancy, and another 20 are seriously injured or disabled.[13] And when a mother dies giving birth, her infant's chances of survival plummet. Motherless newborns are three to 10 times more likely to die than others.[14] Preventing unintended pregnancies through access to family planning could avert 20 to 35 per cent of maternal deaths,[15] saving the lives of more than 100,000 mothers each year.

The rapid spread of the AIDS epidemic further highlights the consequences of gender disparities for reproductive health: Three quarters of all HIV infections are sexually transmitted between men and women—many by husbands to their wives. Although transmission is preventable, the ability of women to protect themselves against HIV is often restricted by imbalances in decision-making power, gender-based violence, economic insecurity and harmful practices. Up to half of new HIV infections are among young people. Young women are at especially high risk. Those who are poor, female and young often have the least power and opportunity to protect themselves.

Gender inequality fuels the epidemic. In many societies, social norms and expectations that idealize male prowess and strength legitimize multiple partners for men and their authority in decision-making. The consequences—for individual men and women, for the children who have lost one or both of their parents to AIDS, and for entire nations—are tragically well known. Limited access to education and health services keeps prevention and treatment out of reach for millions of poor people.

## Adolescents and Youth: The Unmapped Journey

With nearly half of the world's population (almost 3 billion) under the age of 25, young people are crucial to poverty reduction and development. Today's generation of young people is the largest in history. Over 500 million youth (ages 15 to 24) live on less than $2 per day.[16] They are growing up in a different world than their parents: AIDS, information and communications technologies and globalization are powerful forces shaping their lives.

Youth comprise half of the world's unemployed. While work affords some the opportunity to earn, learn and develop new skills, many others are trapped in low-wage, low-skill sectors with few opportunities to advance or to escape poverty.[17] Many of those who begin working in adolescence or as young children are subject to abuse and exploitation, as discussed further in **Chapter 5**.

Adolescence—defined here as from ages 10 to 19—is a critical time to learn and acquire skills and values that can last a lifetime. For those living in poverty it can be a time of diminished freedom and increased risks. Many adolescents are obliged to abandon their schooling to help support their families or because they become pregnant or get married. Adolescent girls are particularly vulnerable to early pregnancy, sexual abuse, child marriage and other harmful practices such as genital mutilation/cutting. In the next 10 years, 100 million girls are likely to be married before the age of 18.[18] Every year, some 14 million adolescent girls give birth.[19] They are also two to five times as likely to die owing to pregnancy-related complications than women in their twenties,[20] and their babies are less likely to survive as well. Poverty leads many to resort to transactional sex to procure bare essentials for themselves and their families. For the 15 million AIDS orphans[21] left on their own to survive and provide for siblings, and for the legions of others around the world abandoned and living on the streets, the challenges and risks are magnified many times over.

The poorest countries have the highest percentage of young people. Yet adolescents and youth have received only limited attention from policymakers and are largely invisible in the MDGs. A growing number of policymakers now grasp the urgency of investing more in the education, reproductive health, well-being and the future prospects of young people, especially adolescent girls, as a matter of both human rights and of national self-interest. Large numbers of poorly educated young people without employment prospects is a recipe for continued poverty, inequality and civil unrest.[22] A large and skilled population of young people entering their most productive years, on the other hand, can give a powerful boost to development, as the economic growth of the "Asian Tigers" has demonstrated.

## Partnering with Boys and Men

Because gender norms and stereotypes limit the possibilities of both women and men, gender equality can be a winning proposition for both— "double happiness" in the words of one campaign to encourage men to take on more domestic responsibility.[23] Men themselves are increasingly challenging notions of "masculinity" that restrict their humanity, limit their participation in the lives of their children, and put themselves and their partners at risk. Many want to become more supportive husbands and fathers, but need support to overcome deeply entrenched ideas about gender relations. Moreover, because they bear responsibility for many reproductive health problems, men play an indispensable role in their solution.

Around the world many innovative programmes are leveraging the positive involvement of men in the struggle for equality and reproductive health. Some initiatives encourage joint participation in decisions about contraception, emergency plans for pregnancy and labour and voluntary HIV testing. Others emphasize men as agents of positive change and encourage them to question gender norms more broadly. Some work with adolescent boys at a formative and potentially risky time in their lives. A few initiatives manage to reach large numbers of men in their places of employment or in military or police institutions. Most programmes, however, are small compared to the scale of the challenge of transforming gender relations. As discussed in **Chapter 6**, stronger efforts to involve men more fully in reproductive health, family life and gender equality are urgently needed.

## Gender-based Violence: A Price Too High

Gender-based violence knows no boundaries— economic, social or geographic. Overwhelmingly perpetrated by men against women, gender-based violence both reflects and reinforces gender inequity. The toll it extorts on the dignity, autonomy and health of women is shocking: Worldwide, one in three women has been beaten, coerced into unwanted sexual relations, or abused—often by a family member or acquaintance.[24] At the start of the 21st century, violence kills and harms as many women and girls between the ages of 15 and 44 as cancer.[25] The costs to countries—in increased health care expenditures, demands on courts, police and schools and losses in educational achievement and productivity—are enormous. In the United States, the figure adds up to some $12.6 billion each year.[26]

Gender-based violence takes many forms, from the domestic confrontations that leave millions of women living in fear to sexual abuse and rape, to harmful practices ranging from female genital mutilation/cutting to "honour killings" and dowry-related violence. In Asia, at least 60 million girls are "missing" due to prenatal sex selection, infanticide or neglect.[27] Each year, up to 800,000 people are trafficked across borders—as many as 80 per cent of them women and girls, mostly exploited in the commercial sex trade.[28] Within borders, the numbers are even higher. **Chapter 7** explores the global prevalence, causes and consequences of gender-based violence, and the steps now being undertaken to combat this global epidemic.

## Women and Young People in Humanitarian Crises

Conflict has erupted in more than 40 countries since the 2000 UN Millennium Summit.[29] Natural disasters are becoming more frequent and are affecting larger numbers of people than ever before. The tsunami in 2004 caused the deaths of 280,000 people and displaced another one million.[30]

The collapse of social systems as a result of conflict or disaster leaves women and young people especially vulnerable. During conflict, rape is commonly used as a weapon of war, leaving millions of women traumatized, forcibly impregnated or infected with HIV. Crises lead to the disintegration of community and family protections. Gender-based violence is a constant risk. The lack of health services often causes infant and maternal mortality rates to increase sharply. Armed groups forcibly recruit children and adolescents as soldiers, or force them to serve as domestic servants or sexual slaves. Women are often left to both fend for themselves and their children and to care for survivors. For these and other reasons, humanitarian crises often lead to long-term economic and social insecurity. Of the 34 countries farthest from reaching the MDGs, 22 are in, or emerging from, conflict.[31]

Peacebuilding and reconstruction offer a chance to correct the inequities that led to conflict in the first place. **Chapter 8** details efforts to address the needs and rights of women and young people in the aftermath of crises. Their participation is essential in establishing equitable and sound poverty reduction action plans in the post-crisis transition. This chapter also highlights the plight of internally displaced persons and describes efforts in some post-conflict countries to make a fresh start in creating gender equitable societies.

## Making Poverty History

The world has an unprecedented opportunity to "make poverty history".[32] With nearly 3 billion people[33] struggling to live on less than $2 a day, over half a

## 2 THE ICPD AND THE MDGS: LINKAGES FOR POVERTY REDUCTION, GENDER EQUALITY AND REPRODUCTIVE HEALTH

### MDG 1: Eradicate extreme poverty and hunger

- Investments in the economic rights of women—equal employment opportunities and wages, credit, agricultural resources, inheritance and property rights—increase productivity, farm yields, and family well-being. Women's control over household resources leads to higher investments in children's health, nutrition and education.
- Many of the poorest countries are those in or emerging from conflict. Investing in women and young people furthers the rebuilding of societies and economies, poverty reduction and lasting peace and stability.
- Reproductive health problems disproportionately affect women and the poor and can push families deeper into poverty.

- Smaller families help reduce hunger and increase investments per child. This leads to a healthier and better skilled labour force, slower population growth, reduced public expenditures, increased savings and investments, and accelerated social and economic development.

### MDG 2: Achieve universal primary education

- When mothers are educated and families are smaller, the likelihood that all children will go to school increases.
- Gender biases keep many girls from school, often to help mothers care for siblings and manage household needs. For many families, the priority is educating boys. Eliminating school fees and supporting poor families can ensure that all children complete their education.

### MDG 3: Promote gender equality and empower women

- Gender inequality slows development. Equal political, economic, social and cultural rights are required to reduce poverty.
- Women's ability to decide freely the number and timing of children is key to their empowerment and expanded opportunities for work, education and social participation.
- Men play a pivotal role in achieving gender equality, poverty reduction and development goals, including improved infant and maternal health and reduced HIV transmission and gender-based violence.
- Violence against women and girls results in high social and economic costs—to individuals, families and public budgets.
- Eliminating child marriage, enabling adolescent girls to delay pregnancy, ending discrimination against pregnant girls, and providing support to young mothers can help ensure that girls complete an education. This can help break the cycle of intergenerational poverty.
- Girls' secondary education provides high payoffs for poverty reduction, gender equality, labour force participation and reproductive health, including HIV prevention and women's and children's health and education status overall.

### MDG 4: Reduce child mortality

- Reproductive health can improve infant survival and health. Birth spacing and maternal health care can help prevent infant deaths. Family planning also prevents unintended pregnancies: Unwanted children are more prone to illness and premature death.
- Screening pregnant women for HIV and other sexually transmitted infections can prevent infant illness, disability and death.
- Empowering adolescent girls to delay pregnancy can prevent many newborn deaths. Babies born to adolescents face higher mortality rates than those born to older women.

### MDG 5: Improve maternal health

- Key reproductive health components—family planning, skilled birth attendance and emergency obstetric care—save lives.
- Family planning can reduce maternal mortality by 20 to 35 per cent.
- Improved quality of care and access to maternal health services (prenatal, during delivery, post-partum) improves women's health and quality of life for them and their families.

### MDG 6: Combat HIV/AIDS, malaria and other diseases

- Reproductive health care includes prevention and management of sexually transmitted infections, including HIV/AIDS.
- Gender discrimination fuels the HIV/AIDS epidemic, placing adolescent girls and women at risk, including within marriage. Reproductive health programmes counsel individuals and couples on prevention, prevent mother-to-child transmission and unwanted pregnancies in HIV-positive women, and offer options should they wish to have children.

### MDG 7: Ensure environmental sustainability

- In developing countries, women are the primary food producers and managers of community and household water and fuel resources. Investments in safe water, sanitation, time-saving technologies and skills training can improve sustainable resource management, food security, nutrition and health, and lessen time spent on collecting water and firewood. This releases girls and women for educational and other productive activities.
- Environmentally-friendly sources of energy can protect women and children from the harmful effects of pollutants and cooking fires.
- Family planning and the prevention of unwanted births, can help stabilize rural areas, slow urbanization and environmental pressures, and ease demands on public services, thereby balancing natural resource use with the needs of the population.

### MDG 8: Develop a global partnership for development

- Decent work for youth—one of the goal's targets—coupled with enlightened socio-economic policies can increase savings, productivity and living standards. Among these policies is family planning, which enables young people to delay having a family until they have acquired the skills and experience to earn a viable income.
- Increased income-earning opportunities offer young women alternatives to early marriage and childbearing and sexual exploitation.
- Global partnership to secure adequate supplies of essential reproductive health drugs and commodities for poor countries—including contraceptives, testing kits and treatments for HIV and other sexually transmitted infections—is critical for achieving poverty reduction, gender equality and health goals.

---

million women dying needlessly every year from pregnancy-related complications, 6,000 young people acquiring HIV daily, and millions of women and girls living in fear of violence, the ethically-acceptable response is self-evident: to fulfil the promises for global action, equality and equity espoused at the United Nations conferences of the 1990s and at the 2000 UN Millennium Summit.

The conclusions of the experts are clear: Investing in gender equality, reproductive health and young people's development has short- and long-term social and economic multiplier effects. Launching national campaigns on violence against women; promoting women's property and inheritance rights; expanding access to reproductive health care and closing funding gaps for supplies and contraceptives; and ensuring that women are involved in the formulation of MDG follow-up policies and strategies are among the high-impact "quick-wins" identified by the UN Millennium Project.[34]

Implementing these strategies calls for a long-term, guaranteed commitment of resources at a consistently higher level than at present. The costs are moderate in relation to the benefits they offer. The investments required to achieve the foundation for human dignity and human security, and for expanding freedoms and choices for the world's poorest people, amount to a fraction of what the world spends on military purposes.[35] The entire MDGs package could be funded if industrialized countries simply fulfilled an agreement made 35 years ago to assign 0.7 per cent of their gross national income to official development assistance. Improved governance and transparency, reduced corruption, increased debt relief and removal of agricultural subsidies in wealthy countries are among the elements of the global compact to end poverty.

The world has reached an unprecedented consensus to end poverty. The strategies and know-how are available. The leadership and resources required can be mobilized. As 2004 Nobel Peace Prize Winner Wangari Maathai told the world in her acceptance speech, "there comes a time when humanity is called to shift to a new level of consciousness, to reach a higher moral ground. That time is now….There can be no peace without equitable development."[36]

# 2 Strategic Investments: The Equality Dividend

> *"The Millennium Development Goals, particularly the eradication of extreme poverty and hunger, cannot be achieved if questions of population and reproductive health care are not squarely addressed. And that means stronger efforts to promote women's rights and greater investment in education and health, including reproductive health and family planning."*
>
> — UN Secretary-General Kofi Annan, Bangkok

Just ten years remain to reduce extreme poverty by half and to meet the 2015 deadline for the Millennium Development Goals (MDGs). The MDGs are closely interlinked—reaching them will depend on the combined, considered efforts of governments, civil society and the international community to mobilize around highly strategic approaches. The consensus and evidence are clear: Investing in gender equality offers invaluable opportunities and substantial returns for reducing poverty.

One of the eight MDGs is gender equality and women's empowerment, itself a pressing human rights concern. Reaching this goal underpins success towards all the others. It will also release a powerful force for development in other areas.

This chapter examines the wider social and economic rationale for promoting gender equality. It shows that when the dampers of gender discrimination on men and women are removed, families, communities and entire countries benefit. It considers the key policy recommendations from the UN Millennium Project[1] for promoting gender equality and attaining the MDGs. Improving education, reproductive health and economic opportunity for women and girls is particularly strategic in this regard. It will be equally important to eliminate violence against women, discussed later in Chapter 7. Increased political participation of women and greater accountability for gender equality will help ensure that these areas are given the attention they merit.

Many countries have made significant progress towards gender equality, especially in the area of policy and legislation, and in health and education. National development policies increasingly place gender equality at the forefront of poverty reduction efforts. But progress has been uneven, and the gap between policy and practice remains wide.[2] To unleash the equality dividend for development, stronger partnerships and the resolve of governments, civil society, the private sector, donors and the United Nations system are required.

## A Poverty of Opportunity and Choices

As the World Bank reports, gender inequality is inefficient and undermines the effectiveness of development policies.[3] Inequality between women and men is often pervasive and deeply entrenched, though its scope and intensity varies among, and within, countries. It begins early, can last a lifetime and is often exacerbated by poverty. Poor families struggle with difficult spending choices to benefit all their children. But girls in various settings end up with less education, health care and skills than their brothers. This "gender gap" often widens later in life, limiting women's opportunities for safe work, fair pay and accumulation of economic assets. Although marriage and childbearing are life-altering decisions with important social and economic ramifications, women and adolescent girls in many parts of the world have limited say in them.

Families are major conduits of sociocultural and gender norms, and it is in the family that the roles and responsibilities of women and men, girls and boys, are largely defined. Families are also the basic economic units of consumption and production:

THE STATE OF WORLD POPULATION 2005   9

Decisions about education, health, nutrition, childbearing and political and economic participation are made within the family. Even with the best intentions, these decisions can undermine the human rights and well-being of women and girls and limit their options and choices, thereby perpetuating poverty. Understanding how families and communities make decisions can offer valuable insights into effective policymaking.[4]

Promoting gender equality can expand opportunities for human development and remove costly obstacles to meeting the MDGs. This is because gender discrimination is based on predetermined and often rigid expectations of the appropriate roles of men and women in political, economic, social and family life, regardless of individual abilities or aspirations. Gender discrimination thus restricts the personal development of both men and women and holds back progress towards poverty reduction and development.

**CRITICAL INVESTMENTS, LARGE PAYOFFS.** Investments that enable girls and women to reach their full potential offer a double dividend, because of women's dual productive and reproductive roles. In addition to their often unpaid vital contributions to household, community and national economies, women bring forth and are the primary caretakers of the next generation. Investments in the education, reproductive health and economic opportunities of women and girls have immediate, longer term and intergenerational payoffs. These three investment areas represent critical and synergistic elements in the development of the human capital of women, and, by extension, of their children.[5]

The East Asian "economic miracle" of unprecedented growth from 1965 to 1990 offers an example of how these elements can work together. Gender gaps in education were closed, access to family planning was expanded and women were able to delay childbearing and marriage while more work opportunities increased their participation in the labour force. The economic contribution of women helped reduce poverty and spur growth.[6] The UN Millennium Project refers to East and South-East Asia as the only regions where there has been "tremendous progress" in the reduction of poverty, hunger and gender inequality.[7]

**THE POWER OF GIRLS' EDUCATION.** All girls and boys have the right to education. Education fosters dignity and a sense of self-worth. It offers opportunities to acquire knowledge and skills and enhances life prospects. Along with nutrition, health and skills, education is a pillar of human capital: These essential elements together enable people to lead productive lives and to contribute to their countries' economic growth and development.[8]

But poverty prevents millions of children, especially girls, from attending school. In the least developed countries, only half of all children complete primary school.[9] While gender gaps in primary education are closing globally, more girls than boys are still out of school.[10] The gaps are wider still within and among countries: In Southern Asia and sub-Saharan Africa, only 69 and 49 per cent of girls, respectively, complete primary school.[11] At the secondary level, even fewer girls are in school—with only 30 and 47 per cent of them enrolled in sub-Saharan Africa and South Asia, respectively.[12] These gender gaps are evident in literacy rates: Worldwide, 600 million women are illiterate compared to 320 million men.[13]

Secondary, or higher, education for women is particularly strategic. According to the UN Millennium Project, it provides the "greatest payoffs for women's empowerment".[14] Secondary education yields higher returns for women than for men, including increased use of maternal health and family planning services and altered attitudes towards harmful practices.[15] Women with secondary education are also more likely than illiterate women to understand the dangers posed by HIV and how to prevent its spread. In Egypt, women with secondary education were four times more likely to oppose the genital mutilation/cutting of their daughters than women who had never completed primary school.[16] Secondary education also plays a more significant role than primary education in reducing violence against women, for example, by empowering women to leave abusive relationships.[17] The social and economic benefits of girls' education are summarized below:

**Girls' education contributes to economic growth.** Investing in the education of girls is one of the most effective ways to reduce poverty. By one estimate, countries that do not meet the MDG target of gender parity in education are at risk of foregoing 0.1 to 0.3 percentage points annually in per capita economic growth.[18] Economic growth rates in sub-Saharan Africa and South Asia could have been nearly 1 per cent a year higher had those countries started with East Asia's smaller gender gaps and made progress in closing them at the rate observed in East Asia between 1960 and 1992.[19]

**Educated mothers increase human capital through their influence on the health, education and nutrition of their children.** Daughters of educated mothers are more likely to attend school.[20] A mother's education also translates into higher immunization rates and better nutrition for her children, both of which increase enrolment and improve school performance. Every year of mothers' education corresponds to 5 to 10 per cent lower mortality rates in children under the age of five.[21]

**Education improves a family's economic prospects by improving women's qualifications and skills.** As better-educated women participate in paid employment, families enjoy higher income and overall productivity increases. In rural economies, the education of women and girls may translate into higher agricultural production. In Kenya, for example, one study estimated that crop yields could rise up to 22 per cent if women farmers enjoyed the same education and decision-making authority as men.[22]

**Education improves reproductive health.** Educated women are more likely to seek adequate prenatal care, skilled attendance during childbirth and to use contraception. They tend to initiate sexual activity, marry and begin childbearing later than uneducated women. They also have fewer children: Every three years of additional education correlates with up to one child fewer per woman.[23] When women have fewer children, the well-being and development prospects of each child are generally enhanced.[24]

CLOSING THE GAP. Many countries have made progress in girls' education. But despite the evidence of its power for reducing poverty and stimulating development, the latest estimates suggest that a number of countries will miss the MDG target for eliminating gender disparity in all levels of education by 2015: At least 21 countries will miss the target relating to primary education, and 27 countries will miss it for secondary education.[25] The earlier timeline—to eliminate gender disparities in primary and secondary education "preferably by 2005" has already been missed by several countries.[26]

In UNFPA's Global Survey on progress since the 1994 International Conference on Population and Development (ICPD), 58 of 142 countries reported an increase in public school spending and only 14 countries launched initiatives to promote girls' education. Of 129 countries reporting, 23 passed laws on equal education for girls and boys, and 16 increased the number of secondary schools for girls.[27]

For poor families, the costs of sending girls to school need to be weighed carefully against the possible benefits, an analysis that often reflects and reinforces gender norms. In societies where women's life options are typically limited to marriage and childbearing, for instance, a girl's education may be considered a luxury, especially after her contribution to household chores, agricultural work and child or elder care is factored in. Moreover, marriage may be seen as a transfer of the investment in daughters to another family, with little benefit to the girl's parents.

To realize the full benefits of girls' education, countries need to overcome the barriers that keep girls from attending school. Effective strategies to close gender gaps in education focus on poor communities and address specific obstacles. The safety of daughters in school and in transit to and from school, for instance, is an important issue for parents. This can be addressed by adding female teachers, improving security measures, reducing travel times by increasing the number of schools and generally making schools more "girl-friendly". (Simply adding a separate washroom for girls can make a difference.) Eliminating school fees and other costs can lower economic hurdles: Bangladesh, Mexico, Uganda, the United Republic of Tanzania, among others, have found success with offers of free school meals, subsidies and scholarships.[28] Efforts to improve enrolment at the secondary level are vital, including special efforts to retain married and pregnant adolescents. At the global level, UNESCO's Education for All and the UN Girls' Education Initiative promote girls' schooling.

It is important to improve the quality as well as the quantity of education. Addressing issues such as shortages of teachers, overcrowded classrooms, and the content and relevance of education are essential to enable young people to acquire the skills they need, whether to prevent HIV infection or seek better jobs. Improved quality also demands gender-sensitive curricula to eliminate gender stereotypes that affect how girls and boys are treated in the classroom and what subjects they study. This enables girls to obtain the most from their education and better equips them to transcend rigid gender norms that undermine their full potential. It may, for instance, encourage them to consider a wider variety of jobs, including non-traditional ones.[29] Skills in information and communication technologies (ICTs) can open up a world of opportunities, especially as countries improve ICT literacy levels and rural infrastructure. Several countries have begun programmes for girls and women. The Islamic Republic of Iran, for example, is offering training in information technology to rural women, especially housewives.[30]

The power of girls' education for poverty reduction, gender equality and development is unquestionable. But education alone is insufficient in the absence of supportive social institutions and systems that expand women's opportunities and freedoms, access to resources and control of decisions affecting their lives. Simultaneous efforts to improve women's reproductive health and economic opportunities can maximize the social and economic dividends of girls' education.

## ESSENTIAL INVESTMENTS IN REPRODUCTIVE HEALTH AND RIGHTS.

Reproductive health is a human right, a building block of human capital and a core aspect of gender equality. It is integral to the well-being of women and their families.[31] Poor women have the greatest need, and as the research presented below shows, they, their families and society as a whole have much to gain from improvements in their reproductive health. Associated problems can push households deeper into poverty.[32] Impoverished women, who typically have the least access to contraception, may find it difficult to determine the number and spacing of their children. This limits their prospects for good health and stable employment and for pursuing better economic opportunities that can raise living standards.[33] A woman's reproductive health status also greatly affects her children—a country's future human capital—and therefore has both short and longer-term socio-economic implications.[34] Though the ICPD goal of universal access to reproductive health by 2015 was not explicitly included in the MDGs, investments in reproductive health are now widely recognized as essential to their achievement:[35]

**Reproductive health care, through family planning services, allows women to delay childbearing so that they can complete their education, participate in the workforce, and acquire skills and experience.** Where contraceptives are widely available, women tend to delay childbearing, spend less time pregnant and complete their childbearing years sooner.[36] For sexually active adolescent girls (married and unmarried), family planning can mean the difference between early pregnancy and an education.

**Reproductive health problems undermine poverty reduction efforts by eroding productivity.** Reproductive health problems are a major cause of ill-health that disproportionately affect adolescent girls and women. They reduce female labour productivity—in some cases by 20 per cent—and cost 250 million years of productive life each year worldwide.[37]

**Giving people the freedom and means to choose the number of children they desire results in smaller families, slower population growth and reduced pressure on natural resources.** The world's population is expected to increase from 6.5 billion today to 9.1 billion by 2050—assuming continuation of the historical increase in family planning use.[38] Most of this growth will occur in countries battling poverty. Satisfying individuals' and couples' unmet demand for contraception is necessary from a human rights standpoint. Reducing unwanted fertility also carries important macro-level implications.

**Reproductive health can provide important economic benefits through the "demographic dividend".** When countries undergo demographic transitions resulting from reduced mortality and fertility rates, population structures change. Families become smaller, with a high proportion of young adults entering their productive life, but with fewer children and elder dependents. With the appropriate social and economic policies in place, this can result in increased savings and greater available resources to invest in each child. For nations, this results in greater investments for generating productivity and economic growth.[39] In East Asia, economists credit the demographic dividend for one third of the region's unprecedented economic growth from 1965 to 1990.[40] Researchers estimate that developing countries can use their demographic dividends to reduce poverty by approximately 14 per cent between 2000 and 2015.[41]

**Access to reproductive health care means large savings for public health and other social services.** Reproductive health problems are largely preventable: Stronger health systems and better access to services can avert many of these problems and their costly consequences. In Thailand and Egypt, every dollar invested in family planning was estimated to save approximately $16 and $31, respectively, in health, education, housing and other social service costs.[42] The costs to national budgets and economies of the AIDS epidemic and high rates of teenage pregnancy are well-known and documented.[43]

### WOMEN'S ECONOMIC RIGHTS AND INVISIBLE LABOUR.

Women are the backbones of their families, pillars of community life, caregivers for the sick and elderly and primary caretakers of the next generation. In addition to managing households and securing and preparing food, many work in farms, factories, marketplaces, mines, sweatshops or offices. Women work more hours on average than men,[44] and do so mostly in the absence of supportive policies, laws, institutions, services, family arrangements and time-saving technologies. Much of their work is unrecognized, invisible and unpaid. Even though women are entering the workforce in increasing numbers, they risk dismissal should they become pregnant and generally

---

> **3 HUMAN SECURITY THROUGH A GENDER LENS**
>
> In an increasingly globalized world, where epidemics, HIV/AIDS, environmental problems and migration defy national boundaries, the concept of national security has begun to evolve beyond a concept of security centred on the state towards a more people-centred concept, that of human security. The UN Commission on Human Security defines this as "freedom from want, freedom from fear, and freedom to take action on one's own behalf". It remains a distant ideal for much of the world's population—especially the 2.7 billion who live in poverty and for those whose lives have been disrupted by violent conflicts or natural disasters.
>
> Freedom from fear eludes the millions of girls and women who are subjected to violence and abuse, often within their homes, on a daily basis. Millions of women have never fully enjoyed freedom to take action because others make decisions about whether they attend school, get married, have children or vote. Many can hardly imagine reproductive security—control over their fertility and the means to identify, prevent and manage reproductive risks. Nor are they free from the fear of unintended pregnancy, HIV infection, of dying of, or suffering from, severe injuries sustained through pregnancy or childbirth. Yet reproductive security remains fundamental to the empowerment of women, gender equality, and family well-being and to the achievement of the MDGs.

---

enjoy less overall income and job security than men. Unequal economic rights disadvantage millions of women in their efforts to improve the quality of their own and their children's lives. Improving women's access to, and control over, economic resources can be a key lever for lifting families and communities out of poverty.

Traditional macroeconomic approaches and development programmes have largely ignored the economic contributions of women, partly because data is generally not disaggregated by sex and fails to account for their unpaid labour. In many rural areas, women and girls spend many hours every day fetching water and fuel, although these efforts rarely appear in national accounts.[45] In Zambia, women spend 800 hours a year collecting water and fuelwood; in Ghana and the United Republic of Tanzania, they spend 300 hours gathering wood.[46] Infrastructure improvements, such as access to conveniently located and affordable safe water and sanitation, modern cooking fuels and better transportation, could ease this burden and release girls to attend school and adult women for other productive and community activities. It could also increase their use of health services.[47] But such improvements may be overlooked unless policymakers explicitly address these gender-specific factors and women have a role in community decision-making.

**ACCESS AND CONTROL OVER ASSETS.** In many regions, restrictions on women's rights to own, use and inherit property, and to qualify for credit, diminish their contribution to agricultural production and overall development. These restrictions also prevent women from investing in the land that they cultivate. Addressing inequitable inheritance and property rights is one of seven strategic priorities recommended by the UN Millennium Project Task Force on Education and Gender Equality.

Rural women are responsible for 60 to 80 per cent of food production in developing countries, but many countries still prohibit a woman from acquiring or disposing of land without her husband's consent. In much of sub-Saharan Africa, for example, widows have virtually no land or inheritance rights.[48] African countries have begun legislating to grant women equal rights to own or use land and inherit property. This is especially relevant in combating AIDS given that women's economic vulnerability limits their ability to protect themselves from HIV.[49] Liberia, for instance, has granted equal inheritance rights to girls and women. Botswana's Abolition of Marital Power Bill now gives women equal decision-making with respect to family assets. Eritrea has trained legal officers to promote women's land rights. Some countries in the Latin American and Caribbean region, including Barbados, Belize and Costa Rica, have also granted women property and inheritance rights within common-law unions.

Still, access to resources is inequitable. Women represent a third, or fewer, of land owners in Latin America, sub-Saharan Africa and South Asia.[50] In these regions, female farmers tend to cultivate smaller plots than men and have less access to agricultural extension services, even where they represent the majority of farmers.[51] In African countries, women receive less than 10 per cent of all loans earmarked for small farmers and only 1 per cent of total agricultural sector credit.[52] When women do obtain resources and financial services, however, productivity can rise. World Bank research in some sub-Saharan African countries found that output could increase by up to 20 per cent if more women had equal access and control over farm income, agricultural services and land.[53]

**HARD WORK, LOWER WAGES.** Mothers are substantial, primary or sole breadwinners for a large proportion of families.[54] In many poor households, women's work is essential for the family's survival. They also tend to reinvest a larger percentage of their earnings into their children and overall family well-being than do men. For example, according to the World Bank, a mother's control of income has a marginal impact on child survival almost 20 times greater than that of the father.[55] In areas where women earn wages and control resources, household incomes and standards of living rise, and families tend to benefit more than when men have exclusive control.[56]

Women's share of non-agricultural employment is rising steadily, but not everywhere. In only 17 of the 110 countries with data do women represent more than half of all wage earners, and this is primarily in

---

**4 | VIET NAM: IMPROVING FAMILY ECONOMIES, ONE WOMAN AT A TIME**

In Dong Loi, a small farming community in the uplands of northern Viet Nam, an initiative combining microcredit and reproductive health services, established by the Viet Nam Women's Union with UNFPA support, is demonstrating that women's leadership can help poor families rise out of poverty. Here, the members of a women's cooperative have seen their household incomes double in two years, largely through the breeding and sale of livestock purchased with loans. Extra funds allow participants to keep their children in school, buy supplies such as fertilizers and seeds, and even purchase computers or other consumer goods.

"Because of this project, the economy of the entire village has improved," says group leader Dinh Thi Nga. "Another reason for our success is that nearly every woman in my group is practising family planning."

The project has taught Dong Loi two important things, Nga adds. "First, women can play important roles in community development if given the chance, and second, in order to do that we need access to credit and training as well as to reproductive health and family planning services. The two are intimately linked to economic development."

more developed countries, Eastern Europe and Central Asia.[57] Secondary or higher levels of education would qualify more women for a more equitable share of good jobs. Often the education or training women receive is not well suited to local markets, limiting their economic participation.[58]

When they are employed, substantially more women than men work in the informal sector, which tends to offer lower wages, with less regulation, safety and security.[59] Women represent about two thirds of self-employed entrepreneurs in the informal sector.[60] Labour laws offer little protection to informal workers, who rarely have access to pension or social security schemes.

Many countries have reformed laws that discriminated against women in employment and unequal pay in the workplace.[61] Nevertheless, women in all sectors are paid less than men—in developed countries, they earn 77 cents for every dollar men earn and, in developing countries, only 73 cents, according to the World Bank. Lower lifetime earnings also decrease retirement savings, leaving older women and widows especially vulnerable to privation in old age.[62]

## Reconciling Productive and Reproductive Roles

The productive and reproductive roles of women are inextricably linked. Though their time and energy may be thinly stretched between family responsibilities and the need to earn money, women increasingly do both. However, public policies have not kept pace with the social changes generated by the increasing workforce participation of women and changing family structures. Nor have they fulfilled women's fundamental right to determine the number and spacing of children.

More and more countries are realizing that women need support to balance work and family life and that raising children is a shared right and responsibility of men and women. Targeted support can enable women to secure better employment and encourage men to enjoy a greater share of reproductive health and child-rearing responsibilities. This, in turn, is likely to contribute to economic growth and poverty reduction.

*"The continuing marginalization of women in decision-making has been both a cause and an effect of slow progress in many areas of development."*

— UN Secretary-General Kofi Annan

International Labour Organization conventions bar discrimination on the basis of pregnancy and motherhood and call for the provision of maternity care.[63] Many countries have taken measures in response. Scandinavian countries established family-friendly policies early on, and European countries are increasingly paying attention to the importance of fathers' roles within the family and providing paid paternity leave.[64] Kenya found that reducing the costs of childcare increases women's participation in the labour force and girls' secondary schooling.[65] Half of the governments reviewing ten years of progress on the commitments agreed at the 1995 Beijing Fourth World Conference on Women report that they have made some efforts to support both women and men in balancing family and work responsibilities.[66] Policies generally do not address fathers' roles and how they relate to the employment of working mothers, who are still primarily responsible for resolving childcare needs.[67] Policies are rarely tailored to the specific needs of particular groups, such as lower-income, indigenous or ethnic minorities.[68] Gender norms also make it more challenging for fathers to take parental leave even when it is available.[69] In Europe, men's careers suffered when they took advantage of family-friendly policies.[70] Leave policies also vary widely in terms of entitlements and financial support. In all cases, national policies addressing the interconnections between reproductive and productive roles should be guided by the right of individuals and couples to choose the number of children they wish to have, and to offer support and flexibility in balancing the demands of family and work life.

Reproductive health programmes that address gender relations and economic empowerment offer greater potential benefits than those that ignore the context in which reproductive decisions are made.[71] Providing opportunities for education and training, and for delaying marriage and childbearing, can enable young women to develop their full potential as economic agents.[72] Because millions of working women have children, employers can help by establishing family-friendly policies encouraging flexible

> ### 5 | FAMILIES IN TRANSITION
>
> Globalization, urbanization, modernization, migration, wars, natural disasters and population dynamics have transformed family life. Fewer extended families live together. Poverty has forced ever-larger numbers of parents and young people to seek work far from their families. In some places, the rapid spread of AIDS has redefined what it means to be a family—including groups of orphaned siblings living together under the care of the eldest or of a grandparent. These changing family structures have important policy implications. Female-headed households are on the rise in both developed and developing regions, comprising a fifth to a third of households in many countries. A growing proportion of these are headed by mothers who are also providing most or all of the economic support. Their children may also need to work in order to help the family survive.
>
> Support networks once provided by extended families are less available to working women today, and social measures have not yet filled the gap. "No single country provides the investment in care services that is required to fully meet the needs of women and their children," the UN Millennium Project Task Force on Education and Gender Equality reports. In the absence of childcare, single mothers face particular challenges, including restrictions on hours or type of employment. Irregular or missing child support further complicates their struggle to provide for their children.
>
> Women traditionally bear the brunt of caretaking for both young and old. As life spans lengthen and populations age, the time and resources required to care for the elderly may outstrip the ability of younger generations to cope. For older women, the cumulative consequences of life-long discrimination in labour markets, inadequate pensions and weak social supports often mean impoverishment and lower standards of life in later years. A lifetime of poor nutrition and reproductive health may result in chronic ill health—particularly for older women living in developing countries. Geographical distance from other family members may contribute to isolation and neglect.

work schedules, and offering childcare facilities and access to health care. In Jordan and Malaysia, employers are now responsible for providing childcare in workplaces.[73] In a number of countries, employers have begun to provide reproductive health and HIV prevention information and services because they understand that good health increases productivity and reduces absenteeism. Business for Social Responsibility, an international NGO with a global membership of 80 major companies (such as Coca-Cola and Sony), has developed a guidebook that details the economic benefits of supporting the reproductive health of female employees.[74]

**POLITICAL RIGHTS, POWER AND PARTICIPATION.**
Women's political participation transforms the process of setting priorities for public policy and helps make governance more egalitarian and inclusive.[75] By exercising this right more fully, women can advance poverty reduction efforts. Research shows that as larger numbers of women enter politics, public agendas change, corruption is reduced and governance improves.[76] Such shifts can accelerate the broad social change required for achieving the MDGs—a key reason why the UN Millennium Project Task Force on Education and Gender Equality identified increased political participation of women as a strategic priority.[77]

However, stereotypes and family responsibilities restrict women's participation in political decision-making, and women remain largely absent from national decision-making bodies. In general, progress is slow and uneven.[78] Women hold only 16 per cent of national parliamentary seats globally, up by less than 4 percentage points since 1990. To date, only 19 countries have met the 30 per cent target set by the United Nations for achievement by 1995.[79] In another 31 countries, women hold between 20 and 29 per cent of seats. Nevertheless, women have made progress in political life since 1990. Quota laws have been a major factor in raising women's national parliamentary representation in Latin America and the Caribbean, in sub-Saharan Africa and in the countries of the former Yugoslavia. Increased representation is also the result of lobbying by women's groups, which continue to mobilize support and build constituencies.[80]

At the local level, women often have greater opportunities to wield power—especially where decentralization is occurring. In both India and France, policies to increase the grass-roots political participation of women led to their entry in large numbers into local decision-making bodies. In India, over a million women serve in local government.[81] A study of *panchayats*, the local government councils in India, found that the inclusion of women members has resulted in profound changes, including councils that are more responsive to local demands for better infrastructure, housing, schools and health care.[82] Research indicates that female-headed *panchayats* drafted policies more sensitive to the needs of women, children and families. Ethiopia, Jordan and Namibia, among others, also report increased women's participation at local levels.[83]

The political participation of women does not necessarily correspond to national levels of poverty: A number of countries in sub-Saharan Africa, the world's poorest region, are ahead of France, Japan and the United States, where women hold only 15 per cent or less of legislative seats.[84] Rwanda has now surpassed Sweden as the country with the highest proportion of women in parliament in the world (see Chapter 8).[85]

## Accountability for Gender Justice

Despite many commitments—the 1994 ICPD, the 1995 Beijing Conference and the 2000 Millennium Summit, among others—gender inequality remains a pressing human rights and development issue. Too often, addressing discrimination is a matter of rhetoric or ad hoc efforts rather than sustained and institutionalized practice. Continuing the "business as usual" approach to gender equality can derail efforts to reach the MDGs. Staying on track for the MDGs calls for accountability on the part of governments, parliamentarians, employers, other key national actors and the international community. Closer partnerships between governments and civil society, including women's groups and other non-governmental, community-based and professional associations, are essential in providing the impetus for change and in promoting continuity during administrative transitions.

### DATA: TRACKING EQUITY AND EQUALITY.

Accountability relies on data for establishing benchmarks and measuring progress. Many countries lack data and analysis disaggregated by sex, age and ethnicity, among other characteristics, that limit policy and programme development.[86] Since gender equality is a core component of the MDGs, good data are essential for effective policies and resource allocation, for example, calculating poverty indicators according to sex rather than only by total household income, as is now the case.[87] More accurate and extensive data will be critical for advocacy to keep gender issues in the public and media spotlight, to improve communities' and policymakers' understanding of gender issues and to stimulate action.

Governments, United Nations organizations, the regional economic commissions and the Demographic and Health Surveys have made progress in gender-sensitive data collection and analysis.[88] While progress has been made in developing data methodologies that capture gender differences, a limited number of countries make use of them.[89] Particularly innovative is the Index of Fulfilled Commitments developed in Chile by women's organizations to monitor governmental accountability in the key areas of citizen participation, economic rights and reproductive health.[90]

> *"The under-representation of women in decision-making structures reflects the level of maturity of the democratic process...and is an indication that a society is less democratic and less egalitarian."*
>
> — Declaration on Gender Equality in Africa, Heads of State and Government of Member States of the African Union, Addis Ababa, Ethiopia, July 2004

Although better data are essential for implementing the MDGs,[91] information alone will not produce changes. The purpose of information and analysis is to help policymakers integrate gender issues into all levels of policymaking, especially in the formulation of national poverty reduction strategies.[92]

**MAINSTREAMING GENDER: PROMISES, PRACTICES AND PROSPECTS.** Gender mainstreaming is essential to the implementation and monitoring of the MDGs. It means assessing the implications of policies and programmes for women and men by taking into account their different roles, needs and perspectives, so that inequalities are not perpetuated and both may benefit.[93] Gender mainstreaming also means examining how gender dynamics affect decision-making within families and communities—including whether girls will be sent to school and whether women have influence over how family resources are spent.[94]

Governments, civil society, women's groups, donors, development banks and the UN System have worked to strengthen their gender mainstreaming efforts. Many governments have established national women's ministries or units.[95] Progress, however, has been uneven and limited to smaller projects in most countries. Resources are generally inadequate, and misconceptions about the nature and purpose of gender mainstreaming hold back change.[96] Gender mainstreaming is often viewed as a woman's issue and segregated in under-funded women's ministries.[97]

On the other hand, some countries, including post-apartheid South Africa and post-war Cambodia (see Box 33), have taken advantage of political transitions to mainstream gender across development strategies. In South Africa, a powerful women's movement; a strong government mandate to mainstream gender; a new constitution; a supportive legal framework; and gender-sensitive budgeting have all contributed to a successful gender mainstreaming strategy.[98] Malawi has embarked on gender training for policymakers, district assembly staff and media representatives, as have many other countries seeking to build and expand capacity in this area.[99] In West African countries, government officials from ministries of planning and public administration, parliamentarians, political party leaders and labour unions have been trained on a gender-sensitive approach with UNFPA support. Specific efforts are being made to work with teams responsible for formulating national poverty reduction strategies. In the Arab States, UNFPA has collaborated with the Centre for Arab Women, Training and Research on integrating gender in development planning and policies, training government officials and improving collection and analysis of sex-disaggregated data.[100]

In the Dominican Republic, with UNFPA support, the Ministry of Women's Affairs has formed partnerships with the Ministry of Defense, the national police, congress, the women's movement, the UN and donors. The Government's commitment to mainstreaming gender is reflected in the creation of Gender Equity and Development Offices in all ministries. Violence against women is being tackled through legislative reform and the formation of coalitions between political parties and among the 700 women who hold local political office.

Achievements include the revision of school curricula so they are more gender-sensitive; a new law on domestic violence; criminal code reform; new migration and anti-trafficking laws; legal protections for elderly women; a data registration system on violence; a shelter for trafficked and returned women; and equipment specifically earmarked for the Integral Health Care Units for Abused Women that are now being set up in the offices of public prosecutors.

In Nicaragua, the Government's Emergency Fund for Social Investment (FISE), the leading channel for disbursing funds under national poverty reduction and development policies, is being assisted by UNFPA to mainstream gender. FISE projects, directed to rural communities, are becoming increasingly "gender democratic". Women are now being encouraged to participate in decision-making within the organizations and businesses they run, own and profit from—including the establishment of schools, mills, dairies, poultry operations and water and sanitation systems.

> "This water project was a priority to all villagers. We chose it in the community assembly, where all adults, men and women, were invited. For the first time, women felt they had their say in community affairs, and I, a woman, was elected as coordinator of the project."
>
> — Ana Marcia Estrada, FISE project coordinator in the village of Cosiguina, Nicaragua

**FOLLOWING THE MONEY: GENDER-RESPONSIVE BUDGETING.** Gender-responsive budgeting is an innovative approach designed to influence policy and improve government accountability towards gender equality goals. It promotes economic efficiency, equality, accountability and transparency.[101] Careful analysis of budgets using sex-disaggregated data can reveal funding gaps so that priorities can be adjusted to advance poverty reduction, gender equality and development.

Various civil society organizations around the world and leading women economists have advanced the field. UNIFEM has provided support to gender budget initiatives in some 30 countries, and other UN agencies and donors have more recently joined in supporting this work, with more than 50 countries now applying this approach.[102] South Africa was among the first to implement gender budgeting in 1995. Rwanda's budget prioritizes gender equality, and all sectoral budgets are prepared with the Ministry of Gender's participation.[103] In Mexico, a well-recognized gender budgeting process was initiated by non-governmental organizations.[104] In Chile, procedures for gender-responsive analysis of policies and budgets were introduced by the Ministry of Finance in 2001, and gender is one of six mandatory areas for reporting by ministries.[105] Botswana offered training on gender-sensitive budgeting to government officials and parliamentarians, as has Malaysia for selected ministries. Guidelines were issued for mainstreaming gender across ministry budgets in the United Republic of Tanzania.[106] UNFPA has supported efforts in countries ranging from Cape Verde to Guatemala to Malaysia.

Gender budgeting has also been applied at decentralized levels of government with some success. In Cuenca, Ecuador, a gender-responsive budgeting exercise supported by UNIFEM led to the adoption of an Equal Opportunities Plan that emphasizes addressing gender-based violence through social, legal and health services. The city's budget for 2003 increased resources devoted to promoting gender equality by 15 times as compared to 2001.[107] In Paraguay, a UNFPA-supported gender budget analysis by the Commission on Social Equity and Gender in the Municipality of Asunción led to a 300 per cent increase in allocations for family planning commodities for the capital's Polyclinic.

In South Asia, a region with large populations living in poverty, India, Nepal and Sri Lanka have launched gender budgeting initiatives with UNIFEM support. India quantified the economic role of women, analysed the impact of programmes on food security, health and women's employment, and reviewed public expenditures in technical education. In a 2004 speech, the Finance Minister announced that the 2005 budget would be formulated with a gender perspective, directing 18 ministries to submit their 2005 budgets reflecting allocations and expenditure on women.[108]

**PUSHING FOR CHANGE: CIVIL SOCIETY'S CRITICAL ROLE.** Promoting gender equality requires stakeholders to engage in strong efforts to alter the status quo. Civil society, and women's groups in particular, have a central role to play in supporting community participation, offering gender expertise and maintaining policy focus and accountability. These groups are also well-positioned to identify and promote gender-sensitive responses to poverty reduction throughout the decision-making process—from involvement in policy design and in setting budget priorities to monitoring results.[109]

One good example is the ten-year partnership between the Latin America and Caribbean Women's Health Network and UNFPA. The Network pioneered a methodology for monitoring ICPD goals and reporting on progress periodically. The database of indicators known as Atenea has become a leading reference for gender-sensitive information on ICPD follow-up. The data and analyses have been used by parliamentarians and government officials, served as the foundation for public policy formulation in Suriname, and formed the basis of reporting on women's rights by civil society organizations.

# 3 The Promise of Human Rights

> *"Sixty years have passed since the founders of the United Nations inscribed, on the first page of our Charter, the equal rights of men and women. Since then, study after study has taught us that there is no tool for development more effective than the empowerment of women. No other policy is as likely to raise economic productivity, or to reduce infant and maternal mortality. No other policy is as sure to improve nutrition and promote health—including the prevention of HIV/AIDS. No other policy is as powerful in increasing the chances of education for the next generation. And I would also venture that no policy is more important in preventing conflict, or in achieving reconciliation after a conflict has ended. But whatever the very real benefits of investing in women, the most important fact remains: Women themselves have the right to live in dignity, in freedom from want and from fear."*
>
> — UN Secretary-General Kofi Annan, UN Commission on the Status of Women

One of the major achievements of the 20th Century was the development of a rich body of international law affirming the equal rights of all human beings. Building on the foundation of the 1948 Universal Declaration of Human Rights, numerous conventions,[1] protocols[2] and agreements have affirmed and expanded its principles. But despite the many agreements embraced and treaties ratified, the reality is that in the early 21st century, women and other neglected groups, especially those whose lives are circumscribed by poverty and discrimination, are not able to exercise their fundamental human rights. The next major challenge is fulfilling the promise of human rights.

Human rights, women's rights among them, are fundamental to poverty reduction and development, yet their importance is not always fully understood. Poverty is characterized by exclusion and lack of power to claim legitimate rights.[3] The 1986 UN Declaration on the Right to Development recognized the right "to participate in, contribute to and enjoy economic, social, cultural and political development, in which human rights and fundamental freedoms can be fully realized". The eradication of extreme poverty as called for by the Millennium Development Goals (MDGs) relies on the fulfilment of the rights of individuals through expanded opportunities, choices and power. The relationship between poverty and human rights is embodied in the UN Millennium Declaration of 2000, in which 189 countries pledged to uphold the Universal Declaration of Human Rights, and to advance the rights of women.

Fulfilling the promise of human rights calls for transformations in the underlying value systems that legitimize discrimination. Internationally accepted standards of human rights provide a framework to guide and measure progress. The dedicated efforts of civil society, parliamentarians and the media in holding governments and other key actors accountable are crucial to maintaining momentum. And the notion that all of humankind is bound by shared human rights has an inherent power, which rights-based approaches to human development can unleash (see Box 6).

Human rights education, and the active participation of those whom development efforts and decisions have passed by, are central to a rights-based approach. Armed with information about rights and equipped with the skills and resources to claim them, individuals and communities can become agents of change and gain control over their own destinies.[4] The empowerment conferred by this sense of entitlement contributes to the momentum and sustainability of rights-based approaches. It is also essential to sensitize those responsible for protecting human rights, including police officers, judges, military personnel and health providers. More such efforts are needed before everyone, especially those who are doubly or triply disenfranchised by poverty, gender and other forms of discrimination, can fully exercise their fundamental rights.

## Human Rights and Poverty Reduction

Expanding freedoms and choices is the goal of human development. Poverty and discrimination diminish freedom by depriving individuals of opportunities to exercise their fundamental human rights. A human rights-based approach to ending poverty and deprivation is at the forefront of UN reform[5] and central to the UN Millennium Declaration.

Because human rights are interdependent and mutually reinforcing, they can become part of a virtuous circle that enables people to overcome poverty. The denial of human rights, on the other hand, can lead to a vicious cycle that entraps individuals in a life of highly restricted choices. A woman whose right to education is denied, for example, is more likely to face compromises to her rights to health, to vote, to marry voluntarily and to choose the number and spacing of her children.

The Office of the High Commissioner for Human Rights provides guidelines to countries on how to apply a rights-based approach in developing poverty reduction policies.[6] They point out that empowering people living in poverty is necessary for effective poverty reduction. They also emphasize that duty-bearers are responsible for upholding international human rights standards (see Box 6).[7]

From a human rights standpoint, addressing poverty is more than a moral obligation. Under international law, both national governments and the wider international community bear responsibility for addressing extreme poverty and the inequities that characterize it.[8] Thus human rights have become a powerful instrument for galvanizing support for the MDGs.[9] Even in situations where governments have explicitly recognized human rights, resource constraints—human, financial and technical—may make it impossible to satisfy the claims of all rights-holders at once. In such circumstances, it may be necessary to set priorities and progressively realize rights.[10] However, under a rights-based approach, no effort must be spared in guaranteeing the core set of rights reflected in the MDGs, such as the rights to personal security, survival, food, shelter, education and health.

Like the MDGs themselves, a rights-based approach gives priority to the most impoverished and marginalized groups whose rights are so often ignored, and calls for a more equitable distribution of resources in their favour.[11] Various resolutions and reports presented to the UN Commission on Human Rights (which is expected to undergo reforms following the UN Secretary-General's recommendations[12]) have called particular attention to the needs of women, especially heads of households and older women, "who often bear the greatest burden of extreme poverty".[13] The report of one independent expert noted that programmes to eradicate extreme poverty "must focus on women" since "allowing women to enjoy all their rights…has a major impact on the enjoyment of these rights for the society as a whole".[14]

## The Human Rights of Girls and Women

Many countries have enshrined the human rights of women in their national legislation. Several prohibit employment discrimination.[15] A number punish gender-based violence, including domestic abuse, and outlaw child marriage and discrimination against girls within the family.[16] About 25 countries have banned female genital mutilation/cutting.[17] Some have taken steps to increase women's awareness of their legal rights and facilitated their access to legal services.[18] More women now serve as judges.[19] Women themselves have been at the forefront of these efforts, galvanizing support and strengthening enforcement.

---

### 6 THE RIGHTS-BASED APPROACH: FROM NEEDS TO RIGHTS

The rights-based approach marks a shift away from an earlier development focus on meeting basic *needs*, which relied on charity or good will. A rights-based approach, in contrast, recognizes individuals as "rights-holders", which implies that others are "duty-bearers". Needs, on the other hand, have no object—there is no person or mechanism designated to meet them.

Under a human rights framework, governments are the primary duty-bearers. Among their duties are the establishment of equitable laws and systems that enable individuals to exercise and enjoy their rights, and to seek judicial recourse for violations under the rule of law. As rights-holders, people can claim their legitimate entitlements. This approach emphasizes the participation of individuals and communities in decision-making processes that shape policies and programmes that affect them.

Despite these achievements, progress is uneven. Across most of the world, women and girls face discrimination. They have fewer social, economic and legal rights than men.[20] Inequalities abound: In some countries, a man can rape a woman with impunity if he then marries her. He can be exonerated for beating or killing his wife if he catches her in an act of adultery.[21] Legal systems are permeated by social norms that reinforce gender inequality, foster mistrust by women[22] and leave many women without effective recourse to justice.

Customary laws and practices sometimes take precedence over constitutional and legal provisions for equality. This is especially so in the areas of family, inheritance and land rights, nationality and personal status.[23] Even where progressive laws are in place, weak enforcement mechanisms and lack of funding often undercut their effectiveness. In many countries, women—especially those who are poor—are largely unaware of their rights and the laws that ostensibly protect them.[24]

### THE FRAMEWORK FOR WOMEN'S HUMAN RIGHTS.
All human rights instruments apply equally to all people, but the two conventions that provide the most explicit protection of the rights of women and girls are the 1979 Convention on the Elimination of All Forms of Discrimination Against Women (CEDAW), and the 1989 UN Convention on the Rights of the Child (CRC).

The UN conferences of the 1990s bolstered the framework for women's human rights. In a historic declaration, the 1993 UN World Conference on Human Rights in Vienna for the first time confirmed women's rights as human rights.[25] The platforms that emerged from the 1994 International Conference on Population and Development (ICPD) and the 1995 Fourth World Conference on Women (Beijing) provide concrete action plans on women's human rights.[26] They form the basis for many national policy and legislative reforms.

When they ratified CEDAW, 180 countries agreed to promote gender equality and combat discrimination against women. The Convention, which is nearing universal ratification, obliges states that are party to CEDAW to abolish discriminatory laws, customs and practices, establish public institutions and take measures to protect women's equal rights. However, the inclusion of gender equality in the MDGs is a reminder that many promises have yet to be kept. Many countries have missed the 2005 target set at Beijing to revoke all discriminatory laws based on sex.[27] Lack of resolve is also suggested by the many reservations by governments to articles of CEDAW that they do not accept as binding. The most problematic are those to Article 2—the core provision on gender discrimination—because these reservations essentially negate the convention's main objective.

Regional instruments also provide protections for the human rights of women. Particularly noteworthy is the 1994 Inter-American Convention on the Prevention, Punishment and Eradication of Violence against Women, the only treaty of its kind exclusively focused on gender-based violence.[28] Another important instrument is the 2003 Protocol to the African Charter on Human and People's Rights that sets out a bill of rights for the continent's women.[29]

Translating these powerful human rights instruments into concrete change in the lives of women and girls depends on sustained and concerted action at the country level. Civil society actors, especially women's organizations, play a critical role in promoting accountability and monitoring implementation and enforcement: Women's groups have pressed for CEDAW implementation by working with government agencies, writing "shadow" reports and publicizing recommendations on compliance. The "Global to Local" programme of International Women's Rights Action Watch trains NGOs on how to implement CEDAW. In Kenya, the United Republic of Tanzania and Uganda, women's groups are using the convention to build a roster of judges to enforce property and inheritance rights.[30] In the Arab States, UNFPA facilitates training on CEDAW and works to further gender-sensitive strategies that enshrine the spirit and letter of the convention.[31] Parliamentarians also play a key role. In Mexico, the Netherlands, Sweden

> *"No individual and no nation must be denied the opportunity to benefit from development. The equal rights and opportunities of men and women must be assured."*
> — 2000 UN Millennium Declaration

> **7 TRAINING YOUNG WOMEN LEADERS ON HUMAN RIGHTS**
>
> The Latin American and Caribbean Youth Network on Sexual and Reproductive Rights, established in 1999, is a youth-led organization with membership in 17 countries. It promotes a vision of development based on young people's perspectives, gender equality and human rights. In collaboration with the United Nations Latin American Institute for the Prevention of Crime and the Treatment of Offenders, the Network has developed a groundbreaking manual on human rights treaties and gender equality. With UNFPA support, it has trained 100 young women leaders on human rights, preparing them to play a greater role in national and local policymaking.

and Uruguay, for example, parliamentary sessions are devoted to reviewing progress on CEDAW and charting follow-up action on the convention's implementation.[32]

## Human Rights: Essentials for the MDGs

Among the core rights identified by the UN Millennium Project are the equal rights of women and girls, including reproductive rights and the right to freedom from violence (see Chapter 7).[33] Furthermore, the right to health, and the rights of people living with HIV, are critical. A rights-based approach to the MDGs can help bridge the equity gap that prevents disenfranchised individuals and groups from enjoying their fundamental rights.

**THE RIGHT TO HEALTH.** All human beings are entitled to a healthy and productive life.[34] The right to health[35] is central to several MDGs, including reducing infant and maternal mortality and combating major diseases. Because health—defined by the World Health Organization as "a state of complete physical, mental and social well-being, not merely the absence of disease or infirmity"[36]—affects productivity, the right to health underpins all the goals for poverty reduction and development. Safe drinking water, basic sanitation, food security and adequate nutrition are necessary preconditions for preserving health. The ability to attain the highest possible standard of health also depends on the *availability, accessibility, acceptability* and *quality* of health services.[37] Poor and rural areas have few health services, and transportation can be costly or simply non-existent. Women and adolescents living in poverty are usually the least able to pay for services or medicines. Services available to the poor are often sub-standard, and discriminatory attitudes and poor treatment can keep impoverished clients from returning. Eliminating these biases, improving the quality of care, engendering health systems, and allocating resources in a way that provides more people the opportunity to enjoy their right to health— including reproductive health—are at the heart of efforts to meet the MDGs.

**HUMAN RIGHTS AND HIV/AIDS.** Over the last decade, the international community has called attention to the rights of people living with HIV to dignity and non-discrimination. As the epidemic increasingly affects women (see Chapter 4), the rights of HIV-positive women and the importance of reproductive rights have become all the more critical to halting its spread. Rights to information and to voluntary family planning, as well as freedom from coercion, are critical in this regard.

The Joint United Nations Programme on HIV/AIDS (UNAIDS) has developed international guidelines to support countries designing national strategies and

> **8 REDUCING STIGMA AND EMPOWERING PEOPLE LIVING WITH HIV/AIDS**
>
> In Central America, more people living with HIV/AIDS are now aware of laws to protect their human rights through their national human rights institutions. Since 2003, UNFPA has partnered with the Inter-American Institute of Human Rights, the Central American Council of Human Rights Lawyers and parliamentarians to strengthen a rights-based approach to HIV/AIDS. Analysis of existing laws in the region showed that gender-differentiated needs, roles and responses to the epidemic were not adequately addressed. The initiative, jointly supported by UNFPA and the International Labour Organization (ILO), also assessed laws governing discrimination in the workplace in order to increase legal access for people living with HIV/AIDS. In Panama, the People's Council (Defensoría del Pueblo) is now included in the national HIV/AIDS programme. In Honduras, a network of human rights and HIV/AIDS lawyers has been created to fight injustice. In Honduras and Panama, a growing number of people living with HIV/AIDS are seeking legal counsel. In Costa Rica, campaigns on HIV prevention and human rights are changing perceptions and working to end stigma and discrimination.

policies to reverse the epidemic.[38] Some countries have passed legislation to protect the rights of people living with HIV/AIDS, for example, to treatment and to non-discrimination in the workplace. Many others have yet to enact laws: Almost half of sub-Saharan African countries and almost 40 per cent worldwide by the end of 2003 had no laws to prevent discrimination against persons living with HIV/AIDS.[39] Few laws address the gender dimensions of the epidemic.[40]

**REPRODUCTIVE RIGHTS.** Reproductive rights, and their centrality to development, were clarified and endorsed internationally for the first time at the 1994 ICPD.[41] This constellation of rights, embracing fundamental human rights established by earlier treaties, was reaffirmed at the Beijing Conference and various international and regional agreements since, as well as in many national laws. The importance of reproductive rights has increasingly been addressed by the international human rights system. Reproductive rights are recognized as valuable ends in themselves, and essential to the enjoyment of other fundamental rights. Special emphasis has been given to the reproductive rights of women and adolescent girls, and to the importance of sex education and reproductive health programmes.[42]

If all individuals and couples could exercise their reproductive rights, progress toward the MDGs would accelerate. The ability to make informed decisions concerning reproductive health, marriage and childbearing without any form of discrimination or coercion is closely correlated with a country's prospects of reducing poverty, improving health and education, raising productivity and living standards, and achieving environmental sustainability. For example, reducing unintended pregnancies through access to voluntary family planning contributes to the reduction of infant and maternal mortality and of mother-to-child HIV transmission. Other ways in which reproductive rights advance MDGs are shown in selected examples provided in Box 9.

*"Reproductive rights...rest on the recognition of the basic right of all couples and individuals to decide freely and responsibly the number, spacing and timing of their children and to have the information and means to do so, and the right to attain the highest standard of sexual and reproductive health. It also includes their right to make decisions concerning reproduction free of discrimination, coercion and violence."*

— ICPD Programme of Action, paragraph 7.3

In UNFPA's 2004 Global Survey on ICPD implementation, 131 countries reported adopting national measures on reproductive rights.[43] However, in many countries, national legislation is still silent and lacks specific measures to effectively safeguard them, with some commendable exceptions.[44] Recent examples of policies and laws, several of which are noteworthy for their comprehensive approach, include Albania, Argentina, Benin, Chad, Colombia, Guinea, Mali and Mexico.[45] Peru and Slovakia passed laws on access to voluntary family planning and guaranteed the right to informed consent regarding surgical contraception.[46] In 2004, El Salvador amended its Labour Code to bar pregnancy testing as a condition of employment. The United Republic of Tanzania's 2004 Employment and Labour Relations Act prohibits discrimination based on gender, pregnancy, disability or marital or HIV status, with specific provisions for paid maternity and paternity leave and breastfeeding breaks.[47]

In some countries, the mandates of national parliamentary and human rights commissions have been expanded to monitor reproductive rights, and complaint mechanisms have been set up. In 2003, ombudsmen from Caribbean countries received training on how human rights apply to reproductive rights, an initiative co-sponsored by UNFPA. Parliamentarians also have played a key role in keeping reproductive health and rights in the public spotlight through supportive declarations at international parliamentary conferences co-sponsored by UNFPA in Ottawa (2002) and Strasbourg (2004).[48]

## Reproductive Rights in Practice

Neglect and violations of women's reproductive rights often happen behind closed doors. Women and adolescent girls may lack the power to negotiate reproductive decisions with their partners and within their families and to navigate health and legal systems. The wider sociocultural and economic environment influences the opportunities and choices

## 9 | REPRODUCTIVE RIGHTS AND THE MDGS

| Elements of Reproductive Rights | Examples of Rights-based Actions | Relevance to specific MDGs |
|---|---|---|
| **Right to life and survival** | Prevent avoidable maternal and infant deaths<br><br>End neglect of and discrimination against girls that can contribute to premature deaths<br><br>Ensure access to information and methods to prevent sexually transmitted infections, including HIV | Promote gender equality and empower women (MDG 3)<br><br>Reduce child mortality (MDG 4)<br><br>Improve maternal health (MDG 5)<br><br>Combat HIV/AIDS, malaria and other diseases (MDG 6) |
| **Right to liberty and security of the person** | Take measures to prevent, punish and eradicate all forms of gender-based violence<br><br>Enable women, men and adolescents to make reproductive decisions free of coercion, violence and discrimination<br><br>Eliminate female genital mutilation/cutting<br><br>Stop sexual trafficking | Eradicate extreme poverty and hunger (MDG 1)<br><br>Promote gender equality and empower women (MDG 3)<br><br>Reduce child mortality (MDG 4)<br><br>Improve maternal health (MDG 5)<br><br>Combat HIV/AIDS, malaria and other diseases (MDG 6) |
| **Right to seek, receive and impart information** | Make information about reproductive health and rights issues and related policies and laws widely and freely available<br><br>Provide full information for people to make informed reproductive health decisions<br><br>Support reproductive health and family life education both in and out of schools | Promote gender equality and empower women (MDG 3)<br><br>Combat HIV/AIDS, malaria and other diseases (MDG 6) |
| **Right to decide the number, timing and spacing of children** | Provide people with full information that enables them to choose and correctly use a family planning method<br><br>Provide access to a full range of modern contraceptive methods<br><br>Enable adolescent girls to delay pregnancy | Eradicate extreme poverty and hunger (MDG 1)<br><br>Achieve universal primary education (MDG 2)<br><br>Promote gender equality and empower women (MDG 3)<br><br>Ensure environmental stability (MDG 7) |
| **Right to voluntarily marry and establish a family** | Prevent and legislate against child and forced marriages<br><br>Prevent and treat sexually transmitted infections that cause infertility<br><br>Provide reproductive health services, including for HIV prevention, to married adolescent girls and their husbands | Achieve universal primary education (MDG 2)<br><br>Promote gender equality and empower women (MDG 3)<br><br>Reduce child mortality (MDG 4)<br><br>Improve maternal health (MDG 5)<br><br>Combat HIV/AIDS, malaria and other diseases (MDG 6) |
| **Right to the highest attainable standard of health** | Provide access to affordable, acceptable, comprehensive and quality reproductive health information and services<br><br>Allocate available resources fairly, prioritizing those with least access to reproductive health education and services | Eradicate extreme poverty and hunger (MDG 1)<br><br>Promote gender equality and empower women (MDG 3)<br><br>Reduce child mortality (MDG 4)<br><br>Improve maternal health (MDG 5)<br><br>Combat HIV/AIDS, malaria and other diseases (MDG 6) |
| **Right to the benefits of scientific progress** | Fund contraceptive research, including female-controlled methods, microbicides and male methods<br><br>Offer a variety of contraceptive options<br><br>Provide access to emergency obstetric care that can prevent maternal deaths and obstetric fistula | Promote gender equality and empower women (MDG 3)<br><br>Reduce child mortality (MDG 4)<br><br>Improve maternal health (MDG 5)<br><br>Combat HIV/AIDS, malaria and other diseases (MDG 6) |
| **Right to non-discrimination and equality in education and employment** | Prohibit discrimination in employment based on pregnancy, proof of contraceptive use or motherhood<br><br>Establish programmes to keep girls in schools<br><br>Ensure pregnant and married adolescent girls, and young mothers, are able to complete their education | Eradicate extreme poverty and hunger (MDG 1)<br><br>Achieve universal primary education (MDG 2)<br><br>Promote gender equality and empower women (MDG 3)<br><br>Combat HIV/AIDS, malaria and other diseases (MDG 6) |

that men and women have in the realm of reproductive health and rights. Rights-based approaches take these factors into consideration. For example, rights-based reproductive health programmes may encourage shared responsibility for reproductive health by counselling couples. They can mobilize communities to understand the risks of child marriage and too early or poorly spaced births, thereby fostering a supportive environment in which decisions are made. Rather than simply making condoms available, a rights-based approach will seek to empower women, to sensitize their partners and facilitate mutual cooperation and negotiation on condom use.[49]

Real progress on the right to health and reproductive rights often occurs when "rights-holders" (clients) and "duty-bearers" (health providers) work together on solutions. An early example was the International Planned Parenthood Federation's (IPPF) widely distributed Charter on Rights of the Client (1992) that considered quality of care from the client's perspective and provided education about rights to information and confidentiality. Informing service providers of their obligations is important as well. The Charter on Sexual and Reproductive Rights, issued by IPPF a few years later, encouraged their affiliates to ensure respect for reproductive rights and to hold governments accountable.[50]

Another good example is UNFPA-supported efforts in Ecuador to implement the 1998 Law on Free Maternity Care. This legislation, like a similar policy enacted in Bolivia, provides free access to a package of pregnancy-related services, family planning and health care for children under five. Though the Government allocated resources for its enforcement, challenges remain. In response, the government has set up local committees charged with managing local health funds in collaboration with the Ministry of Health, municipal authorities, the National Council of Women and community organizations. Service users' committees have also been established, and meet with women from the surrounding communities to raise awareness about the law and discuss and monitor implementation.

## Rights, Gender and Culture: Seeking Convergence

The concept of human rights binds the world's inhabitants into a common humanity. Human rights standards globally adopted make clear the distinction between respect for the rich diversity of the world's cultures and customs and the rejection of harmful practices that endanger women and girls. CEDAW and CRC, among other international agreements, make this explicit, by clarifying that governments should refrain from invoking custom, tradition or religious beliefs to justify harmful practices that interfere with human rights, and that also constitute forms of violence and violations of women's reproductive rights.[51] Nevertheless, cultural relativism, and the label of international human rights as "Western", have been used to legitimize harmful practices and laws that perpetuate gender inequities.[52] Existing standards, however, reflect a clear international consensus to guide national action and accountability.

A number of harmful practices are deeply rooted in tradition. Though many reflect an underlying gender bias, they have been practised by parents and grandparents and passed from one generation to the next. They are thus commonly accepted facets of community life. But culture is not static: It is dynamic and learned.[53] People are not passive products of their cultures but are active participants in interpreting and shaping them. As experience around the world has shown, communities that understand the dangers posed by certain practices, and question them from within their own cultural lens, can mobilize to change or eliminate them.

Culturally sensitive approaches can be effective in promoting human rights and gender equality in diverse national and local contexts.[54] Such approaches

*"The ability of women to control their own fertility is absolutely fundamental to women's empowerment and equality. When a woman can plan her family, she can plan the rest of her life. When she is healthy, she can be more productive. And when her reproductive rights...are promoted and protected, she has freedom to participate more fully and equally in society. Reproductive rights are essential to women's advancement."*

— Thoraya A. Obaid, UNFPA Executive Director

emphasize the importance of understanding the complexities of the sociocultural context in which development processes operate. They assess the roles and perspectives of a range of actors, and look at how changes at both policy and societal levels can be effected. This includes analyzing local power structures and listening to the views of local leaders and custodians of prevailing cultural norms and beliefs. It also includes identifying sub-cultures and ensuring the participation of those whose voices are not traditionally heard, such as women, adolescents, ethnic minorities and others. Culturally sensitive approaches centre on community dialogue and awareness-raising about human rights and gender issues, using language and social symbols that the community can internalize.

Efforts to outlaw discriminatory practices such as child marriage, honour killings, acid burning and the inheritance or "cleansing" of widows, among others, are unlikely to succeed unless they are accompanied by practical measures to promote gender-equitable norms that respect the rights of girls and women. For instance, some countries in sub-Saharan Africa and Asia have outlawed female genital mutilation/cutting, prenatal sex selection or child marriage, but find it difficult to enforce these bans. As long as daughters face discrimination and are devalued, especially in the context of poor families' limited choices, simply outlawing child marriage will not succeed. Similarly, it may be difficult to eliminate female genital mutilation/cutting where it is closely tied to a woman's marriage prospects and social identity. The practice is often encouraged by relatives and signals a girl's entry into a position of greater social recognition and status.

Transformations in gender attitudes and norms are possible, however, especially when the views and concerns of the community are addressed. Successful attempts to reduce female genital mutilation/cutting, for example, have been accompanied by acceptance of non-harmful rituals to serve the same social purpose, thus preserving values important to the community.[55] The participation of socially prominent individuals, including religious leaders, can be crucial in changing social norms. A key element in the Islamic Republic of Iran's dramatic success with expanding access to family planning (the country's total fertility rate has dropped from an average of over seven children per woman to 2.3 over the last two decades[56]) was the full support of imams. They encouraged smaller families and issued religious edicts that endorsed a full range of contraceptive methods, including male sterilization.[57] In Yemen, a guide was produced for imams and other religious leaders that relates family planning and reproductive health to the Koran and stresses the Prophet's teachings on the equality of women and men. In Cambodia, partnerships with Buddhist monks and nuns are helping to address the threat of HIV to young people.[58]

By building on positive belief systems and cultural and religious values espoused by local communities, and raising awareness of the harm caused by gender stereotypes and related practices, culturally sensitive approaches serve to gain ground for women's human rights and gender equality.

## Support for Disenfranchised Groups

Since the 1990s, more emphasis has been placed on securing the rights of historically neglected and marginalized groups. These include persons with disabilities, migrant workers and ethnic, racial and religious minorities and castes, including the *Dalits* or "untouchables" in India, the Roma in Europe and indigenous communities in Latin America and elsewhere. The rights of women and children in humanitarian crises and of adolescents—two groups who represent large and critical sections of their countries' population—will be discussed in later chapters.

Together, these marginalized groups represent a sizeable share of the global population: disabled persons account for 10 per cent (or 600 million);[59] indigenous people, for 370 million living in some 70 countries;[60] international migrants number an estimated 175 million people.[61] People belonging to these groups tend to fare the worst in terms of MDG indicators, especially true in the case of indigenous people who are often among the poorest of the poor. They frequently have inadequate access to clean water and

> "We did not know the law existed. The Users' Committee is helping us to understand that we have rights."
> — Woman from the Province of Manabí, Ecuador

## 10 STRONGER VOICES FOR REPRODUCTIVE HEALTH AND RIGHTS: EMPOWERING WOMEN, EMPOWERING COMMUNITIES

Quality of care is about rights as well as services. When individuals and communities understand their rights, they can demand appropriate care. This demand can, in turn, influence service providers and health systems by improving their understanding of how to supply better services. This is the premise behind the Stronger Voices for Reproductive Health initiative launched in 2001 by UNFPA in collaboration with ILO, UNICEF and WHO, and funded by the United Nations Foundation. By providing people with information about their rights, the initiative has mobilized residents of communities in India, Kyrgyzstan, Mauritania, Nepal, Peru and the United Republic of Tanzania to work together for improvements in their lives.

In four rural provinces or oblasts of Kyrgyzstan, the initiative has expanded awareness about the country's 2000 Law on Reproductive Rights. Communities, providers and local administration officials meet regularly to discuss the law, and local police, teachers and lawyers have been trained on reproductive rights. One of the major changes is that communities are now speaking out against the traditional practice of "bride-napping". Families are rescuing daughters who have been taken as brides against their will and tribal leaders are reviewing bride-napping cases.

*"Because of sexual and reproductive health problems and domestic violence, some families had problems, which were discussed on the village level. There were no common views on such issues. We did not know about the law on reproductive rights. We thought it was forbidden to write about sexual and reproductive health issues. Now we know about the law and our rights."*
— Aldayarova, 37, Kyrgyzstan

*"We never thought that it would happen to our daughter. Zarema went out with this young man only once. After some days...we were informed that she had been bride-napped. Our first thought was to bring her back home. But we respect our traditions, so we decided to leave her in that family for the time being. Later we met Zarema several times. I became more and more certain that she would not be happy in that family. So after two weeks, we brought her back. All participants in the workshops came to one conclusion: that first of all it is necessary to protect the interests and rights of individuals rather than society's....Four more families made the same decision; they did not sacrifice their daughters."*
— Zarema's mother, Kyrgyzstan

Peru's poor, indigenous populations, especially adolescent girls, face economic, sociocultural and gender barriers to reproductive health services. Stronger Voices operates in Lima's most densely populated urban district, San Juan de Lurigacho, where one third of the population is young and living in extreme poverty, and in the Amazonian jungle region of Pucallpa. Working with young people, health providers and parents, the initiative is reducing the stigma attached to adolescents' access to reproductive health services.

Young people are actively speaking up in community public forums. Adolescents and health care providers have held joint workshops to build trust and decide how to make services more youth-friendly. The DiscoAIDS event in Pucallpa, complete with lights, music and videos, drew more than 600 young people and 23 teachers to discuss prevention of sexually transmitted infections and HIV, condom use and peer pressure. Adolescent Health Policy Guidelines were developed by the Government through a participatory process with youth and other civil society organizations.

*"We have to take care of ourselves, make our own decisions, have our own ideas and be more responsible, because we are the only ones who are going to protect us, who are going to look out for us. We are responsible for our future."*
— Adolescent Girl, San Juan de Lurigacho

*"Many patients come once, and if you haven't treated them well, next time they don't come."*
— Health-care provider, Pucallpa

In India, women's self-help groups in Haryana State now sit at the negotiating table with district authorities at health services planning meetings and raise their reproductive health and rights concerns with service providers and panchayats (local village councils). Operating as "watch groups", they monitor the quality of care and safeguard women's rights. Providers are trained to consider client perspectives on the quality of care. The participatory process has broken the "culture of silence" that prevailed in the communities on harmful practices such as prenatal sex selection, violence and child marriage. Women in the community have become more forthcoming in communicating about human rights issues.

*"After the training, I discussed the sexual and reproductive health issue with both of my adolescent daughters, and also with my husband and neighbors. We discussed rights in much detail. Now, in case of any violence against women in our vicinity, we will not tolerate silently as we used to do before."*
— Woman participant in a village of Haryana State, India

other resources and may be pushed into fragile or degraded ecosystems. Compared to the general population of their countries, they have higher rates of infant and maternal mortality, greater vulnerability to HIV, less access to education and/or limited participation in the government and social systems that affect their lives.[62] All of these groups remain largely invisible and voiceless, often ignored by national policies and laws, even though they face multiple forms of discrimination, structural poverty and social exclusion.

Gender discrimination exacerbates inequities. Disabled adolescent girls and women are at particularly high risk of sexual abuse and have limited autonomy and access to education and employment. They also face risks of violations of their reproductive rights, including forced sterilization and infringements on their rights to marry and form a family.[63] Indigenous women are targets of both gender-specific and racially motivated violence. Poverty and limited access to resources further erode their economic and social rights, while patriarchal traditions present obstacles to decision-making and community participation.[64] Migrant women in search of work in cities or abroad are exposed to trafficking and exploitation and can end up living in slave-like conditions as domestic servants.[65]

Fortunately, an international human rights framework that offers greater protection for these vulnerable groups and that increasingly recognizes the added dimension of gender discrimination, has been evolving since the 1990s. In the last decade, legally-binding conventions,[66] world programmes of action,[67] the international human rights treaty bodies and special rapporteurs[68] have brought increasing attention and protections to advance their rights. Practical guidelines and human rights standards for

> **11 INDIGENOUS WOMEN: REGAINING PRIDE AND DEMANDING RIGHTS**
>
> In Ecuador and in other Latin American countries, UNFPA has been working for more than a decade with indigenous communities to address the powerlessness, discrimination and low self-esteem that women experience in their daily lives, whether within their families or when seeking services. Training on human rights issues and new opportunities for dialogue and reflection on gender equality have helped indigenous women regain pride in their cultural heritage. They have been empowered to tackle domestic violence and demand equal rights to political participation and in reproductive decisions—areas in which the voices of indigenous women were rarely heard.

implementation of national policies and programmes have been developed.[69] In some regions, such as in Africa, Asia and the Americas, specific conventions and forums focusing on the rights of indigenous people and of persons with disabilities have highlighted discrimination against these groups.[70] Civil society networks have mobilized and established advocacy groups to protect their rights. The International Indigenous Women's Forum, for instance, is a platform for advocacy and mobilization on their rights.[71] Some countries now explicitly recognize the rights of these groups, in some cases with specific attention to gender equality. National plans on indigenous people in Mexico and Nepal incorporate a gender perspective. Peru established constitutional provisions for their participation in elections.[72]

The unprecedented scale of both migration and trafficking has given rise to particular concern for the rights of migrant women. Many countries are taking measures to support women who have been victims of trafficking, and some governments have established immigration offices, telephone hotlines and access to information.[73] Jordan and the Philippines, with support from UNIFEM, have set minimum standards and special contracts for domestic workers.[74] The Philippines has established bilateral agreements to promote the rights of their female nationals working in domestic service abroad. Pakistan regulates recruitment agencies to prevent abuses, and India pays for domestic workers who escape from abuse abroad to return home.[75]

Nonetheless, the gap between promise and practice remains wide. The convention protecting indigenous people's rights, though adopted in 1989, has been ratified by only 17 countries.[76] The International Decade of the World's Indigenous Peoples ended in 2004 without meeting a key objective—adoption of a draft declaration to protect their rights.[77] Similarly, the 1990 convention protecting migrant workers' rights did not come into force until 2003, after the minimum number of countries required had ratified it.[78]

The 2000 Millennium Declaration explicitly calls attention to the rights of minorities and migrants, as well as inclusive political processes.[79] It provides renewed opportunity for a rights-based approach that can work to end the discrimination and exclusion of neglected groups—factors that underlie poverty and hamper prospects for achieving the MDGs.

# 4 Reproductive Health: A Measure of Equity

*"The differences in reproductive health between the rich and the poor—both between and within countries— are larger than in any other area of health care."*
— UN Millennium Project

Reproductive health problems are the leading cause of women's ill health and death worldwide. When both women and men are taken into account, reproductive health conditions are the second-highest cause of ill health globally, after communicable diseases (see Figure 1). These figures mask huge disparities, both among and within countries. Because reproductive health status depends so heavily on income and gender, addressing this issue becomes a matter of social justice, ethics and equity.

Reproductive health and rights are important ends in themselves. They form a foundation for satisfying relationships, harmonious family life and the dream of a better future. Reproductive health and rights are also keystones for meeting the Millennium Development Goals (MDGs): They offer women and young people greater control over their own destinies and afford them opportunities to overcome poverty. Yet poverty and gender discrimination prevent millions of people around the world from exercising their reproductive rights and safeguarding their reproductive health. The costs are highest for impoverished women and adolescent girls. Multiplied across families, communities and countries, these costs are exorbitant.

Universal access to reproductive health care is achievable, could prevent most reproductive health problems and could also spur progress across various areas of social and economic development, as discussed earlier in this report. Some countries, even those with high poverty levels, have demonstrated what political leadership combined with technical knowledge and resources can accomplish. Countries successful in reducing maternal mortality now include Bangladesh, Bolivia, China, Cuba, Egypt, Honduras, Indonesia, Jamaica, Malaysia, Sri Lanka, Thailand and Tunisia, among others.[1] Bangladesh, a least-developed country, has also made exceptional progress in expanding access to family planning.[2] Political leadership combined with broad social mobilization have characterized the few examples of success in reducing the spread of HIV—principally Brazil, Cambodia, Senegal, Thailand and Uganda.

Reproductive health questions and concerns cut across many aspects of social and economic life and are beyond the capacity of the health sector alone to resolve. But many problems and their costly consequences could be averted if reproductive health were routinely addressed within the context of primary health care as a first line of prevention and care. This will require strengthening health systems, building trust among the communities they serve and expanding access to reproductive health programmes that respond to social, cultural, economic and gender factors.

**COSTLY CONSEQUENCES FOR POVERTY REDUCTION.** A successful fight against poverty requires a healthy population free of reproductive problems. Though almost entirely preventable, reproductive health problems remain widespread in much of the developing world. They ruin lives, burden families, tax health systems and weaken countries. The costs range from the sorrow of a motherless child to the diminished energy and productivity of millions of women. They include maternal deaths, unintended pregnancies, high fertility, abandoned children, unsafe abortions and AIDS, as well as sexually transmitted infections and the cancers, infertility and newborn illnesses associated with them.

At the 1994 International Conference on Population and Development (ICPD), 179 governments pledged to make reproductive health care universally available "as soon as possible and no later than 2015".³ From that conference emerged the global consensus that reproductive rights are central to human rights, sustainable development, gender equality and women's empowerment. Though the goal of universal reproductive health care was not explicitly included as one of the MDGs, there is widespread international agreement that the MDGs can be met only with a redoubling of efforts and resources for reproductive health and rights. Indeed, the UN Millennium Project concludes that reproductive health is "critical to overall success in economic growth and poverty reduction" and remains one of the "key elements of adequate human capital" essential to achieving the MDGs.⁴

Poverty reduction, gender equality and reproductive health go hand in hand. They are interrelated and mutually reinforcing, and all have positive effects that can last for generations. Social and cultural assumptions about appropriate female and male roles strongly affect decisions regarding reproduction and sexual behaviour, which in turn influence prospects for social and economic development. When restrictive norms and stereotypes are transmitted to children, the cycles of gender discrimination, poor health and poverty are perpetuated. The effects show themselves in direct and indirect ways, most dramatically in the incidence of maternal deaths and injuries, and HIV infections.

## Maternal Death and Disability

Maternal death and injury rates throw into sharp relief the impact of poverty and gender inequity on reproductive health. Every minute one woman dies needlessly of pregnancy-related causes. This adds up to more than a half million mothers lost each year—a figure that has hardly improved over the past few decades.⁵ Another eight million or more suffer life-long health consequences from the complications of pregnancy.⁶ Every woman, rich or poor, faces a 15 per cent risk of complications around the time of delivery, but maternal death is practically nonexistent in developed regions.⁷ The lack of progress in reducing maternal mortality in many countries highlights the low value placed on the lives of women and testifies to their limited voice in setting public priorities. The lives of many women in developing countries could be saved with reproductive health interventions that people in rich countries take for granted.

*"Better health and education, and freedom to plan their family's future, will widen women's economic choices; but it will also liberate their minds and spirits."*
— Nafis Sadik, Secretary-General of the ICPD

**POVERTY, DISCRIMINATION AND MOTHERS' SURVIVAL.** Poverty increases the risks inherent in childbearing, and maternal mortality and morbidity deepen poverty. In sub-Saharan Africa, where high fertility multiplies the dangers mothers face over a lifetime, 1 in 16 women is likely to die as a consequence of pregnancy; in some of the poorest parts, as many as 1 in 6 face this risk. By comparison, in industrialized countries the lifetime risk is only 1 in 2,800.⁸ Ninety-nine per cent of maternal deaths occur in developing countries, almost all—95 per cent—in Africa and Asia.⁹

**Figure 1: The Global Burden of Sexual and Reproductive Health Conditions**

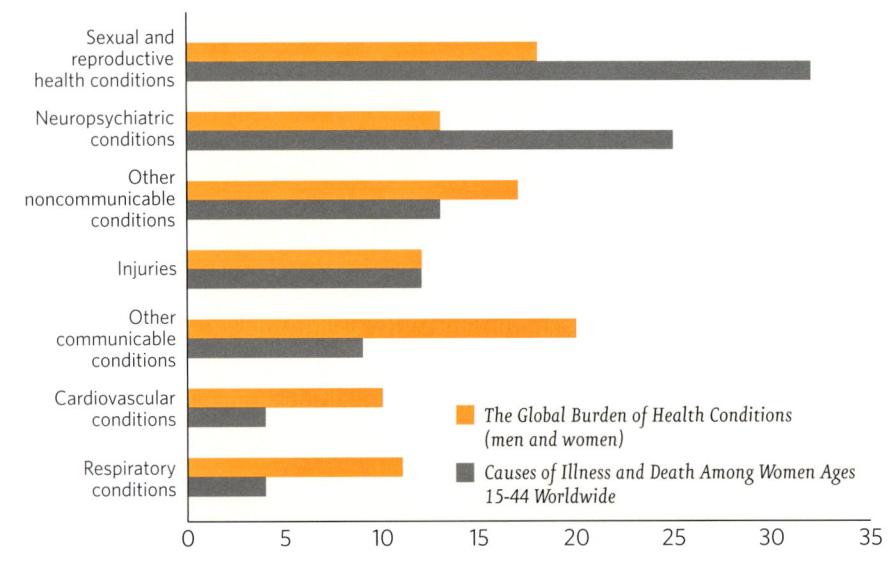

*The Global Burden of Health Conditions (men and women)*
*Causes of Illness and Death Among Women Ages 15-44 Worldwide*

**Source:** WHO, 2002, cited in Alan Guttmacher Institute/UNFPA, 2003, *Adding it Up: The Benefits of Investing in Sexual and Reproductive Healthcare.*

Wealth matters: Two thirds of maternal deaths in 2000 occurred in 13 of the world's poorest countries, and one quarter of these were in India alone.[10] Within countries, the wealthiest women have much better access to skilled obstetric care than the poor (see Figure 2).

Poverty and gender discrimination exacerbate reproductive health problems throughout the life cycle. The foundation for good reproductive health begins early in life. For instance, stunted growth in underfed girls increases the risks of obstructed labour later in life. Malnourished mothers and their babies are vulnerable to premature death and chronic disability. Anaemia, which can lead to post-partum haemorrhage, afflicts 50 to 70 per cent of pregnant women in developing countries.[11]

Gender discrimination related to education, health care and lack of control over economic resources and reproductive decisions further increase pregnancy-related risks. High levels of maternal mortality are associated with gender inequality.[12] Although using contraceptives can prevent 20 to 35 per cent of maternal deaths,[13] limited family planning supplies and services, as well as social norms, often bar women from using them. Inadequate education often leaves women with little or no understanding of childbearing risks and other health matters, including how to navigate the health system or negotiate timely life-saving care within the family. Informing women about their right to free care (where it exists) can be critical. High service costs can push families into poverty and deepen impoverishment. Fees may thus deter families from seeking services, especially when the quality of care provided is considered no better than that of trusted traditional birth attendants.

**PAYING THE PRICE: UNINTENDED PREGNANCY AND UNSAFE ABORTION.** Unsafe abortions are a leading cause of maternal mortality and can result in permanent injuries. Lack of access to family planning results in some 76 million unintended pregnancies every year in the developing world alone.[14] Each year, 19 million abortions are carried out under unsanitary or medically unsound conditions. These result in some 68,000 deaths.[15] Many women who seek abortions are married. They are usually poor and struggling to provide for children they already have.[16] Research

---

### 12 | LIKE MOTHER, LIKE CHILD

Good reproductive health care and the exercise of women's reproductive rights can help ensure that every infant is wanted, loved and has a chance to thrive. Conversely, a mother's poor reproductive health can undermine the health and well-being of her children.

Maternal and infant mortality are closely linked. When a mother dies giving birth, her infant often dies as well. Motherless newborns are three to ten times more likely to die than those with mothers who survive. Surviving children also suffer: Mothers are usually the primary guardians of the health, education and nutrition of their children, and in many cases, also a contributing or main breadwinner. Every year up to two million children lose their mothers for lack of services that are readily available in wealthier nations.

Birth spacing significantly reduces infant mortality. A two- to three-year interval between births reduces the chances of premature birth and low infant birth weight. Birth spacing is credited with reducing child mortality by close to 20 per cent in India, and 10 per cent in Nigeria. Unwanted children in general are more vulnerable than others to illness and premature death.

Routine screening of pregnant mothers for sexually transmitted infections can boost child survival as well, because these infections can cause miscarriages, stillbirth, premature birth, low infant birth weight, blindness, and pneumonia. Syphilis leads to illness or death in 40 per cent of infants afflicted. Voluntary testing for sexually transmitted infections and HIV can lead future mothers to treatments that can protect them and their children.

---

suggests that 1 in 10 pregnancies will end in an unsafe abortion, with Asia, Africa and Latin America accounting for the highest numbers.[17]

Unsafe abortion is one of the main reasons women and girls seek emergency care: In sub-Saharan Africa, post-abortion care takes up one fifth to half of all gynaecological beds.[18] Fearing exposure and judgmental attitudes from providers, many women delay seeking life-saving treatment until it is too late. The many costs of unsafe abortions far outweigh the price of the contraceptives that could prevent such suffering.

Recognizing the impact of unsafe abortion as "a major public health concern", the ICPD Programme of Action urges governments to spare no effort in preventing unwanted pregnancies and reducing "the recourse to abortion through expanded and improved family planning services".[19] The efficacy of this strategy is proven: Access to safe and effective contraception decreases the incidence of induced abortion.[20] In several countries of Central and Eastern Europe, abortion rates declined rapidly with the establishment of family planning information and services, increased supplies of contraceptives and the active involvement of civil society and religious groups.[21] The most dramatic decrease was reported in Romania, where abortion rates dropped from 52 to 11 per 1,000 in women aged 15 to 44 between 1995 and 1999.[22]

**MEN AND PREGNANCY.** Where pregnancy is defined as a "women's issue", the participation of men in the decisions and responsibilities it entails may be limited. Yet helping men and communities appreciate the risks of pregnancy can improve a woman's chance of obtaining life-saving care.[23] In Uganda, educating fathers about safer childbirth discouraged unsafe home deliveries.[24] In India, training physicians to involve men in maternity care resulted in more husbands accompanying their wives to antenatal clinics.[25] In rural China, a survey found that where husbands shared domestic chores and parenting responsibilities, women were more likely to receive prenatal care, to reduce their workloads before giving birth and to deliver under more sanitary conditions.[26] The Mother Friendly Movement in Indonesia—along with the Alert Husband programme—has helped communities recognize the need for maternal support and establish emergency transport for women in labour.[27]

**SAVING WOMEN'S LIVES.** Though safe motherhood has been high on the international agenda for nearly two decades, progress has been uneven, and in some countries maternal mortality rates are considered to be rising.[28] More is known about which strategies are most effective in averting maternal death and injury. They are: family planning to reduce unintended pregnancies, skilled attendance at all births, and appropriate and timely emergency obstetric care for all women who develop complications.[29] Weak health systems, limited transportation in remote and rural areas, shortage of skilled health providers, and the limited availability of contraceptives are among the major challenges. Gender discrimination can make it difficult to muster the political will and resources needed to implement change.

A leading initiative is the Averting Maternal Death and Disability programme to improve emergency obstetric care in developing countries. UNFPA, WHO, UNICEF and many non-governmental organizations have partnered with governments across the developing world to restructure health systems and build capacity. UNFPA supports programmes to expand access to skilled attendance at birth and emergency obstetric care for women in poor and rural areas, including health-provider training now being undertaken in 76 countries.[30] Uganda is tackling several of the challenges commonly faced in reducing maternal deaths, including equipping and staffing health centres with doctors and nurses, and establishing referrals and transportation to handle emergencies. A radio communication system ('RESCUER') and ambulance services have

**Figure 2: Births Attended by Skilled Personnel\* Among the Poorest and Richest Women**

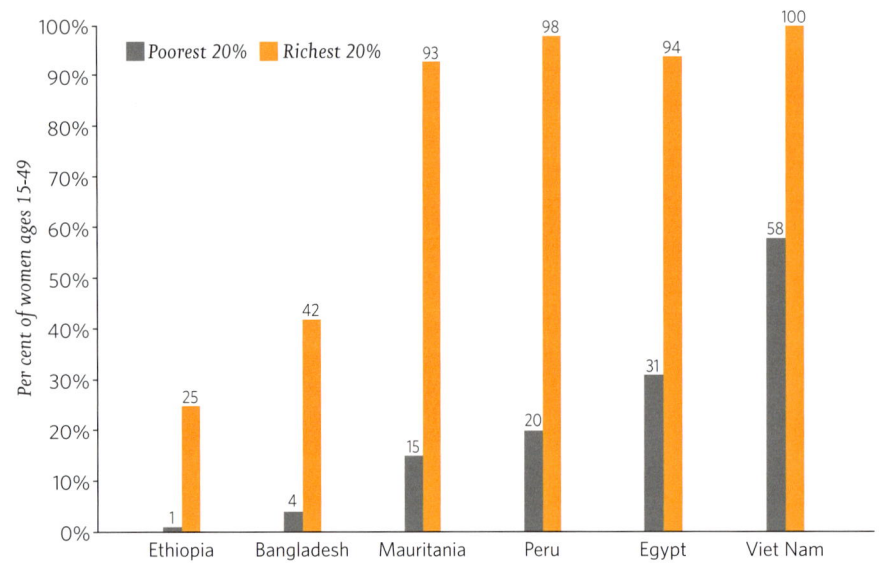

| Country | Poorest 20% | Richest 20% |
|---|---|---|
| Ethiopia | 1 | 25 |
| Bangladesh | 4 | 42 |
| Mauritania | 15 | 93 |
| Peru | 20 | 98 |
| Egypt | 31 | 94 |
| Viet Nam | 58 | 100 |

Per cent of women ages 15-49

\* Defined to include a doctor, nurse or trained midwife.

Source: World Bank, 2004, *Round II Country Reports on Health, Nutrition, and Population Conditions Among the Poor and the Better-Off in 56 Countries.*

been introduced in some areas.[31] In three regions of Nicaragua, the proportion of women who received emergency obstetric care climbed from 37 in 2000 to 50 per cent in 2003.[32] In Senegal, 100 rural women were saved within a year of UNFPA support to a local health centre.[33] In Yemen, the number of female providers has been increased, with 12,000 community midwives trained.[34]

Some countries are dealing with their acute shortage of doctors by delegating obstetric care to other skilled medical practitioners. For example, nurses in Mozambique have been trained to perform Caesarean sections.[35] In Nepal and Afghanistan—a country with one of the world's highest maternal death rates—midwives are being trained to provide skilled attendance at birth.[36]

Communities play a key role in reducing maternal mortality. Trusted local health workers can refer women to the formal health system and encourage them to deliver in safe settings. In poor countries, communities can pool resources to arrange emergency transport for women with complications, for example, by working with taxi, bus or truck drivers and their unions. In Honduras, community-based efforts helped cut maternal mortality by 37 per cent between 1990 and 1997 and increased skilled attendance at delivery by 33 per cent in rural areas.[37] In Senegal, imams have been enlisted to promote safe motherhood.[38]

## The Feminization of HIV/AIDS

Increasingly, "the face of HIV/AIDS is a woman's face".[39] Women have greater susceptibility than men to infection due to social, cultural and physiological reasons, and are now being infected at a higher rate than men. Though the epidemic initially affected mostly men, today approximately half of the 40 million people living with HIV are women. The highest female infection rates are in countries where the epidemic has become generalized and where transmission is primarily heterosexual, often in the context of marriage.[40] Fifty-seven per cent of all people living with HIV in sub-Saharan Africa and 49 per cent in the Caribbean are women, with young women facing the highest risks (see Chapter 5).[41] Seventy-seven per cent of all HIV-positive women in the world are African.[42]

**AT THE EPIDEMIC'S CORE: POVERTY, VIOLENCE AND GENDER DISCRIMINATION.** Gender discrimination, poverty and violence lie at the centre of the AIDS epidemic (see Box 13). Physiologically, women are at least twice as likely as men to become infected with HIV during sex.[43] Women and girls are often ill-informed about sexual and reproductive matters and are more likely than men to be illiterate. They often lack negotiating power and social support for insisting on safer sex or rejecting sexual advances. Gender-based violence is a major risk factor for contracting HIV (see Chapter 7). In addition, poverty forces many women into subsistence sex work or transactional relationships that preclude negotiating condom use. Often these women are unable for economic reasons to leave a relationship, even if they know their partner has been infected or exposed to HIV.[44] Some harmful practices—such as female genital mutilation/cutting, child marriage, and "widow inheritance" (the union of the widow to a relative of the deceased husband)—compound women's risks.

Many people are still unaware of how to protect themselves from HIV. Only about 8 per cent of pregnant women and 16 per cent of sex workers worldwide were reached by prevention efforts in 2003.[45] Though most countries, including those in sub-Saharan Africa, have adopted national strategies to combat the epidemic, millions of women and men—indeed, the vast majority—are still without services or treatment.

**GENDER MATTERS.** Gender-sensitive approaches to preventing HIV are central to halting the epidemic. They can also catalyse broader social transformation. Women can gain more control in decisions affecting their lives with the support and cooperation of male partners, providers, communities and governments. Young men

> *"The toll on women and girls… presents Africa and the world with a practical and moral challenge, which places gender at the centre of the human condition. The practice of ignoring gender analysis has turned out to be lethal."*
>
> — Stephen Lewis, UN Secretary-General's Envoy to Africa, Barcelona International AIDS Conference

who learn to respect women and understand their responsibilities in halting HIV/AIDS are more likely to use a condom. Husbands can be enlisted to protect their wives and future children against HIV and other sexually transmitted infections.

Preventing HIV among women of childbearing age is crucial. Voluntary family planning should be integral to any and all strategies to halt the epidemic: Ethics and human rights demand that women who are HIV-positive can make informed family planning choices, including to prevent unwanted pregnancy. Access to antiretroviral treatment can help safeguard a woman's well-being and prevent the tragedy of HIV transmission to her children.

Prevention, care and treatment programmes have gradually opened up discussions on gender, sexuality and reproductive issues. In 2004, UNAIDS launched the Global Coalition on Women and AIDS, a worldwide alliance of civil society groups, networks of women living with HIV/AIDS, governments and UN organizations. Its platform calls for education, literacy and economic rights for women; equal access to antiretroviral treatment; access to sexual and reproductive health services; changes in harmful gender stereotypes; and zero tolerance for gender-based violence.[46]

**REPRODUCTIVE HEALTH AND RIGHTS OF HIV-POSITIVE WOMEN.** Most HIV-positive women in developing countries have no access to antiretroviral treatment, neither for themselves nor to prevent transmission to their children. In addition, many assume that

---

### 13 | HIV/AIDS: WHAT DOES GENDER HAVE TO DO WITH IT?

About three quarters of all new HIV infections are sexually transmitted between men and women. The attitudes and behaviours of men are critical to prevention efforts: Men hold overwhelming power in decisions on sexual matters, including whether to use condoms. In many societies, women are expected to know little about such matters, and those who raise the issue of condom use risk charges of being unfaithful or promiscuous. Violence against women and adolescent girls, and the fear of it, further erode women's negotiating position.

- AIDS emerged in the 1980s as a disease that primarily affected men; but the proportion of infected women compared to men has risen steadily, from 35 per cent in 1990 and 41 per cent in 1997, to 48 per cent in 2004.

- Among HIV-positive women, many are married and have had only one partner—their husbands.

- In parts of Africa and the Caribbean, the two regions with the highest HIV prevalence, young women (ages 15 to 24) are up to six times more likely to be infected than young men their age.

- Young women are the most affected group in the world: They represent 67 per cent of all new cases of HIV among people aged 15 to 24 in developing countries. In sub-Saharan Africa, young women represent 76 per cent of young people living with HIV. Up to 38 per cent of unmarried adolescents ages 15 to 19 years have engaged in sex for money or goods in some sub-Saharan African countries where AIDS is rampant.

#### Marriage: Safety or Risk for HIV?

Most people think marriage is "safe", but in many places it poses significant risks of HIV infection for women. The following figures, from both national studies and smaller-scale surveys of women, are indicative:

- More than four fifths of new HIV infections in women occur in marriage or long-term relationships with primary partners.

- In sub-Saharan Africa, an estimated 60 to 80 per cent of HIV-positive women have been infected by their husbands—their sole partner.

- At least 50 per cent of Senegalese women living with HIV reported only one risk factor—living in a "monogamous" union.

- In Mexico, more than 30 per cent of women diagnosed with HIV discover their status after their husbands are diagnosed.

- In India, some 90 per cent of women with HIV said they were virgins when they married and had remained faithful to their husbands.

- In Cambodia, 42 per cent of all new HIV infections occur from transmission by husbands to their wives. One third of new infections are to the babies of these women.

- In Thailand, 75 per cent of women living with HIV were likely to have been infected by their husbands.

- In Morocco, up to 55 per cent of HIV-positive women were infected by their husbands.

HIV-positive women will not have sexual relations and should not have children.[47] As a result, these women are often denied information and services to prevent pregnancy and mother-to-child HIV transmission, as well as access to quality prenatal and obstetric care. In societies where women are expected to produce children, HIV-positive women who opt to have none must contend with both the social disapproval of being childless and the suspicions and prejudice surrounding their status. Protecting the reproductive rights of HIV-positive women, including preventing coerced abortions or sterilization, is a critical human rights issue.

The International Community of Women Living with HIV/AIDS, created to address the lack of support provided to HIV-positive women, has led a Voices and Choices initiative in Central America, West Africa, Thailand and Zimbabwe that promotes women's rights to sexual and reproductive health.[48] In Argentina, FEIM, a leading women's NGO, disseminates the women's Bill of Rights developed at the 2002 International AIDS Conference and trains health personnel on human rights and contraception for HIV-positive women.[49]

In Kenya and South Africa, the "Mothers 2 Mothers 2 Be" project links HIV-positive new mothers with HIV-positive pregnant women for advice on issues from family planning to income generation.[50] Such "peer-led" counselling has helped HIV-positive women understand their reproductive health options and to cope with the challenges they face.

---

- Studies show that married women would often rather risk HIV infection than ask their husbands to use a condom, thereby confronting them over infidelity. In two districts of Uganda, only 26 per cent of women said it was acceptable for a married woman to ask a husband to use a condom.

*"I didn't understand how I, as a submissive woman, could be infected, having been faithful to the one man in my life."*
— HIV-positive woman from Burkina Faso

### It's Not as Simple as "ABC"
The "ABC" approach to HIV prevention counsels people to **A**bstain from sex, **B**e faithful to one partner, or use **C**ondoms. ABC programmes have indeed expanded awareness. However, unless both women and men can make free and informed decisions, "ABC" messages may overlook critical factors that millions of women must confront:

- Can an adolescent girl insist that her older husband use a condom or be faithful?

- Can a battered woman who depends on her partner or husband to support her and her children raise the subject of fidelity or condom use?

- Can a young wife insist on condom use when she is pressured to produce a child in order to be accepted by her new husband and in-laws?

- Can a sex worker struggling to feed her children refuse a client who does not want to use a condom, especially if he pays twice or more the usual rate?

- Can an adolescent girl who is sexually coerced or raped protect herself from infection?

- Does counselling abstinence until marriage keep young people safe when most are sexually active before they turn 20?

### Disproportionate Vulnerabilities, Disproportionate Burdens
Women and adolescent girls face high risks of HIV infection. They also provide much of the care for others who have acquired or are affected by the disease, including husbands and orphaned children. Women and girls represent 75 per cent of those caring for people living with AIDS. Taking care of the sick erodes the ability of women to generate income, thus limiting their opportunities for economic participation. The impact is especially severe in countries where women comprise the majority of farmers and produce most of the food. In the United Republic of Tanzania, women caring for sick husbands spent half as much time farming as they had previously. The loss of a husband's income, the costs of health care for ill relatives, and additional responsibilities can plunge women and their children deeper into poverty.

Women with AIDS are also the last and least likely to seek or receive care. By the time a husband dies, family resources have usually dwindled to the point where women are either unable or unwilling to seek medical care. Inheritance laws and customs that favour the husband's relatives may leave widows and their children impoverished. The additional financial pressure may force women and girls into exploitative and risky sex work or relationships, further fuelling the epidemic.

### 14 TRANSFORMING LIVES IN SWAZILAND

In the drought-stricken Lumombo region of Swaziland, women's active role in food distribution has led to benefits for the whole community. Non-governmental organizations supported by UNFPA and the World Food Programme trained women who led food distribution projects to address issues affecting the rural poor: sexual abuse, exploitation, AIDS and family planning. Community Relief Committees, which were 80 per cent women, reached out to men through discussion on these issues in community meetings, on food distribution days, at church, during home visits and when visiting the sick.

The project resulted in increased reporting to police by women and children of sexual abuse, a surge in requests for HIV testing, and a ten-fold increase within a year in the number of people receiving antiretroviral treatment. One major success is that rural leaders now give women authority to speak in community meetings—which is unprecedented—because women are seen not only as food distributors but also as sources of knowledge.

"I have never felt so important in my community. Before I was chosen to be a member of the food distribution committee, I was a nobody, and now people come to me for advice and help," said a woman who is now a recognized community leader.

**WOMEN'S ACCESS TO HIV/AIDS TREATMENT.** Programmes to prevent mother-to-child HIV transmission provide the only access to antiretroviral drugs for many HIV-positive women. In developing countries, most programmes focus on preventing transmission to the child and offer no benefits to the mother. In 2003, only 2 per cent of pregnant women testing HIV-positive worldwide received antiretroviral drugs to improve their own health.[51] In Africa, only 5 per cent of pregnant women are offered HIV prevention services.[52] Some emerging programmes emphasize the health and well-being of both child *and* mother.[53]

For wealthy people living in wealthy countries, antiretroviral drugs have largely transformed HIV into a manageable, chronic disease. But only 12 per cent of people in low and middle-income countries had access to treatment by the end of 2004.[54] Concerned that women, especially those not pregnant, might be denied access to treatment as it becomes available, women's groups, WHO and UNAIDS have called on governments to set national targets for equal access.[55]

**SHAME, BLAME AND AIDS.** Stigma kills. The shame associated with AIDS is a major obstacle to its prevention, and the stigma that surrounds people living with HIV is compounded by discrimination against women. Hundreds of thousands of HIV-positive women avoid testing and treatment services for fear of abandonment and other repercussions from husbands, families, communities and health providers.[56] Lack of confidentiality in testing services is a well-grounded concern. Women sometimes discover their HIV status last—after their husbands or in-laws.[57] Only 5 per cent of HIV-positive people are aware of their status,[58] and testing during pregnancy is often the only way that a family learns of HIV in its midst. Even if they contracted HIV from their husbands, women are sometimes blamed for "bringing AIDS home" and may face violence or ostracism as a result.[59] Health care providers sometimes deny HIV-positive women proper care during and following delivery. Women may refuse or discontinue treatment after negative interactions with staff.[60]

Many developing countries are combating stigma by opening up discussions about the disease, a key step in encouraging people to seek testing and treatment. One such programme supported by UNFPA is a regional initiative in seven Arab States on HIV awareness-raising. In Uzbekistan, a popular television soap opera airing since 2003 focuses on issues encountered in daily life, including substance abuse, HIV prevention and discrimination against people living with HIV/AIDS. In eight African and six Asian countries, UNFPA supports partnerships between radio networks and community-based health organizations to produce dramas on HIV and AIDS.[61] Multiple partners are supporting many similar initiatives across the developed and developing world, using the mass media and community-based dialogue to overcome the shame and discrimination that perpetuates the epidemic.

**THE OTHER EPIDEMIC—SEXUALLY TRANSMITTED INFECTIONS.** Sexually transmitted infections (STIs) and reproductive tract infections are among the most common causes of illness worldwide. An estimated 340 million new cases of *curable* STIs are reported every year.[62] When *incurable* infections (including HIV) are taken into account that number effectively triples.

Women are more susceptible than men to these infections, for sociocultural and physiological reasons, and disproportionately suffer severe consequences, including cervical cancer and infertility. About 70 per cent of women with STIs present no symptoms (compared to 10 per cent of men),[63] making diagnosis in women more difficult. When symptoms do appear, women tend to accept them as unimportant.[64] The presence of STIs can also increase the risk of HIV infection two to nine times.[65] Yet only 14 per cent of people with STIs in sub-Saharan Africa had access to treatment in 2003.[66] In addition, because sexually transmitted infections, including HIV, are most prevalent among young people, preventing these infections can have long-term benefits for the labour force and lead to higher productivity.[67]

## Reaping the Rewards of Family Planning

The freedom to choose how many children, and when, is a fundamental human right. Better access to safe and affordable contraceptive methods is key to achieving the MDGs. Family planning has proven benefits in terms of gender equality, maternal health, child survival, and preventing HIV. Family planning can also reduce poverty and promote economic growth by improving family well-being, raising female productivity and lowering fertility (see Chapter 2).[68] It is one of the wisest and most cost-effective investments any country can make towards a better quality of life. Limited access to contraception, on the other hand, constrains women's opportunities to pull themselves and their families out of poverty.

Drawing on earlier human rights conventions, the 1994 ICPD and the 1995 Fourth World Conference on Women placed reproductive health, including voluntary family planning, at the centre of initiatives to promote the human rights of women. This was a departure from earlier efforts that focused more on curbing rapid population growth, in some cases at the expense of women's rights. Citing ethical values and human rights principles, both conferences asserted that freedom to make reproductive decisions is essential for achieving gender equality and sustainable development.

*"Gender inequality and gender roles are in many settings the most important underlying influences on vulnerability to HIV. In fact, the AIDS epidemic cannot be understood, nor can effective responses be developed, without taking into account the fundamental ways that gender influences the spread of the disease, its impact, and the success of prevention efforts."*

— UN Millennium Project, *Combating AIDS in the Developing World*

**BARRIERS TO ACCESS: POVERTY AND GENDER DISCRIMINATION.** Since reliable methods became available in the 1960s, the use of modern contraception has risen steadily to 54 per cent of all women currently married or in union. The figure rises to 61 per cent when traditional methods are taken into account.[69] As a result, fertility rates continue to fall. In the developing world, the total fertility rate—average number of births per woman—has fallen from over six in the 1960s to under three per woman today. However, fertility remains high in the least-developed countries, at five children per woman.[70]

The combination of high fertility and pervasive poverty in developing countries intensifies the latter by slowing economic growth and increasing costs for health, education and other basic needs, lowering female productivity, and reducing income and savings. Falling fertility, on the other hand, can accelerate poverty reduction, especially when combined with supportive social and economic policies.[71]

Some of the world's poorest countries have made slow or only halting progress over the past 30 years in increasing contraceptive access. In 21 of the poorest countries in sub-Saharan Africa, the total fertility rate has remained high, or declined only slightly, since the 1970s.[72]

Contraceptive use is uneven both among and within countries. It varies according to income, education, ethnicity, proximity to clinics and the strength of family planning programmes. In Africa, only 27 per cent of married women are using any method of contraception, and only 20 per cent are relying on more effective modern methods. And in some parts of the continent, the proportion drops to under 5 per cent for modern methods.[73] The wealthiest women are four times more likely to use contraception than the poorest: In some countries, the rate is 12 times higher (see Figure 3). Globally, some 201 million women lack access to effective contraceptives but many would practise family planning if given the option.[74]

> **15** **COMMON GENDER-BASED BARRIERS TO CONTRACEPTIVE USE**
>
> - At the *policy and legal* level, decision-makers may not place high priority on funding contraceptive services because they view family planning as a "women's programme". Some countries restrict certain methods. Laws may require a woman to have her husband's permission to use some methods, and adolescents under a certain age may be required to get parental consent.
>
> - In *health facilities*, biased service providers may fail to offer a range of contraceptive options, on the basis that a woman will not understand them or would choose "wrongly". Some providers incorrectly believe that certain contraceptive methods cause infertility and only provide them to women who have already had children.
>
> *"[The nurse] told me that if I did not want the pill, then she would not recommend anything."*
> – Zambian woman
>
> - At the *community level*, contraceptives may be frowned upon as contributing to female promiscuity, a concern not expressed for men.
>
> - At the level of *individuals and couples*, some women may fear their husbands' disapproval, or even retribution for contraceptive use. Many couples have difficulty discussing the subject.
>
> *"My husband knew about the pills. I told him, and he was always against them. We almost broke up over it."*
> – Guatemalan woman
>
> - *Young women*, if married, may be expected to "prove" childbearing ability to their husbands and families; if unmarried, they may be expected to remain abstinent.
>
> *"I tried to get some tablets, but I was chased from the clinic. I think it was because I looked very young."*
> – Zimbabwean secondary school student
>
> - *Men* are often excluded from family planning programmes because they are designed for women and operate as part of maternal and child health services.

In addition to the macro-level social and economic benefits of family planning, studies have found that women who plan their families reap personal, psychological and economic rewards. In Bolivia, contraceptive use was associated with working for pay outside the home. In Cebu, the Philippines, the average income growth for women with one to three pregnancies was twice that of women who had undergone more than seven pregnancies.[75] Family planning programmes also produce tangible and sizeable savings for governments.

Several factors affect demand for contraception. Social, cultural and gender-related obstacles can prevent a woman from realizing her childbearing preferences (see Box 15). Women who cannot read or have limited education may know little about their own bodies, much less about family planning. Misconceptions and myths about pregnancy and contraceptive methods abound.[76] Men tend to want more children and to want them earlier than women do, and in many cases have greater decision-making power to determine family size.[77] Social norms surrounding fertility and virility, and the overall low status of women, keep many women and men from seeking family planning.

**Figure 3: Contraceptive Use According to Wealth**

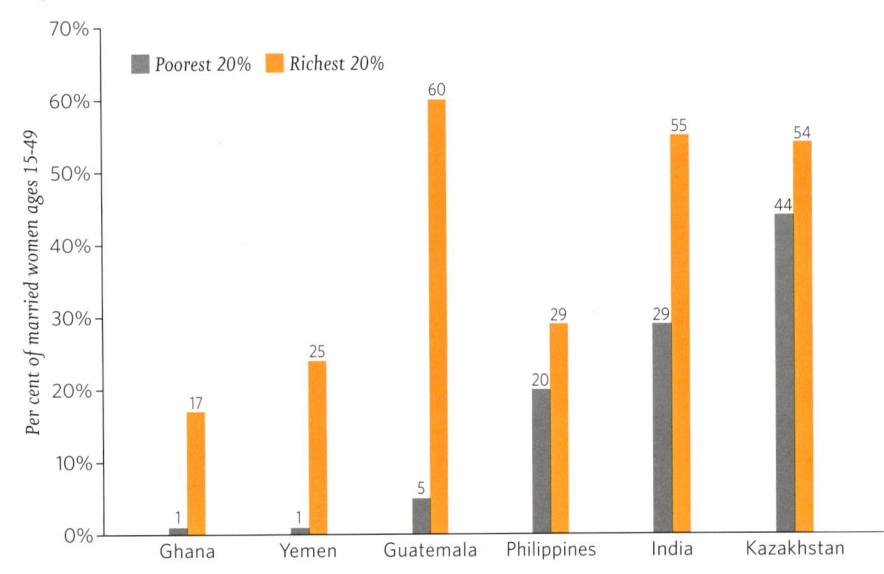

Per cent of married women ages 15-49

| Country | Poorest 20% | Richest 20% |
|---|---|---|
| Ghana | 1 | 17 |
| Yemen | 1 | 25 |
| Guatemala | 5 | 60 |
| Philippines | 20 | 29 |
| India | 29 | 55 |
| Kazakhstan | 44 | 54 |

**Source:** World Bank, 2004, *Round II Country Reports on Health, Nutrition, and Population Conditions Among the Poor and the Better-Off in 56 Countries.*

### 16 | WHERE ARE THE CONDOMS?

Approximately five billion condoms were distributed in 2003 for HIV prevention. But many more—an estimated 13 billion—were needed to help halt the spread of HIV and other sexually transmitted infections. In 2003, donor support paid for the equivalent of one condom a year for each man of reproductive age living in the developing world. In sub-Saharan Africa, the region receiving the largest share of support, donor contributions provided six condoms a year for each man.

The shortage of condoms is alarming. They are the only effective means of protecting sexually active people from HIV infection. If used consistently and correctly, condoms also serve as a means of contraception for people with limited access to health care and more effective methods. The projected cost of the number of condoms that will be required to halt the AIDS epidemic is expected to reach $590 million by 2015. This is about three times current condom costs. Brazil, China and India are self-sufficient in contraceptives, but other developing countries must import them, paying with scarce foreign exchange required for food, medicine and other necessities.

### 17 | CHANGING LIVES IN COMMUNITIES OF ZIMBABWE

Zimbabwe has one of the highest HIV prevalence rates in the world: 25 per cent of the population. Close to one million women are HIV-positive. Young women represent two thirds of all new HIV infections among young people 15 to 24. UNFPA Zimbabwe is working to improve the social and economic status of women as a way to give them greater power to protect themselves.

In Ruheri District, women are trained in communication and negotiation skills, and spread the gender equality message at weddings, parties, schools, food distribution points and public forums. Men's initial resistance, based on concerns that changes would promote promiscuity, was overcome through dialogue with key groups and traditional leaders. In 2004, the project exceeded expectations with a 50 and 20 per cent increase in the distribution of male and female condoms, respectively, reaching a total of 47,423 people.

In Mutare, commercial sex work is a fact of life. Authorities decided 13 years ago to train sex workers as peer educators on the prevention of HIV and sexually transmitted infections (STIs). They are encouraged to use and distribute condoms to their clients and fellow workers, inform the larger community about prevention and refer people to treatment. In 2003, the project reached 1,177,128 women and 736,981 men. Clinic nurses report a steady decline in STIs—of between 6 to 50 per cent, varying by neighbourhood—with more than 5.7 million condoms distributed. This initiative has changed lives: the majority of peer educators have left sex work for entrepreneurial activities. As Caroline, a former sex worker, said, "If it were not for this project, I would have died of AIDS a long time ago."

**GROWING DEMAND, GROWING SHORTAGES.** Many developing countries face critical shortfalls of contraceptives and condoms. Reasons include rising numbers of users (from population growth), growing demand (from a desire for smaller families), the spread of HIV/AIDS (requiring substantial resources), and declining levels of donor funding.[78]

A number of developing countries are able to cover contraceptive costs, but most lack the foreign exchange and manufacturing capacity to meet their own needs without donor support. The cost of contraceptives and condoms is estimated to rise from $1 billion to $1.6 billion between 2004 and 2015, with a large gap still existing between projected costs and donor funding. Meanwhile, the AIDS epidemic means that shortfalls—not only in male and female condoms, but in other reproductive health supplies such as STI treatments and HIV test kits—have become all the more pressing.

**EXPANDING CONTRACEPTIVE CHOICE.** The ICPD called for universal access to "a full range" of family planning methods. However, in most countries, one or two methods dominate. Three methods—female sterilization, intrauterine devices, and oral contraceptives—account for most contraception worldwide.[79] Contraceptives under development, including a male hormonal method, may soon add to the mix of choices available in wealthier nations. But it will be many years before these become available in developing countries.[80] Until an HIV vaccine and microbicides become available, expanding access to the female condom offers the only female-controlled alternative protection from HIV. As it still requires male cooperation, men need to be informed and sensitized to its use.[81]

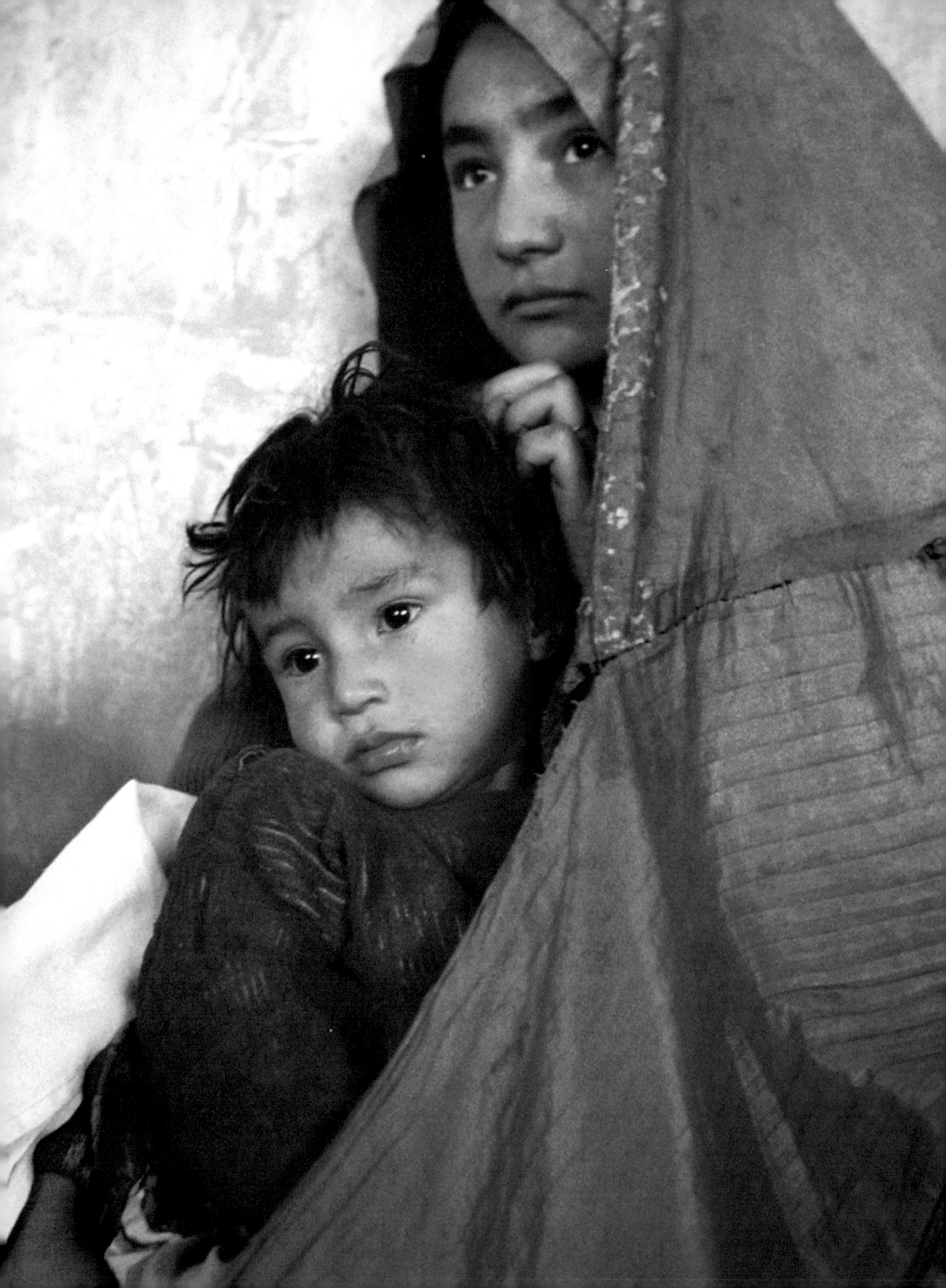

# 5 The Unmapped Journey: Adolescents, Poverty and Gender

*"Some groups think we are too young to know. They should know we are too young to die."*

— Hector, 20 years old, Honduras, member of UNFPA's Global Youth Partners programme

Today's generation of young people is the largest in human history. Nearly half the world's population—more than 3 billion people—are under the age of 25. Eighty-five per cent of youth live in developing countries.[1] Many of them are coming of age in the grip of poverty and facing the peril of HIV and AIDS. Nearly 45 per cent of all youth—515 million—survive on less than $2 a day.[2]

Within the world of the young, adolescents are at a particularly formative stage. These 1.2 billion adolescents between the ages of 10 and 19[3] are brimming with energy and possibilities. Their minds are open to acquiring knowledge, learning skills and absorbing values. Their attitudes are still being shaped. They need vocational and life skills and access to reproductive health information and services, both for their own well-being and to participate more fully in their countries' development.

Adolescents are not mentioned in the UN Millennium Declaration and are largely invisible in the Millennium Development Goals (MDGs). Nevertheless, because they represent such a sizeable share of the world's poor, they both affect and are affected by all of the goals. Throughout the next 10 years, today's adolescents will participate in achieving the MDGs. By the 2015 deadline, today's 10-year-olds will be 20 and ready to fully take on the role as agents of development. Policy decisions regarding the education, health, employment and human rights of today's young people will also affect the next wave of 1.2 billion children who will be adolescents in 2015.[4] Decisions taken—or opportunities missed—today will reverberate for generations to come.[5]

## Adolescence: Opportunities and Risks

The experience of adolescence is diverse and depends on many factors including one's sex, place of residence, socio-cultural context, economic circumstances and marital status. A major determinant is whether an adolescent is protected and harboured by a nurturing family, or trying to survive with little or no help, like many AIDS orphans. This generation is also growing up in an increasingly globalized world, which poses a new set of challenges and possibilities.[6]

While millions of adolescents enjoy loving and supportive environments and benefit from expanding opportunities and freedom, millions of others face threats to their safe and healthy passage into adulthood. Poverty compounds the challenges and risks of adolescence and obliges many parents to put their children to work, often in harm's way. Many girls and boys do not get the chance to obtain an education.

In urban areas, boys may be forced by poverty to survive on the streets. In conflict situations, adolescent boys and girls are often recruited as soldiers or domestic and sexual slaves by armed rebel forces (see Chapter 8). Adolescent girls also face risks of exploita-

---

**18 | DEFINING TERMS**

Use and meanings of the terms "young people", "youth", and "adolescents" vary in different societies around the world, depending on political, economic and sociocultural context. This report uses the following United Nations definitions:

- Adolescents: 10-19 year olds (early adolescence 10-14 and late adolescence 15-19)
- Youth: 15-24 year olds
- Young People: 10-24 year olds

tion and abuse and are being trafficked into sexual slavery on an unprecedented scale (see Chapter 7).[7]

**FOR GIRLS, DIMINISHED OPPORTUNITIES AND INCREASED RISKS.** Gender-based expectations greatly influence the experience of adolescence.[8] Girls are often left at a disadvantage. As they enter puberty, bias against girls puts them at higher risk than boys for dropping out of school, sexual violence and child marriage. Boys' freedoms and opportunities may expand, while girls' experiences are often the opposite.[9] During this period, differential treatment may become more pronounced, with girls schooled to become wives and mothers, and boys groomed to become providers. Girls are typically expected to be compliant, while boys are encouraged to project strength and control. The expectations placed on boys may contribute to aggressive or risky behaviour, with harmful effects for them and others (see Chapter 6).

For many girls, particularly those living in poverty, adolescence means more risks and fewer freedoms. New research from South Africa's most populated province, KwaZulu-Natal, finds that while poverty has a negative influence on the health and behaviour of all young people, its impact is greater on young women, who have less access to information and less negotiating power to influence decisions, including to protect themselves from HIV.[10] Girls are more likely than boys to drop out of school, either because of pregnancy or to help with household and child-rearing responsibilities or to care for ailing relatives.[11] This is reflected in lower literacy rates for young women: Of the 137 million illiterate youth in the world, 63 per cent are female.[12] Adolescent girls face higher risks of harmful practices and poor reproductive health and are especially at risk of contracting HIV. In some societies, girls are forbidden to socialize with boys and are restricted from playing or moving about outside the home. For the millions of girls who marry young, childhood comes to an abrupt halt.

Adolescents' perception of their own value and potential is strongly influenced by family members, friends, schools, communities and the media. Parents and other adults in the community can provide supportive guidance and foster inter-generational understanding as adolescents navigate the new chal-

---

**19 THE LIVES OF AFRICA'S RURAL GIRLS**

Participatory research conducted in Burkina Faso, Mali and Senegal informed the efforts of Family Care International and UNFPA to address the needs and rights of rural adolescent girls. It revealed some important insights into their lives:

**Education:** Girls in Mali believe in education, but 72 per cent of rural girls have never attended school. Education is often cut short by forced and child marriage, the cost and distance of secondary schools and the custom of rural girls spending a year in the city working as domestic servants to earn money for their wedding trousseaux. "Our village has never produced a girl with a diploma. For us, education is a remote dream," said an 18-year-old girl from Mali. "A girl does not really need to be educated, as she will leave in any case to establish a family elsewhere, and then the advantages of her education will benefit others," said a parent. This perception was widely echoed in the community.

**Reproductive Health:** Girls in the three countries often receive confusing and frightening information about puberty and menstruation. Reproductive health services and information about puberty and family planning are rudimentary. Fewer than 30 per cent of rural girls and women give birth with the assistance of a skilled attendant, and many are afraid to use the local medical facilities. "We don't go to the maternity to have our babies," said a married girl in Mali, "because the midwife is tough on us and shouts at us during the delivery. Plus, there is never any medicine and the beds are dirty. We prefer to have our babies at home."

**Livelihoods:** Rural girls work hard to contribute to the household economy, but their prospects of economic security are limited by their lack of education, child marriage and childbearing, lack of mobility and the poverty of their rural environments.

---

lenges in their lives. Raising girls and boys to respect each other, to aspire equally to educational and work opportunities and to expect fair treatment in relationships and marriage helps build strong families and advance development goals.

**A MISSING LINK IN POLICIES AND BUDGETS.** Many public programmes focus on children's health and primary education, but the needs of adolescents rarely attract attention. The resulting policy gaps deprive adolescents of much-needed support. At the same time, countries risk losing the returns of their earlier investments in children. For instance, while primary education has been the focus of international efforts, secondary and higher education—especially for girls—provide especially high returns for poverty reduction, economic growth, reproductive health and the MDGs overall.[13]

Adolescents have often been left out of poverty reduction policies, although this may be changing: 17 of the 31 countries that completed a Poverty Reduction Strategy Paper (PRSP) between 2002 and 2003 devoted considerable attention to youth.[14] However, only six identified youth as a specific group living in poverty.[15]

Though many countries have developed youth policies or programmes, few give youth concerns the concerted and sustained attention they deserve. Budgets are limited, and the share of funding for young people is rarely tracked or quantified. Countries lack reliable sex-disaggregated data on adolescents and youth, including poverty research or information documenting the macroeconomic and developmental benefits of investing in adolescents.[16] A nine-country evaluation sponsored by UNFPA found that when governments did collect reliable data on young people, policy attention soon followed.[17]

**ACCOUNTABILITY TO YOUNG PEOPLE.** Traditionally, adolescents have been left out of decisions that affect their lives. However, national governments, NGOs and UN agencies increasingly include young people in decision-making and advisory groups at both global and national levels. UNFPA, for example, set up a Youth Advisory Panel in 2004 as a forum for youth participation. The panel advises the Fund on how best to address young people's needs and rights in the national development plans and programmes it supports.[18] The International Planned Parenthood Federation includes youth as members of its board of directors.[19]

In Nicaragua, a countrywide consultation with adolescents, supported by UNFPA and UNICEF, led to the government's adoption of a comprehensive youth policy.[20] Panama's 1999 National Youth Pact drew public commitments from presidential candidates and contributed to the development of a national youth plan, a process supported by UNFPA.[21] National consultations in Tunisia, held every five years and led by the President, have involved tens of thousands of youths. In India, UNFPA collaborated with the national parliament and UNAIDS on a youth parliament special session on HIV/AIDS that involved some 3,000 students in 2004. During the special session, youth leaders deliberated or proposed legislation in the presence of senior political leaders.

A rights-based approach to poverty reduction requires attention to the needs of the most vulnerable and the most marginalized. However, the voices of neglected groups of adolescents are rarely heard during policy deliberations. With the support of UNICEF, groups of abused and trafficked youth from slums and brothels in Bangladesh influenced the formulation of the country's national plan of action against the sexual abuse and exploitation of children.[22] UNFPA has also supported pioneering work to give a voice and extend reproductive health education and services to particularly excluded groups. These include youth with disabilities in Jamaica;[23] Roma youth in Bulgaria; ethnic youth in Laos;[24] and indigenous adolescents in Panama.[25]

Removing legislative barriers to the participation of youth advocacy groups, and institutionalizing relevant mechanisms, can be a key step. In Bulgaria, for example, youth parliaments are attached to local governments. In Costa Rica, the 2002 General Law on the Young Person authorized the National Youth Assembly, a network of local youth committees, to draw up a national youth policy. UNFPA provided lead support to extensive consultations by the Vice Ministry of Youth with young people across the country, which led in turn to the inclusive, rights-based policy that Costa Rica adopted in 2003.[26] Mozambique's Youth Policy, drafted in 1996, led to the legalization of youth organizations and to the creation of the National Youth Council that gave voice to its 120 constituent youth organizations in governmental discussions. Kenya has formally established a Children's Parliament, with representatives under 21 serving as ministers for each area of government.[27]

**INVESTING IN YOUNG PEOPLE.** How many of today's young people will grow up to be healthy and productive citizens? How many will slip further into ill health and economic want? Failure to make the necessary invest-

> **20  MUNICIPAL HOUSES FOR ADOLESCENTS AND YOUTH: EMPOWERING COMMUNITIES IN NICARAGUA**
>
> Nicaragua, a country with 65 per cent of its population under age 25, has one of the highest adolescent fertility rates in the Americas. Only six of every 10 adolescents attend school and only half of these make it to secondary school. Since 1998, UNFPA has worked with local partners to establish Adolescent and Youth Houses (Casas) in 21 municipalities that cover 25 per cent of the country's adolescent population.
>
> The Casas promote the rights, citizenship and participation of young people and the importance of community empowerment and intergenerational dialogue. Adolescents receive information on and training in reproductive health, violence, drug abuse and vocational skills, and carry out community and media outreach on reproductive health and rights.
>
> Enabling young people to take charge of their own destinies has paid off. Those trained as leaders and peer counsellors are playing a more active social role in their communities. Young people have changed their attitudes about harmful gender stereotypes and roles. From 1999 to 2003, practices to prevent pregnancy increased from 66 to 83 per cent and contraceptive use jumped from 52 to 80 per cent.
>
> *"The Municipal Adolescent House is a place where I feel important and where I learn to make others feel important too. . . . It's a place where I learn to organize activities and where I never finish learning. In a few words, it's an opportunity."*
>
> — Michael, adolescent from Estelí Municipality

ment in today's young people will have long-term repercussions on individual lives, health systems, security, demographics, economies and development.[28] However, action now to address gender disparities, poverty and powerlessness can secure the future. The UN Millennium Project Task Force on Education and Gender Equality recommends that adolescent girls living in poverty should be a priority for those investments.

**The 1.5 billion young people who represent 29 per cent of the population of less developed regions are entitled to a fair share of resources.**[29] This argument carries even more weight in the poorest countries, where young people's share of the population is greatest;[30] in countries with high socio-economic structural inequities; and in post-war countries, where many young people served as combatants or lost their parents.

**Investing in young people is not only a priority for furthering human rights and poverty reduction, but could also bring about a "demographic bonus".** The population of the 50 poorest countries is projected to more than double by 2050, from 800 million in 2005 to 1.7 billion people.[31] With higher investments in their education, reproductive health, job skills and employment opportunities, these young people can be a source of increased productivity.[32] Enabling young couples to choose when to marry and have children will give them greater control over their own lives and will probably lead to smaller families and slower population growth. A larger workforce and relatively fewer older and younger dependents offers a unique opportunity for investment and economic growth, as East Asian countries have found (see Chapter 2). Conversely, failure to respond to the needs of youth could further entrench poverty and stall development for decades to come.

**Appropriate investments in young people can reduce the risk of violence and civil disorder.** Violent crime disproportionately involves young men.[33] Based on data from 145 countries, research shows that sizeable population groups of young men with few opportunities for education and decent employment increase the risk of civil unrest and armed conflict.[34] Investing in education can reduce the risks, but only when it is buttressed by the creation of jobs for large numbers of educated youth.[35]

Investments in young people can not only avert personal risks but save billions of dollars in lost productivity and direct public expenditures—the consequences of school drop out, teen pregnancy, substance abuse, crime, and HIV/AIDS. They will also yield long-term dividends to societies and economies.[36]

## Reproductive Health in the Lives of Adolescents and Youth

International human rights agreements adopted over the last fifteen years uphold adolescents' reproductive health and rights. The 1989 Convention on the Rights of the Child, the most universally accepted human rights instrument, guarantees the rights of children and adolescents, including freedom from discrimination, abuse and exploitation; participation in decisions affecting their lives; privacy; and access to education, health information and services for their well-being. All of these rights have direct implications for adolescent reproductive health. In 1994, governments pledged for the first time to address the reproductive health needs and rights of adolescents at the International Conference on Population and Development (ICPD). At the 1995 Fourth World Conference on Women in Beijing, governments reaffirmed this commitment and placed special emphasis on the girl child. The 1995 World Programme of Action for Youth to the Year 2000 and Beyond cemented a global agenda for action in critical areas that directly affect progress toward the MDGs. The committees overseeing compliance with international treaties have also issued recommendations on adolescents' reproductive health and rights, and expressed particular concern for the situation of adolescent girls.[37]

Several countries have adopted policies and laws to address adolescent reproductive health. In Albania, reproductive health education and services for adolescents are free.[38] Kyrgyzstan protects the right of young people to reproductive health care.[39] Benin's law calls for separate reproductive health services for adolescents.[40] Panama recognizes the right of pregnant adolescents to health care, information on their rights and continued education.[41] Colombia now specifically protects the right of adolescents—including for those displaced by internal conflict—to contraception.[42] Many countries have established a minimum age for marriage, as called for by the 1962 Convention on Consent to Marriage, Minimum Age for Marriage and Registration of Marriages.[43] Anti-trafficking and anti-violence policies and laws, such as those of Bangladesh, Niger and the Philippines, also prohibit child marriage and the forced marriage of women and girls in exchange for money or goods.[44]

In the last decade, a growing global youth movement and the AIDS epidemic have contributed to a surge in efforts to provide reproductive health education and services for young people. The pressing need to make reproductive health services more youth-friendly and youth-driven is widely acknowledged. Communities are being more effectively engaged, for example, through outreach efforts to remove the stigma associated with reproductive health services for adolescents. The important role of parents is being leveraged by educating them about the risks their children face and about their needs and rights to information that can affect their well-being and, in the case of HIV, their very survival. In a district in Ghana, "Time with Grandma" is an initiative operating from within the cultural framework to reach out to adolescent girls through traditional "queen mothers". These women, who are leaders in their communities and role models for young people, are now being trained to mentor the younger generation on reproductive health issues.[45]

A broad spectrum of government, civil society, youth groups and international partners is working to expand young people's access to reproductive health care. UNFPA helped initiate the first-ever youth-friendly reproductive health services in countries from Bosnia-Herzegovina to Lao PDR.[46] Its Reproductive Health Initiative for Youth in Asia, supported by the European Union, is empowering neglected groups in a region that is home to 70 per cent of the developing world's young people.[47] Using theatre, comic books, peer education, games and talk shows, the initiative has reached out to young people in rural areas, commercial sex workers, street children and factory workers. Influential adults, such as parents, community leaders and health providers have been enlisted to strengthen the impact of messages. In Cambodia, the initiative reaches more than 250,000 young people directly and 1.2 million more through the radio programmes it sponsors.[48]

The Y-PEER programme has coordinated and strengthened the efforts of nearly 200 peer education projects that reach some 1.7 million young people in

---

**21 | SAVING YOUNG MOTHERS' LIVES IN BANGLADESH**

In Manikganj, a farming community 70 km outside the capital of Bangladesh, UNFPA supports the Ministry of Health in making Mother and Child Welfare Centres accessible to poor women. Hamida, 25, gave birth to her second child last year in the UNFPA-supported local centre: *"Before this centre upgraded its services, women with complicated pregnancies had to go to a hospital in Dhaka. Some of them didn't make it on time."* She told of a school classmate, married at 15 and pregnant at 16, who bled to death in a horse cart on the way to the hospital. *"If she had access to these services, she would still be alive today."*

27 countries of Eastern Europe and Central Asia. Y-PEER uses Internet-based communications to share information, resources and lessons learned and has translated its peer education training manual into 15 regional languages.[49]

In the Arab States, UNFPA supported a successful regional initiative with Boy Scout and Girl Guide Associations to extend reproductive health education through their community development programmes. Over 4,000 girl guides and boy scouts were trained, and collaboration with ministries of health and education strengthened attention to young people's reproductive health needs.[50]

Full-blown national and regional programmes remain the exception, however. Most projects remain small in scale, leaving the reproductive health needs of most adolescents—especially the poorest and most marginalized—neglected.[51]

**THE COSTS AND RISKS OF EARLY PREGNANCY.** An estimated 14 million adolescents between 15 and 19 give birth each year.[52] Uncounted others have babies at even younger ages. One quarter to one half of adolescent girls in developing countries are mothers before they reach 18.[53] The highest rates of adolescent fertility are found in sub-Saharan Africa and South Asia.[54] Based on data from 56 countries, girls aged 15 to 19 from the poorest groups are three times more likely than their better-off peers to give birth in adolescence, and have twice as many children[55] (see Figure 4). High rates of early childbearing in many developing countries result primarily from the practice of child marriage.[56]

Adolescent girls between the ages of 15 and 19 are twice as likely to die during pregnancy or childbirth as women in their twenties. For those under 15, the risks are five times higher.[57] And for every girl who dies in childbirth, many more will suffer injuries, infections and lingering disabilities, such as obstetric fistula.[58] Fistulas are reparable if services are available, and UNFPA has led a global campaign to bring hope into these girls' lives (see Box 23).

**UNPLANNED PREGNANCIES.** Too many adolescents face the life-altering consequences of unplanned pregnancies. In Latin America and the Caribbean, for example, 35 to 52 per cent of adolescent pregnancies are unplanned.[59] The reasons vary. They include lack of knowledge about the basic facts of reproduction and lack of information about contraceptives, contributing

---

> **22 | TEENAGE PREGNANCY AND NEWBORN SURVIVAL**
>
> Enabling adolescent girls to delay childbearing saves lives. Every year four million newborns die within the first month of life, many because their mothers were simply too young to give birth: babies with adolescent mothers are 1.5 times more likely than those with older mothers to die before their first birthday. Adolescents are at highest risk of premature delivery. Because their bodies are generally not fully developed and ready for childbirth, adolescent girls are also more likely to suffer obstructed labour. The risks are higher for poor girls whose growth was stunted due to malnourishment. In the absence of medical intervention, the infant usually dies. Access to life-saving emergency care when complications arise is fundamental to the survival of young mothers and their newborns—and to reaching the MDGs on infant and maternal mortality.

---

**Figure 4: Childbearing Among the Poorest and Richest Adolescents**

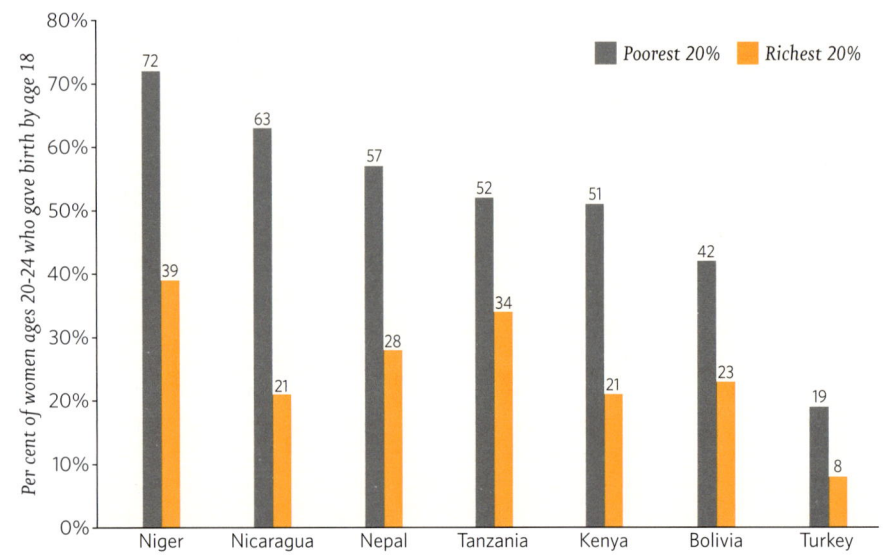

| Country | Poorest 20% | Richest 20% |
|---|---|---|
| Niger | 72 | 39 |
| Nicaragua | 63 | 21 |
| Nepal | 57 | 28 |
| Tanzania | 52 | 34 |
| Kenya | 51 | 21 |
| Bolivia | 42 | 23 |
| Turkey | 19 | 8 |

Per cent of women ages 20-24 who gave birth by age 18

**Source:** Rani, M. and E. Lule, 2004, "Exploring the Socioeconomic Dimension of Adolescent Reproductive Health: A Multicountry Analysis" *International Family Planning Perspectives* 30 (3): 112.

to contraceptive failure. Some unplanned pregnancies are a consequence of rape, sexual abuse and incest, though these possibilities are often ignored, even when very young pregnant adolescents visit a clinic.

Unwanted pregnancies result in an estimated five million unsafe abortions among adolescents every year.[60] In sub-Saharan Africa, where 40 per cent of all unsafe abortions among adolescents in developing countries occur, data from seven countries revealed that 39 to 79 per cent of those treated for abortion-related complications were adolescents.[61] Half of the 10,000 Nigerian women who die from unsafe abortions each year are estimated to be adolescents.[62] In Argentina and Chile, one third of maternal deaths of 15- to 19-year-olds were found to be abortion-related.[63]

Like adult women, adolescent girls encounter gender-related obstacles to informed choice about reproductive health, as discussed in Chapter 4. These obstacles are compounded by their low social status as young people. Adolescent girls are subject to sexual violence and coercion. They often hesitate to seek services because of stigma or mistrust until they are faced with an unintended pregnancy or life-threatening complications from an unsafe abortion. They also have little money to pay for services and transportation. Achieving the MDGs will require attention to the specific reproductive health needs of adolescent girls.[64]

## Young People and HIV/AIDS

Almost a quarter of people living with HIV are under the age of 25.[65] Young people now represent half of all new cases. An estimated 6,000 young people are infected every day—one every 14 minutes. The majority are women and girls.[66] In sub-Saharan Africa, 63 per cent of those who were HIV-positive in 2003 were between the ages of 15 and 24.[67] In the Russian Federation and other countries of Eastern Europe and Central Asia, more than 80 per cent of those living with HIV are under the age of 30, a majority of them young men.[68] In these regions, as well as in Southeast Asia and China, HIV is spread primarily by drug injection and commercial sex work. One third of new cases of curable sexually transmitted infections every year are contracted by young people under 25.[69]

**YOUNG WOMEN FACE HIGHEST RISK.** In the 1980s, HIV/AIDS disproportionately affected men. Now, the face of the epidemic is increasingly that of a young woman. Women between 15 and 24 are 1.6 times more likely than young men to be HIV-positive. In sub-Saharan Africa, young women living with HIV outnumber HIV-positive young men 3.6 to 1.[70] About 70 per cent of all young people living with HIV are women in the Caribbean, the Middle East and in North Africa.[71]

---

**23 | CAMPAIGN ON OBSTETRIC FISTULA: RESTORING ADOLESCENT GIRLS' LIVES AND DIGNITY**

Fatima was married at 14. Soon after, she became pregnant. After a gruelling six days of labour, the young Nigerian gave birth to a stillborn baby. For the following 10 years, Fatima explained, "the whole community rejected me. Anywhere I went, they laughed at me."

Fatima is a survivor of a devastating childbearing injury known as obstetric fistula—a preventable and treatable condition that affects at least two million women and girls worldwide. Caused by prolonged and obstructed labour, a fistula is a hole that forms between a woman's vagina and bladder and/or rectum, leaving her with chronic incontinence. In nearly all cases, the baby dies. Unable to stay dry, women with fistula are often abandoned by their husbands and families, blamed for their condition and ostracized by their communities. Fistula typically affects girls and young women living in poor and remote rural areas with inadequate or non-existent health services, as well as those who deliver at home without professional care.

Fatima is one of hundreds of girls and women who have received surgical treatment through the global Campaign to End Fistula, launched in 2003 by UNFPA and a large number of partners. The campaign works in more than 30 countries in sub-Saharan Africa, South Asia and the Arab States to prevent fistula and treat women and girls. It is also helping them reclaim their place in society by starting to expand their access to skills training, literacy classes and counselling in the post-operative healing process. After her surgery, Fatima smiled, pleased that now she is "being invited by friends and neighbours to weddings and naming ceremonies."

In Nigeria, the campaign supported a two-week project in February 2005 that treated 545 women and provided training to dozens of doctors, nurses and social workers in surgery and post-operative care. After participating in a health education session, a number of men who accompanied their wives and daughters to surgery are now committed to helping other girls and women. "Even if I have to use my own money, I will help other women come to the hospital," said Muhammadu Abubakar of Nigeria, who accompanied his niece.

Women are more vulnerable to the infection than men, for biological, sociocultural and economic reasons (see Chapter 4), but adolescent girls and young women face additional risks. The reproductive tracts of girls under 14, for example, are more susceptible to tearing, because they are not yet fully mature. This increases the risks of HIV infection and other sexually transmitted infections. Younger women and girls are especially vulnerable to sexual violence and exploitation, and are at a disadvantage in negotiating the terms of sexual relations, including the right to say "no" and to insist on condom use. Harmful practices, such as child marriage and female genital mutilation/cutting with unsterile instruments, expose them to additional dangers.

**THE ROLE OF YOUNG MEN.** No discussion of female vulnerability to HIV is complete without mentioning men, whose behaviour drives the epidemic and whose inclusion in prevention efforts is critical to their success. In many countries, having sex with many women is a measure of a young man's virility. Many young men are also exposed to high risks of HIV for a variety of reasons, including through injecting drug use, in prisons, and through their occupations. For instance, most soldiers and many migrants in search of work are young men, in situations that take them away from their families and partners and may lead them to engage in commercial sex. Programmes that allow boys and young men to discuss their concerns in a non-judgemental and supportive environment and that encourage a sense of equality with women are critical, as discussed in Chapter 6.

**LACK OF INFORMATION, MEANS AND SKILLS FOR PREVENTION.** In many of the worst-affected countries, frank discussion of gender equality, contraception, HIV prevention and related issues remains taboo. Studies from around the globe testify to an alarming degree of misinformation and lack of knowledge about the disease, particularly among young women and girls.[72] Misconceptions can give young people a false sense of security and lead them to underestimate the risk of infection. Empowering young people to abstain as a choice, delay sexual initiation, reject unwanted advances, as well as providing them with

---

**24 | 'SUGAR DADDIES' AND SURVIVAL**

Poverty drives many young women to survival sex. This exchange of sex for money or school fees or to help support their families sometimes takes the form of "sugar daddy" relationships found in the Caribbean and sub-Saharan Africa. Sugar daddies are typically older men, married and well off, who support younger women financially in exchange for sex. Increasingly, they seek out adolescent girls owing to the belief that they are less likely to be infected with HIV. The greater the age and economic differences, the more unlikely it is that condoms will be used. Older men tend to have had multiple partners and more exposure to HIV.

Studies of pregnant teens in countries of sub-Saharan Africa revealed that 73 per cent of the girls interviewed had sexual partners who were over age 30. In Haiti, one study found that one third of adolescent girls reported entering sexual relationships out of economic necessity. Of these, 95 per cent had children by several fathers, placing both the women and their infants at higher risk of HIV. In Kenya, one study found 47 per cent of sugar daddies' partners were adolescents. In response, some countries such as Gambia, Uganda and Zimbabwe, have launched campaigns to alert young women.

---

access to condoms, knowledge of their proper use and the ability to negotiate safer sex, can, taken together, make the difference between life and death. Even though most people become sexually active during adolescence,[73] adolescent girls and boys have difficulty obtaining condoms and many do not know how to use them properly.[74] The majority of young people lack effective access to prevention programmes.[75] Better quality programmes are also needed, including those that tackle poverty and the harmful gender stereotypes that drive the epidemic.

**WORKING WITH YOUNG PEOPLE TO HALT THE EPIDEMIC.** The importance of preventing HIV among young people has come into sharper focus since the ICPD. At the 2001 UN General Assembly Special Session on HIV/AIDS, for example, young people were recognized as a priority group for prevention.[76] Working *with* young people can be as important as working *for* them. UNFPA and the Joint United Nations Programme on HIV/AIDS (UNAIDS) sponsor the Global Youth Coalition on HIV/AIDS, a network of some 600 youth leaders from 66 countries.[77] In 2003, UNFPA launched its Global Youth Partners initiative to empower young leaders from developing regions to improve HIV prevention through advocacy and dialogue with decision makers.[78]

Examples abound of youth activism and of communities, organizations and governments working to stop the epidemic from harming young people. In the Russian Federation, UNFPA supports *Juventa*, an innovative municipal programme with 12 clinics in St. Petersburg alone. Offering a confidential telephone hotline, education and medical services, and links with employment programmes for marginalized youth, these youth-friendly clinics, which opened in 1993, now reach 240,000 youth a year. Their "trusted doctors" provide counselling and services to commercial sex workers.

Mass media and entertainment can capture the attention of young people and embed messages in an appealing format. South Africa's Lovelife programme embarked on an innovative multimedia campaign to reach 12–to–17–year olds before they become sexually active.[79] A multimedia initiative in Nicaragua, known as "Sixth Sense", uses radio, a youth-led television soap opera and print materials on young people's rights. It has earned top ratings with young and adult audiences alike in hundreds of media outlets.[80] MTV's "Staying Alive" is the largest global HIV/AIDS campaign, covering 166 countries and territories. Its 2004 campaign, focused on girls and women, was supported by UNFPA, UNAIDS, the World Bank, Family Health International and the Kaiser Family Foundation.[81]

**EMPLOYMENT AND INCOME KEY TO PREVENTION.** Poverty and gender discrimination are at the root of many HIV infections because they limit young people's options. When people have few alternatives or little hope for the future, their possibilities and motivation for taking action to protect themselves against HIV beyond daily self-preservation and survival are limited. Providing adolescents with the skills and resources they need to make a decent living and improve their prospects can help stem the epidemic.

Some pioneering initiatives are addressing the underlying poverty and gender dimensions of the spread of HIV. In Mali, Save the Children UK introduced microcredit for rural adolescent girls to prevent their migration to cities in search of domestic work. In India, with support from the Population Council and CARE, adolescent girls living in slums acquired marketable skills, began saving money and gained self-esteem.[82] In Benin, a government programme combines job training with HIV and pregnancy prevention.

In Senegal, UNFPA, UNICEF and the World Health Organization have helped educate some 10,000 adolescent girls and young women with emphasis on literacy, gender and human rights, reproductive health services, income-generating opportunities and computer literacy and training.[83] In Mozambique, a large-scale programme known as *Geração* Biz brought together ministries, UN agencies and donors to give displaced youth greater access to reproductive health, HIV prevention and training and employment opportunities.[84]

UNESCO has been supporting integrated programmes for poor adolescent girls in South Asia that cover literacy, reproductive health and HIV/AIDS, legal education, and training in income-generation and microfinance. A science programme focusing on basic health, safe water, agriculture and renewable energy has trained 4,250 adolescent girls in 176 villages; 10 per cent of them are now employed or have started their own microbusinesses.[85]

## Child Marriage

Most countries have declared 18 as the minimum legal age of marriage, but parental consent and custom often override these laws.[86] Despite the sanctions on child marriage, more than 100 million girls are expected to marry in the next decade.[87] While it has decreased globally over the last 30 years, the practice is still common among the poorest of the poor and in rural areas.[88] It is highest in South Asia, Western and Middle Africa.[89] Where young girls are perceived as an economic liability, their marriage may form part of a family's survival strategy. More than two thirds of adolescent girls are married in Bangladesh, Niger and the Democratic Republic of the Congo, and more than half in Afghanistan, India and Nigeria.[90] In six West African countries, about 44 per cent of women had married before 15.[91]

**AN EXPERIENCE OF FEAR AND UNCERTAINTY.** While parents may hope to protect girls' economic and personal security through marriage, it frequently has the

### 25 | IN AFRICA, YOUTH LEAD THE WAY ON HIV/AIDS PREVENTION

Since 2000, youth have been active in the fight to prevent HIV in four high-prevalence countries through the African Youth Alliance (AYA), co-led by UNFPA, Pathfinder International and PATH, and supported with a generous grant from the Bill and Melinda Gates Foundation. The programme also engages communities, including cultural and religious leaders, in creating a supportive environment for gender equality and reproductive health. Survey results show AYA increased young people's knowledge of HIV/AIDS, sexually transmitted infections and pregnancy risks, and gave them greater confidence in negotiating condom use. The programme's emphasis on making services more "youth-friendly" resulted in dramatic increases in utilization, with two million young people visiting between 2003 and 2004 and, of those, 17,000 sought voluntary HIV counselling and testing.

The initiative has spurred change at many levels, including on gender issues. In Botswana, 36 faith-based organizations identified adolescent reproductive health as the core strategy of the broader church response to HIV/AIDS. The Ministry of Education is reviewing regulations that expel pregnant girls from school. AYA has also campaigned against sexual violence through "War Against Rape" school clubs. In Ghana, AYA's innovative community-based paralegal initiative has resolved cases of rape, domestic violence, child trafficking, child marriage and the abduction of adolescent girls. Through the Pregnant and Parenting Teen Centre, more than 300 young women have received life-skills training.

In the United Republic of Tanzania, AYA increased the number of young women accessing reproductive health services by organizing girls-only soccer games that included sessions on HIV prevention before the matches. On the issue of child abuse, national media campaigns by the Clouds FM radio station led to the hiring of a law firm to forward cases to the courts. Widely publicized debates on the impact of child marriage influenced the government to order that girls under 18 be allowed to return to school after the delivery of their babies. In Zanzibar, parliamentarians have called for amending an act that imprisons pregnant girls.

In Uganda, Anglican and Muslim leaders have publicly declared support for voluntary HIV counselling testing and condom use, respectively, for married young couples. Emphasis on the availability and confidentiality of services has encouraged young people to seek HIV testing. Christian and Muslim communities are now enforcing the marriage age of 18, requiring girls to produce birth certificates. The King of Busoga called for the reintegration of young mothers into the school system.

*"I never had the opportunity to be heard, understood and appreciated prior to AYA. When you live in an environment that deprives you of your basic rights and discriminates against you because you are young, you need a platform to voice your thoughts, and AYA is more than that. It taught me how to advocate for my rights but most importantly for the rights of other young people, especially girls...."*
— Ngasuma Kanyeka, young woman from the United Republic of Tanzania

---

opposite effect. Marriage often marks an end to their education. A global analysis found that girls with primary school or less were more likely to be married in adolescence.[92] For many girls, marriage is fraught with fear and uncertainty: The decision is made for them and they may have little advance notice before the wedding day. After the ceremony, married girls usually move to their husbands' homes, sometimes in another village, far away from family and familiar surroundings, and are pressured to produce children. They typically describe their first marital sexual experience as distasteful or painful and frequently mention the use of force.[93]

**MARRIED GIRLS—HIGH-RISK FOR MATERNAL MORTALITY AND HIV/AIDS.** Despite the large number of married adolescent girls, policies and programmes often fail to address their vulnerability to HIV or other reproductive health needs. Studies in Kenya, Uganda and Zambia confirm that married adolescents have higher rates of HIV infection than their sexually active unmarried peers.[94] Isolation and powerlessness are additional problems. Young wives often have limited autonomy or freedom of movement. They may be unable to obtain health care because of distance, expense or the need for permission from a spouse or in-laws. These barriers can aggravate the risks of maternal mortality and morbidity for pregnant adolescents.

Ending child marriage is closely correlated with reaching the MDGs. Child marriage denies girls the right to an education and the opportunity to realize their full potential. Married adolescent girls have limited power to influence childbearing or contraceptive decisions, with implications for infant health and survival, maternal mortality, HIV, high fertility and poverty reduction. In Bangladesh, if the mean age of childbearing increased by five years, population growth would fall by 40 per cent,[95] which would improve the country's chances of reducing poverty and sustaining development.

Recognizing the rights of adolescent girls and the implications for poverty reduction, UNFPA and its partners launched a global initiative in 2004 to end child marriage.

## Young People and Employment

Expanding young people's access to "decent and productive work" is one of the MDG targets.[96] With half the world's unemployed between the ages of 15 and 24, the challenge is considerable.[97] This is especially so in poor countries of Asia, sub-Saharan Africa and the Middle East, where youth populations are still growing.[98] The world's highest youth unemployment rates are in sub-Saharan Africa, the poorest region.[99] Furthermore, when young people do find work, many are trapped in low-wage jobs with few opportunities to learn skills. Most of these jobs are in the informal economy where the pay is too low to overcome poverty.[100] Though young women have entered the labour force in large numbers over the last 30 years, their unemployment rates exceed those of young men in all developing regions—with the exception of East Asia and sub-Saharan Africa.[101]

**CHILDREN AND ADOLESCENTS AT WORK—TOILING AND EXPLOITED.** The International Labour Organization (ILO) recommends a minimum working age of 16, but concedes that this is not always possible in rural settings where a family's economic survival depends on the labour of younger members.[102] Some 352 million children and adolescents between the ages of 5 and 17 were economically active in 2000, 171 million of them working in hazardous situations.[103] In Ethiopia, about half of 10- to 14-year-olds are economically active, and in Bangladesh, more than a third.[104] AIDS is a major cause of rising child labour in sub-Saharan Africa, where 29 per cent of children between the ages of 5 and 14 work, the highest proportion in the world. Most of these young workers have lost one or both parents to AIDS.[105]

In many developing countries, girls and young women are sent to work for wealthier households to supplement family income. Most are denied an education, fair pay and decent working conditions. Many are at risk of sexual and physical abuse and of being trafficked within their own country or across borders.[106] UNICEF estimates that there are five million domestic servants working in South Asia, mostly girls. Roughly one in five children under 14 work as domestics in India, and 300,000 in Dhaka, Bangladesh, alone.[107]

**EXPANDING DECENT EMPLOYMENT.** Youth employment is receiving increased attention. In 2002, the Youth Employment Summit (YES) Campaign was launched, supported by UNFPA and a number of partners. YES focuses on fostering young people's entrepreneurial skills and self-employment opportunities. National networks in 60 countries are devising strategies with international support, and the Youth Employment Network, a partnership of the World Bank, the ILO and the UN, is assisting 10 focus countries to develop youth employment action plans.[108]

Harnessing the energies, potential and citizenship of young people represents an invaluable opportunity to nurture agents of gender equality and socio-economic development. The socio-economic, national security and demographic implications of failing to invest in young people are far-reaching. The policies that countries and the international community develop will benefit not only this generation, but the next wave of children entering adolescence in 2015.

---

*"I married when I was 12 years old and I had a baby two years later. I had a lot of problems because I was very young. I did not want to get married."*

— Bangladesh

*"I was promised to a man before I was 10…. When the time came I was just handed over to my husband's family and when I saw him I realized he was older than my daddy."*

— Burkina Faso

From "Too Brief a Child: Voices of Married Adolescents" (video), UNFPA

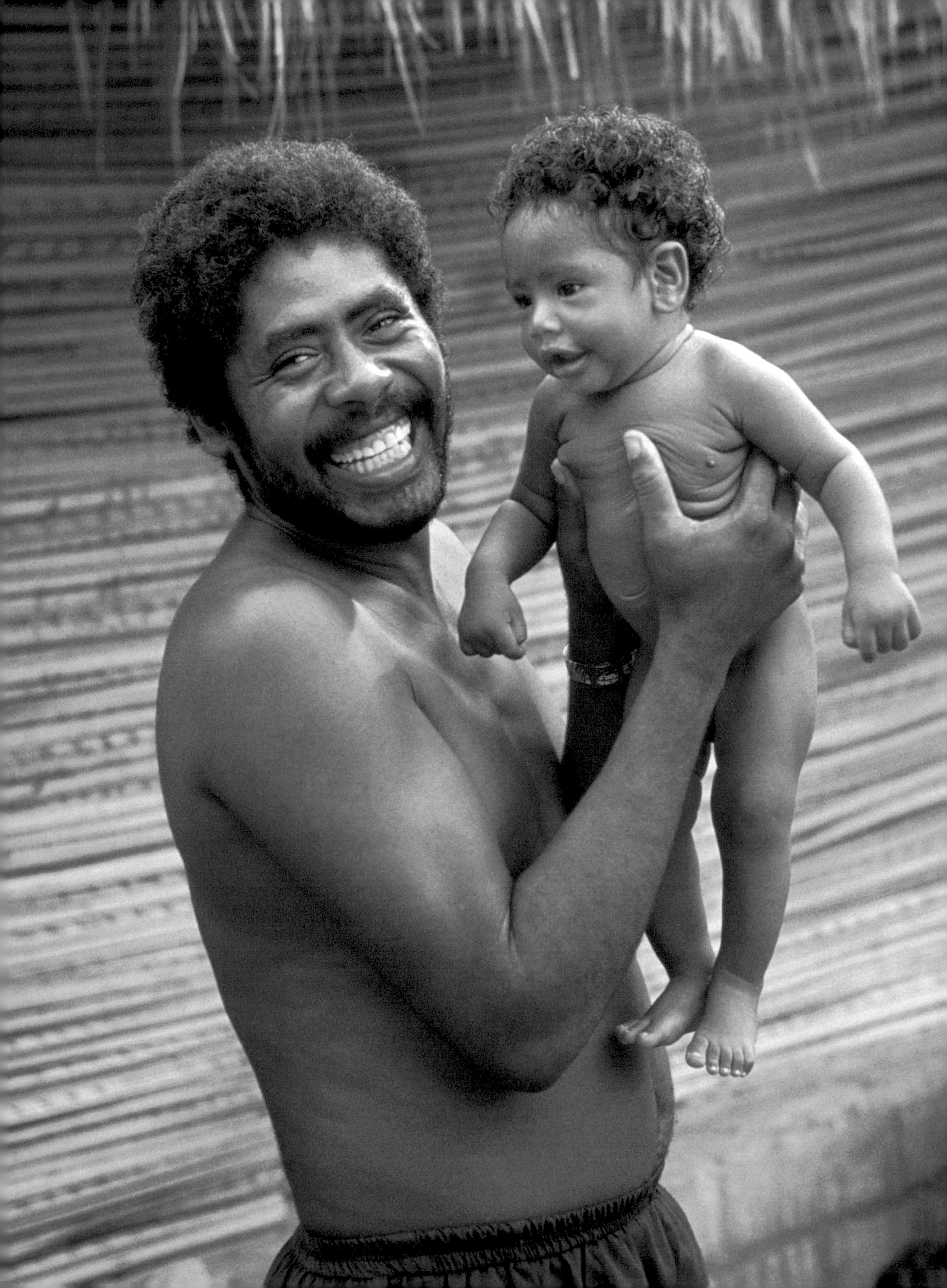

# 6 Partnering with Boys and Men

*"Changes in both men's and women's knowledge, attitudes and behaviour are necessary conditions for achieving the harmonious partnership of men and women. Men play a key role in bringing about gender equality since, in most societies, men exercise preponderant power in nearly every sphere of life, ranging from personal decisions regarding the size of families to the policy and programme decisions taken at all levels of Government. It is essential to improve communication between men and women on issues of sexuality and reproductive health, and the understanding of their joint responsibilities, so that men and women are equal partners in public and private life."*

— ICPD Programme of Action, Para 4.24

In the past, development efforts have tended to focus on either men or women, but rarely on both. For decades, development assistance often took the form of providing technologies, loans and training to men. Starting in the early 1970s, analysts pointed out the need to pay more attention to women as agents of development.[1] The initial effect was to direct more resources to women and, later, focus attention more broadly on gender dynamics and inequalities. The movement for gender equality itself has undergone a similar shift over time, from an early emphasis on women alone to the recognition of the need to engage men in the process.

The 1994 International Conference on Population and Development (ICPD) was unprecedented in its call for countries to promote men's support in the struggle for gender equality and encourage their involvement and shared responsibility in all areas of family life and reproductive health. The Millennium Development Goals (MDGs) give little explicit attention to men's roles, although the need to involve men in their realization is apparent. As a matter of principle, men, especially those who are marginalized by poverty or other circumstances, have needs and rights that deserve greater attention. As a practical matter, men wield preponderant power across all areas of public and private life. Their cooperation is essential not only in the domestic and community spheres, but also in the wider realm of national politics, finance and governance. Gender equality, and the social transformation it implies, is most likely to be achieved when men recognize that the lives of men and women are interdependent and that the empowerment of women benefits everyone.

## Men's Roles in Achieving the Millennium Development Goals

Men's partnership is clearly essential to achieving gender equality and can influence all of the other MDGs both directly and indirectly. Partnering with men is an important strategy for advancing reproductive health and rights, which are so closely linked to the MDGs. The AIDS epidemic sharply underscores men's critical role: In the absence of a vaccine or cure, changes in male behaviour are central to preventing the spread of HIV. Men play a decisive role in many other respects. Husbands often make decisions about family planning, their wives' economic activities and the use of household resources, including for doctors' and school fees. These decisions influence the well-being and prospects of the whole family. The care and support of an informed husband also improves pregnancy and childbirth outcomes and can mean the difference between life and death in cases of complications, when women need immediate medical care.

Supportive fathers can play a large role in the love, care and nurturance of their children. Often they are the primary providers for their families. Researchers have begun analyzing the links between paternal absence and poverty. Children's psychological, social and cognitive development can suffer from paternal abandonment and lack of affective and material support.[2] Fathers who neglect their financial responsibilities leave women with children more vulnerable to poverty.[3] Some mothers are forced to bring, or send, their children to work instead of to school.[4] Research in Central America and the United States has found that repercussions of paternal abandonment or neglect range from poor educational performance and school drop out (including early entry into the workforce to help families make ends meet), to teen pregnancy, drug and alcohol abuse. In the United States, fatherless children were more prone to suicide.[5]

The many benefits of a father's supportive involvement in family life underscore the pressing need for effective policies. Social norms and institutions that assume women are primarily responsible for children's well-being and care may discourage men from getting involved during pregnancy and childbirth. Yet this early involvement is associated with men's later roles and responsibilities as fathers.[6]

Gender-based expectations can keep men from enriching the lives of their children and their own lives as well: Studies confirm that for many men, fatherhood enhances well-being and confers a sense of purpose and fulfilment. Some studies have found that fatherhood may also reduce men's criminal behaviour and other forms of risk-taking.[7] Furthermore, fathers with more gender-equitable and responsible attitudes about childrearing are more likely to pass on those values to their sons and daughters and to spend more time with them.[8]

## The Impact of Gender Roles on Men

Although the lives of women and men are shared, their expectations, opportunities and behaviours often diverge widely. Understanding these differences is essential when crafting effective policies and programmes. Men cannot be considered a homogenous group: Norms vary depending on a range of socio-economic, cultural, ethnic and other factors, both among and within societies.[9] Nevertheless, the ideal of masculinity is widely associated with bravery, strength, independence and sexual activity.[10]

From an early age, boys are taught, in tacit and explicit ways, the ideals that their mothers, fathers, peers and society expect from them as future men. This ideal of "manhood" can shape the attitudes and behaviour of boys and men. The societal concept of masculinity is connected to self-identity, sense of belonging and self-worth. Where one ideal of masculinity is dominant, it is likely to be transmitted first within the family and then reinforced by the community, by other men and women, by opinion leaders and by the media. Consequently, boys and men face pressure to meet that ideal. Often they internalize the expectations and attitudes that go along with the ideal, at the cost of damage to themselves and others. Societal expectations may also restrict men's ability to see themselves as caring, non-violent and responsible partners.[11]

> "I now realize how important it is for us fathers to teach our sons to respect their mothers and sisters, and how we must provide equal opportunities to our daughters."
>
> — Older man from Laos, following a gender training session sponsored by the European Union/UNFPA Reproductive Health Initiative for Youth in Asia (RHIYA), in Luang Namtha

The ideal of men as successful providers, in control and authoritative, influences the ways in which they relate to their wives, children and other men and women. For example, unemployment can undermine a man's ability to prove himself the "breadwinner". Some men fulfil this role by migrating in search of work, even though they must leave their circle of family and friends. When their aspirations are thwarted by lack of opportunity, or when they find themselves away from their families in unfamiliar places, some may seek gratification in alcohol, drugs or risky sexual encounters. In Eastern Europe, declines in men's life expectancy in the 1990s were attributed to stress and depression caused by unemployment in the transition economies. Their distress was reflected in high rates of alcoholism, domestic violence, suicide and cardiovascular diseases.[12]

Many societies tacitly condone male risk-taking and use of violence to exert authority. Boys and men are often socialized to accept violence as appropriate male behaviour, a means to display their manhood and to protect their "honour". This is reflected in high levels of violence, both among men and against women. Boys may first encounter violence within their own families, in the form of domestic abuse.

While young men are often perpetrators of violence, they are also its primary victims: In some Latin

American countries, adolescent boys (15 to 19 years of age) represent 69 per cent of homicide victims.[13] Research from several countries suggests that as many as 10 per cent of young men have experienced unwanted advances and early sexual abuse. Young men also frequently force sex on girlfriends, dates or casual sexual partners, according to research in Mexico, Nigeria, Peru and South Africa. A significant proportion of young males in Cambodia, Peru and South Africa reported active involvement in gang rape.[14] To help young men avoid such harmful behaviours, it is first necessary to understand the inter-related social, cultural and economic factors that drive them.

**THE SEXUAL AND REPRODUCTIVE LIVES OF MEN.** For much of its history, population studies and reproductive health, unlike other development fields, focused almost exclusively on women, specifically on their fertility and reproductive lives.[15] Very little information was collected about men. As a result, few reproductive health services and programmes reflect the specific needs and perspectives of men. However, analysis of national surveys of men aged 15 to 54, undertaken over the past 10 years in 39 developing countries, now provides a better understanding of male sexual behaviour and how it differs from women's.[16]

The data reveal that men's age of sexual initiation tends to be earlier than women's, and that they have more sexual partners, both outside and within marriage.[17] Marriage is relatively infrequent among men in their early twenties or younger. However, young men tend to have more sexual partners than older men, which reinforces the need to give special attention to this age group for HIV prevention. In almost all of the developing countries surveyed, the majority of men aged 20 to 24 report sexual initiation before their 20th birthday. Although this varies significantly by region, in some countries up to 35 per cent report sexual initiation before their 15th birthday.[18]

Reproductive health and contraception remain primarily women's responsibility. A large percentage of married men aged 25 to 39, particularly in sub-Saharan Africa, report that they have not discussed family planning with their partners. Male methods—condoms and vasectomy—account for only a small percentage of global contraceptive use, except in a few industrialized countries and in China.[19]

The proportion of men aged 15 to 49 who know that condom use prevents HIV varies widely—from 9 per cent in Bangladesh to 82 per cent in Brazil. Condom use is rising in many places among sexually active men, particularly those with higher levels of education and those who live in urban areas. This may have to do with availability: Fewer than half of men living in rural areas of Chad, Guinea, Mali, Mozambique and Niger knew of a source for obtaining condoms.[20]

A troubling proportion of men with sexually transmitted infections do not inform their sexual partners. In some developing countries, at least 3 in 10 men aged

---

**26 | MEN IN TRANSITION IN CENTRAL AMERICA**

Research on fatherhood pioneered by the Central American University with UNFPA support identified factors that influence men's roles as fathers. A total of 4,790 fathers, other men and women were surveyed in Costa Rica, El Salvador, Honduras and Nicaragua. Three types emerged:

**'Traditional men'** (51 per cent of men surveyed) assume that men are "by nature" at the top of the family hierarchy. They see themselves as providers and disciplinarians— through force if necessary. They believe that affection and understanding towards their children can erode their authority and respect and consider sexual relations outside of marriage (by husbands) to be acceptable. These men tended to be 50 years or older, poor, illiterate or with minimal education and living in rural areas.

**'Modern men'** (39 per cent) are affectionate with their children and share responsibility for their upbringing, regardless of couple dissolution. They reject the use of violence, view contraception as a shared responsibility and support women's roles outside the domestic sphere. Most were between the ages of 20 and 49, with secondary or higher education, and lived in cities. Many of the "modern" or "transitional" men were younger fathers exposed to new ideas and norms about gender equality and sharing reproductive health and rights and responsibilities with women.

**'Men in transition'**, the remaining 10 per cent, fall somewhere in between. They express uncertain and at times conflicting notions of male identity.

Higher levels of educational attainment are closely correlated with more gender-equitable attitudes. This confirms research from the Economic Commission for Latin America and the Caribbean suggesting that completion of secondary education is critical to poverty reduction and the social and economic transformations necessary to attain the MDGs.

15 to 54 did not tell their partners: In Benin and Peru, 6 in 10 did not. Of sexually active young men aged 15 to 24 in Benin, Mali, Niger and Uganda who had had a sexually transmitted infection in the past 12 months, only half or fewer informed their partners.[21]

## Reaching Out to Boys and Men

Spurred initially by the ICPD's call to involve men and then by the urgency of the AIDS epidemic, innovative projects have reached out to men in bars and brothels, in barbershops and truck stops, at sports fields and youth centres, in military barracks and police academies, in mosques and churches, and in classrooms and clinics.

They have addressed men in their roles as sons, fathers, husbands, sexual partners, elders, educators, health providers, journalists and policymakers. They have used comic books and rap music, Internet sites and hotlines, peer educators and group counsellors, games and theatre productions, radio and talk shows. Several countries are increasingly addressing men's parenting role.[22] Because men are more likely to listen to other men, projects have enlisted respected community figures from high-ranking political officials to religious leaders. Clerics in Saudi Arabia have banned fathers from forcing marriage on their daughters, traditional monks in Cambodia have spoken out on HIV prevention, and national and state officials in Brazil have encouraged men to help end violence against women.[23] In 2005, UNFPA organized a regional conference of Islamic associations from 17 African countries. Imams and other religious leaders adopted a declaration urging the promotion of women's rights and reproductive health as "indispensable to saving the lives of our sisters and daughters and to reducing poverty in Africa".[24]

These varied efforts reflect several approaches to working with men.[25] The most common and earliest approach focuses on **men as clients** and aims to make reproductive health information and services more accessible and attractive to men.[26] This includes overcoming the idea that reproductive health is a woman's concern and the fact that services are often designed for, or are, primarily used by women. Men often report shame in seeking health services and are likely to do so only as a last resort.[27]

The **men as partners** approach recognizes men's influence on reproductive health options and decisions[28] and encourages men and women to deal jointly with issues such as contraception, emergency plans for labour and delivery, voluntary HIV counselling and testing, and post-abortion counselling. This approach may go beyond reproductive health to engage men in wider issues, such as gender-based violence and female genital mutilation/cutting.

A third approach, emphasizing **men as agents of positive change** involves men more fully in promoting gender equality and social change. It offers men opportunities to reflect on their own history and experiences, to question gender attitudes and to recognize how gender inequities harm their partners and themselves.

> *"If you sell the image of a health service as maternal-child care, obviously a man will not go. He says to himself, how am I going to go to a service designed for women? I am not pregnant. Obviously they will not go."*
>
> — Respondent in the UNFPA-sponsored study on men's perspectives in Nicaragua

Programmes working to involve men more effectively face a dilemma that raises ethical and human rights issues. Programmes that overlook existing power imbalances between men and women may have the unintended consequence of reinforcing inequities and male control over women's decision-making. This is especially critical in the area of reproductive health. This is why a clear and explicit gender-responsive approach is necessary in order to develop policies and programmes.

## Reinterpreting Masculinity

The social pressures to perform and codes of honour that men and boys grow up with can encourage them to compete, resort to violence or take sexual risks to demonstrate their "manliness".[29] Taught to hide their fears and emotions, they may find it difficult to reveal their true feelings and concerns. Although such gender norms are often rigid and limiting, they are not static. Positive alternatives can be cultivated.[30] The notion of strength, for example, can lead to violent behaviour, but it can also find expression in resisting peer pressure or in protecting oneself and loved ones. Sometimes the way the message is framed can make a big difference: In several Latin American countries telling young men that they have the right to be involved in their children's lives has had a positive impact, whereas framing their involvement as a duty had the opposite effect.[31]

Research shows that many men in all parts of the world express an interest in supporting and becoming more involved in the reproductive health of their partners. But negative feedback from other men, family members and employers, and resistance by health providers, may prevent men from putting their interest into practice.[32] They may be uncomfortable with rigid gender norms, but unable to challenge them on their own, without the support of peers and a conducive social environment.

Some programmes have shown that with opportunities and encouragement men are motivated to adopt more equitable and healthful attitudes and behaviours.[33] For example, young men spontaneously formed pressure groups to oppose female genital mutilation/cutting as a result of a UNFPA-supported Reproductive, Educative and Community Health Project in Uganda, which was carried out in partnership with the Sabiny Elders Association.[34] At the National Association for People Living with HIV/AIDS in Malawi, nine out of 10 male members confessed that they were unable to disclose their HIV status to their wives. Following the establishment of support groups for young couples, fully 65 per cent of young men who were previously unable to admit they were HIV-positive brought their wives.[35] Also in Malawi, the Men for Gender Equality Network sponsors men's clubs that build awareness of gender equality issues. Viet Nam has entered into the territory of shared domestic responsibilities, with a campaign whose slogan is: "If you share housework with women, happiness will be doubled."[36]

The ReproSalud project implemented by Movimiento Manuela Ramos in Peru trained male educators to help men in poor and indigenous communities to think critically about gender norms and reproductive health. Their workshops demonstrated

*"I'll be a different husband [from the way my father was]. I'll share domestic chores, support her outside the home, give her freedom. I won't tie her down."*

— Victor, 25, group member of the Conscientizing Male Adolescents project, Nigeria

that men value the opportunity to discuss violence, alcoholism, sexuality and fatherhood and to contemplate living differently.[37] Significant behavioural changes were observed as well. Local health facilities reported dramatic increases in the use of services. One nearby hospital, for example, reported a 400 per cent increase in family planning visits within a year. Community members were enthusiastic about the changes brought about by this initiative.

The Men as Partners programme, initiated by EngenderHealth in South Africa, seeks to curb the transmission of HIV through workshops, radio and Internet dialogues, involving frank discussions between men and women about gender norms and relationships. Workshops are often facilitated by men motivated by their own exposure to domestic violence and AIDS, and convinced of the need for change. EngenderHealth, which initiated the programme, has now broadened it through partnerships with other groups, such as the South Africa Men's Forum, and by another component that focuses on young men.[38]

## The Formative Years

Reaching boys and young men early offers the greatest opportunity to instil gender equitable values. Boys who grow up around positive male role models are more likely to question gender inequities and harmful stereotypes.[39] There is also an urgency about addressing youth: Men ages 15 to 24 exhibit the riskiest behaviours relating to HIV transmission, including multiple sexual partners and injecting drug use.[40] Unfortunately, the typical school curriculum does not provide the opportunity for young people to learn relationship skills, discuss norms and peer pressure and raise doubts and questions.[41] In any case, reaching impoverished or marginalized adolescents boys who may have left school, but are at risk of HIV, drug abuse and violence, requires moving beyond the school setting.

Kenya's Chogoria Hospital's "Climbing to Manhood" programme takes advantage of traditional male rites of passage, and boys' heightened receptivity

> **27 PUTTING MEN ON THE AGENDA**
>
> In the context of the MDGs, national policies offer an important but commonly overlooked opportunity to take male perspectives and roles into account. Some countries have begun addressing men's roles in poverty reduction, gender equality and reproductive health through policy and legislative means.
>
> Cambodia's policy on women, the girl child and STIs/HIV/AIDS calls for attention to men's roles. It states that "the spread of HIV/AIDS among women and girls can be slowed only if concrete changes are brought about in the sexual behaviour of men" and explicitly places it on the agenda for policy-makers and service-providers.
>
> Viet Nam's 2002 Poverty Reduction Strategy Paper observes how few men are aware of their roles and responsibilities regarding family planning, and proposes policies to encourage male contraceptive use. Botswana's family planning policy places men first on a list of "special groups" and provides guidelines for catering to them as clients.
>
> Many countries' youth policies are paying more attention to young men. Concerns about young Jamaican men, for instance, have led to an emphasis at the policy level on male education, male role models and fathering. Jamaica's 1994 National Youth Policy calls for promoting "gender equity and the transformation of societal norms and cultural practices of masculinity and femininity".
>
> In general, developed and developing countries alike have paid only limited attention to supporting men's roles as fathers. In the past 20 years, however, policies and programmes in countries of Western Europe, North America and Australia have been adopted to encourage men's role as fathers, including paternity leave. Several Latin American countries have passed legislation obligating fathers to provide care and financial support for their children, though limited budgets and enforcement have restricted their effectiveness.
>
> Costa Rica's innovative Law of Responsible Fatherhood passed in 2001 frames paternal obligations in terms of the right of children to know their parents and to be supported by them and, in so doing, removes some of the stigma for children born out of wedlock. The legislation, which established procedures for mothers to present legal claims and mandates genetic testing where paternity is in question, is credited with a drop in the number of children who are unrecognized by their fathers—from 29.3 per cent in 1999 to 7.8 per cent in 2003. The law also calls for sensitization campaigns, annual budgetary appropriations to cover the costs of DNA testing and the formulation of a national policy on the promotion of responsible fatherhood.

during this period of seclusion, to address sexual behaviours, drugs and relationships.[42] Masculinity at Play, a pilot programme initiated by the Pan American Health Organization, taps into the youthful enthusiasm of boys for sports. Soccer coaches in several Latin American countries have been trained to incorporate lessons about gender equity, adolescent rights and responsibilities and healthy lifestyles into soccer training for boys aged 8 to 12.[43] In Uganda, the African Youth Alliance reached over 500,000 young people in 2003 and 2004 with reproductive health and HIV prevention education and services. Its outreach activities proved especially effective for 10- to 14-year-old boys, who do not typically visit health facilities.

The Conscientizing Male Adolescents project in Nigeria, run by male community members, uses structured dialogues to encourage critical thinking in young men aged 14 to 20 who have demonstrated qualities of leadership. Discussion topics cover gender-based oppression and violence, power dynamics within the family, intimate relationships, sexual and reproductive health, human rights and democracy.[44]

In Egypt and India, the Centre for Development and Population Activities (CEDPA), an international NGO, enables young men to challenge gender inequities while also expanding their options. Its programme works with young men through vocational training classes, remedial tutoring classes, gyms, clubs and other community organizations.[45]

Pioneered in Brazil, Programme H trains health and education professionals to work with groups of young men on violence prevention, paternity and sexual and reproductive health. The workshops encourage reflection on traditionally defined notions of masculinity and the adoption of more gender-equitable attitudes and practices. Programme H is being replicated with UNFPA support in Costa Rica, Honduras, Nicaragua and Panama and is also expanding to countries in Africa and Asia.[46]

## Accelerating Progress

When it comes to poverty reduction, gender equality, reproductive health, halting the AIDS epidemic and eliminating violence against women (see Chapter 7), the benefits of involving men are clear. Recent initiatives, policies and laws are demonstrating success. However, budgetary constraints loom large and sociocultural resistance to greater equity persists. Though many innovative programmes have emerged over the past decade, they are generally small in scale.

Achieving the Millennium Development Goals will require involving men more directly and on a larger scale. Reproductive health and gender programmes in the armed services and police provide a model. Countries in every region have worked with UNFPA to take advantage of established military health and educational infrastructures to reach large segments of the population, especially young men who represent the majority of army recruits, and who are a key audience for prevention of sexually transmitted infections, including HIV.[47] A project with the Botswana armed forces used the urgency of HIV prevention as an entry point for raising awareness about other aspects of reproductive health and rights. In northwest Namibia, military and police officers, as well as soccer coaches and managers, were trained on reproductive health issues. The project, which took advantage of local brew shops to disseminate its messages, is credited with reducing gender-based violence and increasing requests for voluntary testing and counselling, as well as for condoms.[48]

In Latin America, UNFPA has helped to institutionalize reproductive health, gender equality and HIV prevention programmes in the armed forces in nine countries over the last decade. In Ecuador, reproductive health education in military schools and services was expanded to include officers' families. Gender stereotypes have shown signs of changing, and fathers' relationships with their adolescent children have improved.

In Nicaragua, reproductive health programmes are now officially mandated at all levels of the military's health services and training courses. A thousand army conscripts have been trained to serve as Brigades on Sexual and Reproductive Health and educate their communities once they are released from duty. Female military employees report greater respect from colleagues and more support for and knowledge of women's reproductive rights. Demand for condoms has also risen.[49]

Other ways to scale up men's involvement include reaching employees in the workplace and taking advantage of national health infrastructures. In Haiti, the NGO Group in Struggle Against AIDS has reached 20,000 men at utility companies and bottling plants.[50] Bangladesh has tested integrating services for men into rural Health and Female Welfare Centres. If an expansion of the pilot project results in significant improvements, the Ministry of Health plans to scale up coverage nationwide to 3,700 health centres.[51]

Both the 2005 UN Secretary-General's progress reports on the Beijing Conference and the UN Declaration on Commitment to HIV/AIDS reiterate the need to transform social norms affecting boys and men and to involve them as partners in promoting women's human rights, halting the epidemic and caring for HIV-positive family members.[52] A greater emphasis on men raises some important issues. Since women bear a disproportionate burden in reproductive health and childbearing, efforts directed at men should not come at the expense of women or deflect scarce resources from programmes that women desperately need. One solution is to involve men in ways that benefit both sexes and promote gender equality as an explicit aim. The results of various initiatives suggest that efforts to reach both men and women could further progress toward international development goals. This implies mobilizing sufficient resources and political will to accelerate momentum towards a more gender-equitable world, as called for by the UN Millennium Project.

> *"I learned to talk more with my girlfriend. Now I worry more about her...it's important to know what the other person wants, listen to them. Before [the workshops], I just worried about myself."*
>
> — Young Brazilian participant in Programme H

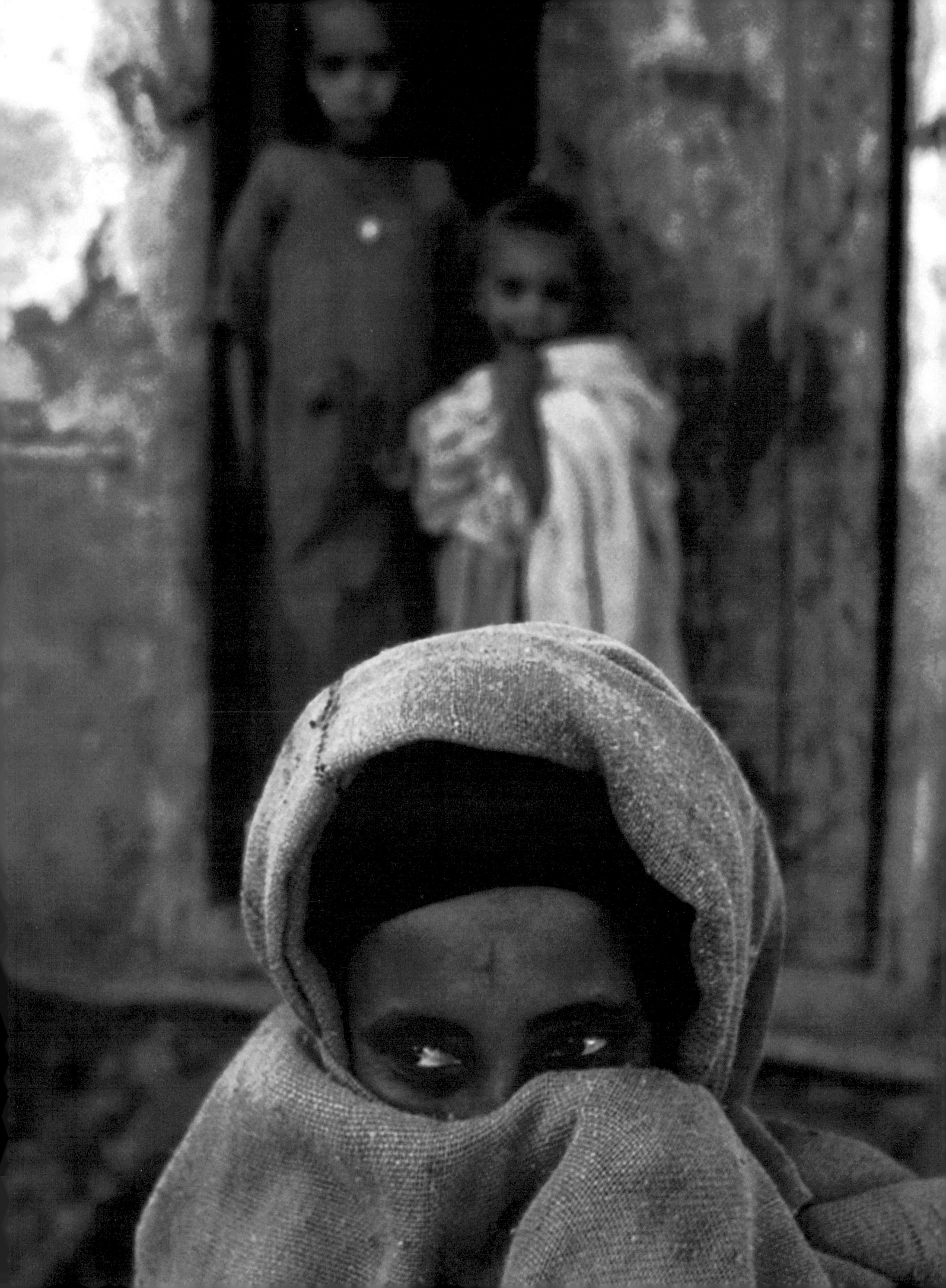

# 7 Gender-Based Violence: A Price Too High

*"[A] woman who lives in the shadow of daily violence ....is not truly free."*
— UN Secretary-General Kofi Annan, *In Larger Freedom*

Gender-based violence is perhaps the most widespread and socially tolerated of human rights violations. The cost to women, their children, families and communities is a significant obstacle to reducing poverty, achieving gender equality and meeting the other Millennium Development Goals (MDGs). Violence is a traumatic experience for any man or woman, but gender-based violence is preponderantly inflicted by men on women and girls. It both reflects and reinforces inequities between men and women and compromises the health, dignity, security and autonomy of its victims.

Worldwide, an estimated one in five women will be a victim of rape or attempted rape in her lifetime.[1] One in three will have been beaten, coerced into sex or otherwise abused, usually by a family member or an acquaintance.[2] More often than not, the perpetrators go unpunished. Each year, hundreds of thousands of women and children are trafficked and enslaved, millions more are subjected to harmful practices. Violence kills and disables as many women between the ages of 15 and 44 as cancer. And its toll on women's health surpasses that of traffic accidents and malaria combined.[3]

The consequences of gender-based violence are devastating. Survivors often experience life-long emotional distress, mental health problems and poor reproductive health. Abused women are also at higher risk of acquiring HIV.[4] Women who have been physically or sexually assaulted tend to be intensive long-term users of health services.[5] The impact of violence may also extend to future generations: Children who have witnessed abuse, or were victims themselves, often suffer lasting psychological damage.[6]

The cost to countries is high as well: Increased health care expenditures; demands on courts, police and schools; and losses in educational achievement and productivity. In Chile, domestic violence cost women $1.56 billion in lost earnings in 1996, more than 2 per cent of the country's GDP.[7] In India, one survey showed women lost an average of seven working days after an incident of violence.[8] Domestic violence constitutes the single biggest health risk to Australian women of reproductive age, resulting in economic losses of about $6.3 billion a year.[9] In the United States, the figure adds up to some $12.6 billion annually.[10] International financial institutions have also begun to take note. The Inter-American Development Bank, for example, is addressing gender-based violence through its lending portfolios.[11]

## The Magnitude and Many Forms of Gender-Based Violence

Gender-based violence may involve intimate partners, family members, acquaintances or strangers. Though it was long regarded a private matter, it is now recognized by the international community as a violation of human rights, rooted in women's subordinate status (see Box 28). The action plans from the 1994 International Conference on Population and Development (ICPD) and the 1995 Fourth World Conference on Women (Beijing) recognized the elimination of gender-based violence as central to gender equality and the empowerment of women. The term comprises domestic violence, sexual and psychological forms of abuse as well as harmful practices, such as female genital mutilation/cutting. It also includes prenatal sex selection and female infanticide—extreme manifestations of the low social value placed on girls (see Box 29). Systematic rape, increasingly used as a tool of terror during armed conflict, has prompted the adoption of major international agree-

## 28 | WHAT IS VIOLENCE AGAINST WOMEN?

In 1993, the UN Declaration on the Elimination of Violence against Women offered the first official definition of gender-based violence:

Article 1: Any act of gender-based violence that results in, or is likely to result in, physical, sexual or psychological harm or suffering to women, including threats of such acts, coercion or arbitrary deprivations of liberty, whether occurring in public or in private life.

Article 2 of the Declaration states that the definition should encompass, but not be limited to, acts of physical, sexual, and psychological violence in the family, community, or perpetrated or condoned by the State, wherever it occurs. These acts include: spousal battery; sexual abuse, including of female children; dowry-related violence; rape, including marital rape; female genital mutilation/cutting and other traditional practices harmful to women; non-spousal violence; sexual violence related to exploitation; sexual harassment and intimidation at work, in school and elsewhere; trafficking in women; and forced prostitution.

The 1995 Beijing Platform for Action expanded on this definition, specifying that it includes: violations of the rights of women in situations of armed conflict, including systematic rape, sexual slavery and forced pregnancy; forced sterilization, forced abortion, coerced or forced use of contraceptives; prenatal sex selection and female infanticide. It further recognized the particular vulnerabilities of women belonging to minorities: the elderly and the displaced; indigenous, refugee and migrant communities; women living in impoverished rural or remote areas, or in detention.

---

ments to protect women and punish perpetrators (see Chapter 8).

Domestic violence is by far the most common form of gender-based violence. Based on survey data, between 10 per cent of women in some countries and 69 per cent in others are subjected to domestic violence.[12] In about one fourth of cases, sexual abuse also occurs.[13] Sexual violence may involve physical and psychological intimidation, unwanted sexual advances or acts, date and marital rape and blackmail. It may also play on a woman's financial insecurity, through threats of job dismissal or exploitation, such as the offer of food or shelter in return for sex. Denial of contraceptive protection is also considered a form of sexual violence.[14] Although abused women often live in terror, many are trapped by fear of community disapproval or reprisal. These fears may be justified; studies from developed countries show that a significant number of intimate partner homicides occur when a woman tries to leave an abusive partner, or soon thereafter. In Australia, Canada, Israel, South Africa and the United States, between 40 and 70 per cent of female murder victims were killed by their male partners.[15]

Human trafficking, sometimes called the "largest slave trade in history", is overtaking drug smuggling as one of the world's fastest growing illegal enterprises.[16] The United States Department of State 2005 Trafficking in Persons report estimates that between 600,000 and 800,000 individuals are trafficked each year for forced labour, the majority for commercial sexual exploitation. Approximately 80 per cent are women and girls, and up to 50 per cent are minors.[17]

Some two million children, mostly girls, are believed to be sex slaves in the multibillion-dollar commercial sex industry.[18] Trafficking estimates within countries run even higher.[19] In 2000, the alarming rise in sexual trafficking prompted the UN General Assembly to adopt a protocol to the UN Convention against Transnational Organized Crime to protect women and children.[20] In 2005, the Council of Europe also adopted a convention on trafficking.[21] A growing number of developed and developing countries have adopted anti-trafficking laws and policies.[22]

### UNDER ASSAULT: ADOLESCENT GIRLS AND YOUNG WOMEN.

Younger women and adolescent girls are especially vulnerable to gender-based violence. Nearly 50 per cent of all sexual assaults worldwide are against girls 15 years or younger.[23] High numbers of young women report that their first sexual experience was coerced.[24] In the Caribbean, this figure is estimated at 48 per cent of

> *"Day in and day out I am verbally and physically abused by my husband and in-laws for not bringing in enough dowry....There is nothing I can do about it."*
>
> — Jamna, 19, bride of six months, India

young women.[25] Studies from Jamaica, Mali, the United Republic of Tanzania and Zimbabwe revealed that between 20 and 30 per cent of adolescent girls had experienced sexual violence.[26] Forced sexual relations are especially likely within the context of child marriage.[27] In Burundi, the UNFPA-supported NGO centres offering support for victims of sexual violence found that 88 per cent of the women seeking care in 2004 were young women. In Thailand, intimate partner violence is a leading cause of death for women and girls between the ages of 15 and 24.[28]

Women who have been sexually abused once are more likely to suffer it again: 60 per cent of women whose first sexual experience was forced experienced sexual violence later in their lives.[29] Sexual abuse and incest in childhood can have life-long effects on sexual behaviour and reproductive health.[30] Abused adolescent girls are more likely to undergo early and repeated pregnancies and abortions, and to contract sexually transmitted infections, including HIV. Adolescent girls and young women are also the prime targets of traffickers and of armed groups during conflicts and are also subjected to harmful practices such as child marriage and female genital mutilation/cutting.

*"People from that area would take any girl like me. They don't have many females there. I was sold and had to live with him… It was a frightening experience. I could not escape and I had no money even for a phone call. I always wanted to return home."*

— 19-year-old girl from China, sold to an older man by her brother

### HIDDEN BY A CULTURE OF SILENCE.
Violence against women has long been shrouded in a culture of silence. Reliable statistics are hard to come by, as violence is underreported because of shame, stigma and fear of retribution.[31] It is not uncommon for women to be blamed for their own rape and for bringing dishonour to their families. The World Health Organization found that 20 to 70 per cent of the women interviewed in its multi-country research were talking about their abuse for the first time.[32]

---

**29 | MISSING GIRLS**

Discrimination against girls may begin in the womb. In some countries, a strong preference for sons has led to the elimination of millions of girls through prenatal sex selection. Baby girls also die through deliberate neglect and starvation. In Asia, at least 60 million girls are "missing". In some countries, sex selection is more common in cities, where technologies such as amniocentesis and ultrasound are readily accessible and open to misuse. In others, it occurs more commonly in rural areas, where the preference for sons is strong. Governments have banned the practice, and passed laws against discrimination and abandonment of girls, but the practice is deeply rooted. In many places, it is reinforced by the perception that daughters are an economic liability, either because of low expected contributions to family income or large dowry requirements. Sex selection has become a lucrative business for doctors and producers of medical equipment.

Sex ratio at birth is slightly skewed in favour of boys due to biological reasons. For every 100 girls born there are normally 103 to 107 boys. However, since boys and men normally have higher mortality rates than girls and women throughout life, in most countries of the world, women outnumber men. A country's sex balance can be a telling indicator of its social well-being. The shortage of women and girls in some Asian countries has potentially alarming social repercussions, including increased demand for trafficking in women, whether for marriage or for sex work, and the worsening of their status overall.

Eliminating the practice requires changes in the way girls and women are valued by society. In India, UNFPA supports the Government in a comprehensive approach that includes building media interest, creating community-based networks to advocate against the practice, sensitizing health providers and involving youth and other key stakeholders. In Haryana State, where the sex ratio imbalance is one of the highest, *jagriti mandalis* ("forums of awakening") function as women's social action groups that promote the rights of daughters. These groups have convinced families and doctors not to practice sex selection. In China, where the government aims to normalize its sex ratio imbalance by 2010, UNFPA has worked with the government, academia, and media to raise awareness and increase capacity. The National Population and Family Planning Commission is offering a "Girl Care" initiative in poor communities in 13 counties. Incentives such as pension plans or monetary rewards designed to offset school fees are being offered to the parents of girls. In 2004, UNFPA and the Ford Foundation organized an international conference on prenatal sex selection, drawing media and policy attention to strategies for eliminating the practice.

### 30 RECLAIMING LIVES, FIGHTING TRAFFICKING IN NEPAL

Lured by a relative's false promises, Maya (not her real name), now 35 years old, left Nepal for a brothel in Kolkata, India when she was a young woman. For 14 years, she was forced to have sex with 10 men a day. When she contracted HIV, she was sent back to Nepal, depressed and suicidal. She spent 35 days receiving counselling at a women's shelter in Nuwakot, Nepal, run by Beyond Trafficking: The Joint Initiative in the Millennium Against Trafficking in Girls and Women (JIT). As her confidence increased, Maya began training other women on trafficking and HIV prevention. JIT, a collaborative effort between the Nepalese government and the UN System Task Force Against Trafficking, works to help women like Maya recover and participate more fully in society, not only as survivors, but also as resourceful community members.

One of the reasons women remain silent is that in many societies violence against women is accepted as a "normal" aspect of gender relations.[33] In some countries, a large proportion of women believe wife beating may be justified for reasons such as refusing to have sex or not preparing food on time (see Figure 5). Studies in Peru and South Africa have found that both girls and boys interviewed believed the victim of a sexual assault was to blame and may even have provoked her own assault.[34]

Financial dependence, subordinate social status and a lack of legal rights and legal counselling services in many societies limit the ability of women to protect themselves or leave abusive situations. Abused women tend to be isolated and kept from social interaction or income-earning activities that might give them the option to end the abuse. Threats of deprivation can trap them and their children in abusive situations. Withholding the means to family survival or financial security, or damage to property or business, constitutes a form of violence. However, such intimidation is rarely legally recognized, with some exceptions, such as in Costa Rica, the Dominican Republic, Guatemala and Honduras.[35]

Even where laws against gender-based violence do exist, enforcement and legal systems may not be supportive.[36] Sometimes they re-victimize women. Such laws often lack budgetary appropriations, leaving critical gaps between intention and reality. In Latin America and the Caribbean, where most countries have passed laws on domestic violence, an analysis of ministry budget lines reveals insufficient funding to implement them properly.[37]

## Violence Against Women and the MDGs

The UN Millennium Project affirms that "freedom from violence, especially for girls and women" is a core right and essential to the ability to lead a productive life.[38] Gender-based violence directly jeopardizes the achievement of the MDGs related to gender equality and the empowerment of women, infant and maternal health and mortality, and combating HIV/AIDS. It can also affect educational attainment. A study in Nicaragua found that 63 per cent of the children of abused women had to repeat a school year and left school on average four years

**Figure 5: Women Who Believe Wife Beating is Justified for at Least One Reason***

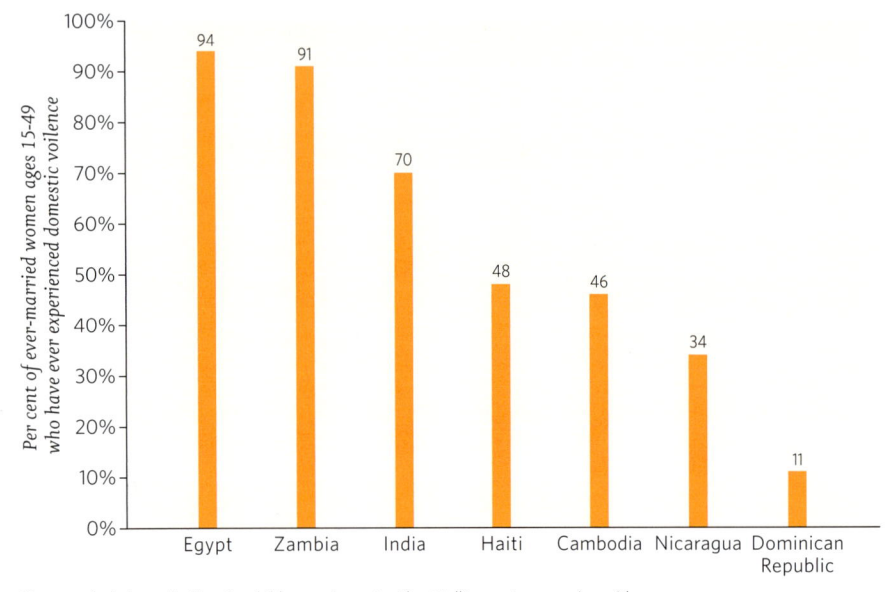

Per cent of ever-married women ages 15-49 who have ever experienced domestic violence:
- Egypt: 94
- Zambia: 91
- India: 70
- Haiti: 48
- Cambodia: 46
- Nicaragua: 34
- Dominican Republic: 11

*Reasons include neglecting the children, going out without telling partner, arguing with partner, refusing to have sex, not preparing food properly/on time, talking to other men.

**Source:** Kishor, S. and K. Johnson, 2004, *Profiling Domestic Violence: A Multicountry Study*, Calverton, MD: ORC Macro, Measure DHS+:66

earlier than others.[39] Gender-based violence imposes obstacles to the full participation of women in social, economic and political life. Illustrating the importance of this issue is the call of the UN Millennium Project Task Force on Education and Gender Equality for a global campaign on violence against women under the leadership of the UN Secretary-General.[40]

**CONSEQUENCES FOR REPRODUCTIVE HEALTH.** Violence against women compromises reproductive health and pregnancy outcomes. Consequences include: unwanted pregnancy, unsafe abortion and maternal mortality; miscarriage and stillbirth; delayed antenatal care; premature labour and childbirth;[41] foetal injury and low birth weight.[42] Abused women also face higher risks of contracting HIV and other sexually transmitted infections. Exposure increases directly with rape and indirectly through fear of negotiating condom use. The fact that violent men tend to have more partners outside of marriage adds to the risks.[43] Sexual coercion is now considered a significant factor in the continuing rise of HIV among young women (see Chapter 5).[44] Brutal rape, such as reported in situations of armed conflict, can result in fistula, perforated sexual organs and other related injuries.[45] The physical consequences of female genital mutilation/cutting include great pain, excessive bleeding, shock, painful sexual intercourse, risks of HIV or other infections from the use of unsanitary tools, chronic pelvic inflammation and even death. Psychological effects include anxiety and depression.[46]

About one in four women is abused during pregnancy, which endangers both mother and child.[47] In some districts of India, 16 per cent of deaths during pregnancy were attributed to domestic violence.[48] Violence during pregnancy quadruples the risk of low birth-weight and doubles the risk of miscarriage.[49] In Nicaragua, abuse of expectant mothers accounts for 16 per cent of low-birth-weight infants.[50] Clinical studies, for example, in Hong Kong SAR, China,[51] and Uganda,[52] found that about 30 per cent of women who had abortions reported abuse as the main reason for terminating their pregnancies.

*"I hate early marriage. I was married at an early age and my in-laws forced me to sleep with my husband and he made me suffer all night. After that, whenever day becomes night, I get worried thinking that it will be like that. This is what I hate most."*

— Ethiopian girl, age 11, married at age 5

**ADDRESSING ABUSE THROUGH REPRODUCTIVE HEALTH PROGRAMMES.** Reproductive health services offer a strategic venue for offering support to women who have suffered violence. A visit to a reproductive health centre may be a woman's only chance to obtain help. Even in sub-Saharan Africa, where public health infrastructures are very limited, the overwhelming majority of women receive some antenatal care or family planning information.[53] Addressing violence against women in reproductive health settings may also be cost-effective. Violence is a cause of recurring health problems and prevents a woman from protecting herself against unwanted pregnancies and sexually transmitted infections. Routine screening of women in reproductive health settings can help reduce the risks for both women and infants.

At the 1995 Beijing Conference, governments promised to "integrate mental health services into primary health care systems…and train primary health workers to recognize and care for girls and women of all ages who have experienced any form of violence".[54] During the 1990s, more countries began providing integrated services to address gender-based violence. Malaysia was among the first to establish "one-stop crisis centres" that offered both medical and legal services.[55] Affiliates of the International Planned Parenthood Federation (IPPF) in Brazil, Colombia, the Dominican Republic and Peru expanded their reproductive health services to include a gender-based violence component. An assessment of an IPPF multi-country project found that detection and referral rates of abused women rose dramatically within the first year.[56] UNFPA has tested similar pilot interventions in reproductive health settings in 10 countries. In some, the interventions led to an increase in the availability of health facilities offering on-site screening and care for abused women. It also expanded the network of services available to women beyond the health sector.[57] Governments are also increasingly making emergency contraception available as a component of post-rape care.

> **31  A LIFE FREE OF VIOLENCE—IT'S OUR RIGHT**
>
> An initiative launched in 1998 by eight UN agencies, including UNFPA, shows how campaigns can help sustain long-term collaboration among governments, civil society, women's groups and the UN system. The UN Inter-Agency Campaign on Women's Human Rights in Latin America and the Caribbean, "A Life Free of Violence—It's Our Right", was endorsed by 22 governments and kept the issue on the agenda of policymakers and in the public eye.
>
> The campaign used mass media, including a magazine called "Maria Maria," a touring photo competition and public service announcements, to spur national and regional action on violence against women. In 2001, a symposium on gender violence, health and rights in the Americas brought together representatives of health ministries, women's organizations and civil society from 30 countries to identify strategies to meet the public health challenge of violence against women. The symposium's Call to Action placed women's rights to personal security squarely on the agenda of health systems, and urged governments and civil society to take comprehensive legislative, financial and social action. Regional entities and UN agencies continue their collaboration, supporting and monitoring progress at regional and country levels.

**EDUCATION, SAFETY AND ECONOMIC ASSETS.** Although gender-based violence affects women of all classes, poverty and lack of education are additional risk factors.[58] Increasing educational levels can help prevent violence by empowering young women. Quality educational programmes can also serve as a vehicle for sensitizing young men to respect women's rights.

Making schools safe for girls is an essential step for achieving the MDG education targets. In some countries, parents keep their daughters out of school for fear of sexual abuse or rape. Some countries are taking action. For example, the Government of Panama with UNFPA support developed a national programme to prevent sexual abuse of girls in schools.[59] Women and girls living in poverty are often more vulnerable to rape, possibly because their neighbourhoods and commutes to work or school are more dangerous. Successful public responses include Montreal's "Between Two Stops", which allows women to get off a bus as close to their destination as possible at night, and Bangkok's "Lady Bus" service.[60]

Economic assets also seem to have a protective effect. In Kerala, India, a survey found that 49 per cent of women without property reported physical violence, compared to only 7 per cent of women who owned assets.[61] In some cases, anti-violence efforts are focusing on women's economic empowerment. In Algeria and Morocco, UNFPA is supporting efforts to include such initiatives in existing services for survivors.[62] In Venezuela, UNFPA has supported the efforts of the National Women's Bank, *Banmujer*, to integrate violence prevention into its credit services. The National Women's Institute, a member of the network of government and non-governmental organizations established to provide relevant services for victims of abuse, operates a hotline to report violence. Bank officers regularly receive refresher training on gender-based violence and reproductive health to better meet the non-financial needs of female clients. Promoting women's economic rights, including their rights to property and inheritance, as recommended by the UN Millennium Project, can help women avoid and end abusive relationships.[63]

## Mobilizing for 'Zero Tolerance'

For decades, women's rights advocates and international agencies such as the United Nations Development Fund for Women (UNIFEM) have worked to promote a culture of zero tolerance for violence against women. An increasing number of communities, coalitions and countries are mobilizing around the cause.

Some 25 countries have signalled their commitment by developing national action plans on eliminating violence against women.[64] Many countries are also adopting laws on various forms of gender-based violence. For example, Tunisia criminalized sexual harassment in 2004. Niger's 2003 law defines rape and sexual harassment and prohibits any form of slavery of women and children.[65] A 2003 law passed in Kyrgyzstan was initiated by non-governmental organizations. They gathered 30,000 signatures in a first-of-a-kind, grass-roots effort to promote anti-violence legislation. Jordan has removed impunity for honour killings. More countries have criminalized rape within marriage.[66]

Gender-based violence is a multi-dimensional problem that demands a multi-faceted response. In India, Family Counselling Centres, set up by the Madhya

> **32 CAMPAIGNING AGAINST SEX TOURISM AND SEXUAL EXPLOITATION IN PANAMA**
>
> With support from UNFPA, the Panamanian National Directorate for Women launched a mass-media campaign against sexual exploitation on 25 November 2004, the International Day to Eradicate Violence Against Women. The campaign targeted the general public, government officials, the media and tourists and publicized a law on sex tourism passed in 2000. It aired radio messages from celebrities, distributed posters to neighbourhood shops, cybercafés, hotels and casinos, and gave information packets to government decision makers and journalists. In the presence of the media, the First Lady and high-level officials passed out postcards promoting safe tourism instead of sex tourism to tourists at the national airport.

Pradesh police department and supported by UNFPA, provide counselling and legal services in cases of violence related to dowries, harassment by in-laws, child marriage, rape and abuse.[67] UNFPA has also worked closely with the Network of African Women Ministers and Parliamentarians to scale up their national advocacy efforts for stronger laws and enforcement.[68] In Kenya, counselling services help girls who run away to escape genital mutilation/cutting or forced marriage to return home without risk.[69] China has produced a manual on domestic violence for social workers.[70] Disseminating legal information in a language that is easily understood is essential to ensure that communities, women and potential perpetrators—especially those who are illiterate, living in poverty, or from different linguistic backgrounds—are informed about rights and penalties under the law.

In Honduras, almost one in six women over age 14 reports having been the victim of physical violence. A groundbreaking initiative is training police officers to become more gender-sensitive when they intervene in cases of domestic violence. The partnership involving the Ministry of Security, the National Police, the National Institute for Women's Affairs and UNFPA has reached its goal of training all national police institute graduates—some 1,500 per year. The curriculum on gender-based violence is now part of the regular police training programme. The 2004 regional conference on good governance and gender equality convened by ECLAC recognized the initiative as a "best practice" and it was praised as the second highest achievement of the President's administration in his annual report. Since the project began in 2002, the number of domestic violence cases reported to authorities has increased significantly. This has been the result of the collaborative efforts of many other organizations and institutions who mobilized to address the issue. At the regional level, the Gender Council of the Commission of Heads of Police in Central America and the Caribbean, with UNFPA support, continues its work to improve responses to violence against women through gender-sensitive training and protocols.

**NATIONAL CAMPAIGNS: 'QUICK WINS'.** National campaigns against gender-based violence are one of the "quick-win" solutions recommended by the UN Millennium Project. These are relatively inexpensive, high-impact initiatives that are expected to reap development benefits within three years.[71] In some countries efforts are already under way. For example, the "Stop Violence Against Women" campaign was initiated in 2004 in Turkey with UNFPA support. The government enlisted celebrities and athletes to appear on public service ads aired on 15 television channels. Turkish Football Federation T-shirts with an anti-violence motto were produced, and religious leaders delivered speeches at Friday prayers in all the mosques. The private sector has been involved in the campaign, both as sponsors and champions for the cause.[72] In Latin America and the Caribbean, a UN inter-agency campaign generated sustained progress on the issue (see Box 31) and bolstered other efforts. Thailand launched its "Love and Peace in the Home" campaign.[73] In Burundi, UNFPA has played a leading role in a national campaign addressing sexual violence against women, including sponsoring research on the

> *"Before the training, I felt very depressed and always thought about the violence I had suffered. I lived with fear. I was scared to share my experience with others. Now I feel more empowered. As a police officer, I can better understand and help a woman who is a victim of domestic violence because of my first-hand experience."*
>
> — Female police officer who was herself a victim of abuse, Centre for Police Training, Department of La Paz, Honduras

magnitude of sexual violence among displaced populations. In 2004, the campaign saw a 53 per cent increase in the number of women victims of sexual violence seeking services at NGO centres supported by UNFPA. The centres also provide legal assistance for raped women through the Burundian Association of Women Lawyers and the ITEKA Human Rights League.

## Men Take a Stand

Some initiatives are building momentum by enlisting groups of men to promote a culture of "zero tolerance" for gender-based violence. The White Ribbon Campaign, for example, founded in Canada and the largest effort of its kind in the world, is based on the idea that all men and boys must take responsibility for ending violence against women. Participation is open to any man who is opposed to violence against women. Wearing a white ribbon is a personal pledge never to commit, condone or remain silent about violence against women. The organization encourages reflection that leads to personal and collective action among men, distributes education and action kits to schools, addresses public policy issues and works with women's organizations.[74] In 2004, a national campaign to stop violence against women was launched in Brazil by men's and women's groups backed by ECOS, a research organization focusing on gender and sexuality. As part of the campaign, well-known comic actors appeared in a video stating that violence against women is "not funny".[75]

A Philippine NGO, Harnessing Self-Reliant Initiatives and Knowledge, developed a model of gender-sensitive training on gender stereotyping, violence against women and other related issues. Some of the participants have formed groups aimed at reaching other men and intervening with abusive partners.[76] In Cambodia, Men Against Violence Against Women supports annual campaigns against gender-based violence and works to provide young men with role models.[77]

Although its toll is increasingly acknowledged, responses to the problem of gender-based violence remain inadequate. Several initiatives have had limited impact due to a lack of comprehensive policies and action plans, and limited data and research on which to base and monitor them. Weak enforcement mechanisms and insufficient resources to implement them are common. Policy and legal frameworks to address violence against women as a human rights and public health concern need to be developed, upgraded and fully implemented. Because gender-based violence is so widely tolerated, successful action ultimately requires social transformation. Elements of successful and comprehensive approaches include: strengthened legal systems; investments in the safety, education, reproductive health and rights, and economic empowerment of women; gender-sensitive education from an early age; public health systems that provide appropriate care and support for victims; mobilizing communities, opinion and religious leaders, and the media; and engaging young and adult men to take a strong stand on the issue.

Inadequate budgets[78] and competing priorities have contributed to inaction on this issue. Yet the costs of effective measures to reduce violence are insignificant in comparison to the human, social and economic impact on present and future generations. In Tajikistan, for example, the UN Millennium Project estimated that a mere $1.30 per capita per year would make a difference to implement a set of gender-specific interventions that includes those to combat gender-based violence.[79] In the United States, the 1994 Violence Against Women Act has provided an estimated net benefit of $16.4 billion, proving that prevention costs far less than inaction.[80] Investments in prevention and women's protection have high and cost-effective payoffs, and are critical to the Millennium Declaration's pledge "to create an environment…conducive to development and to the elimination of poverty".[81]

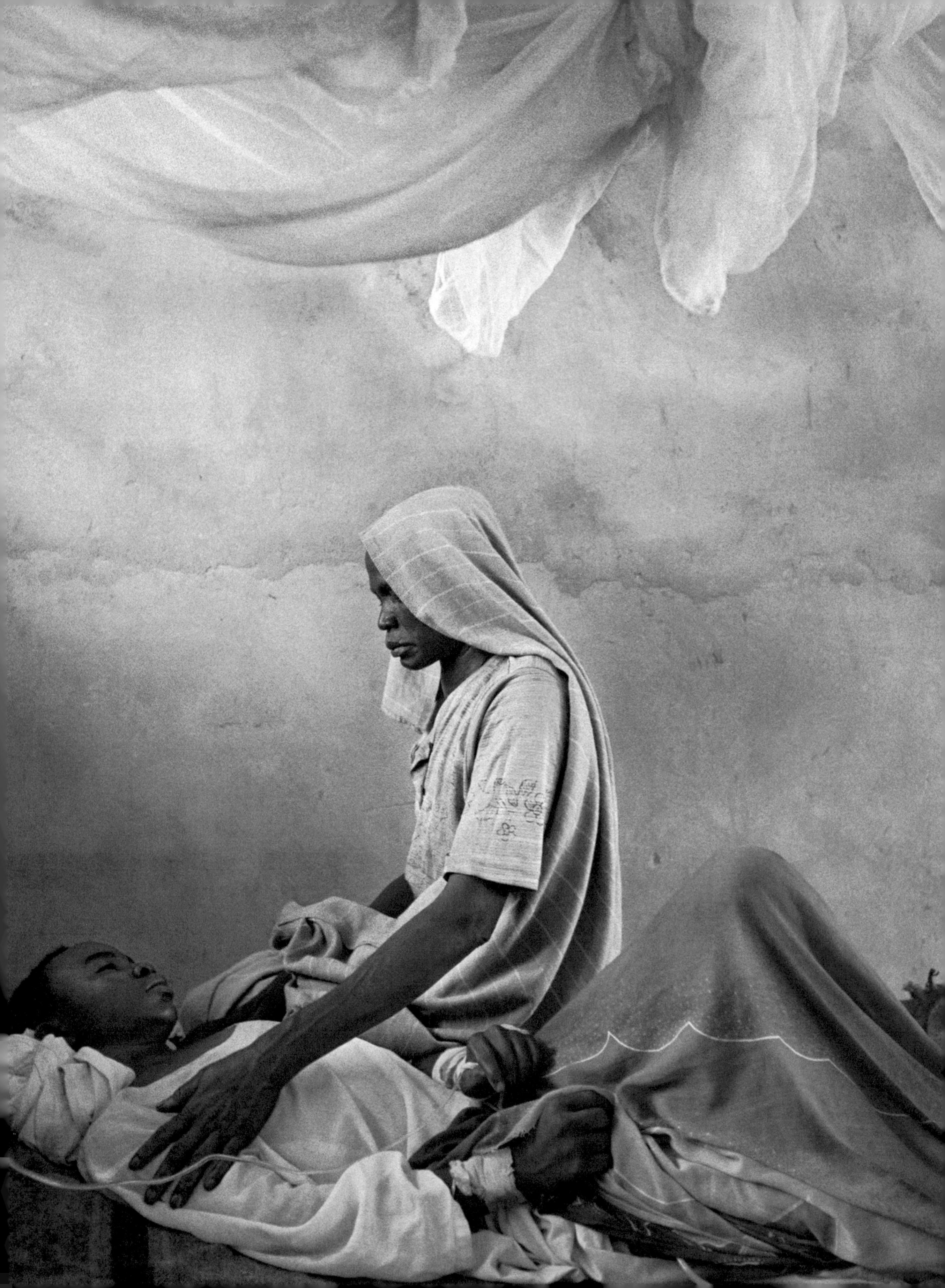

# 8 Women and Young People in Humanitarian Crises

*"During the transition to peace, a unique window of opportunity exists to put in place a gender-responsive framework for a country's reconstruction. The involvement of women in peacebuilding and reconstruction is in fact a key part of the process of inclusion and democracy that can contribute to a lasting peace".*

— Noeleen Heyzer, Executive Director, United Nations Development Fund for Women (UNIFEM)

Since the 2000 UN Millennium Summit, conflict has erupted in 40 countries.[1] In 2004, a single natural disaster—the tsunami in East Asia—killed more than 280,000 people and displaced more than one million.[2] In the wake of war or disaster, educational and health systems collapse, gender-based violence increases, HIV and other sexually transmitted infections spread, and infant and maternal mortality rates often skyrocket.

The large number of these humanitarian crises stands in the way of the Millennium Development Goals (MDGs). Of the 34 poor countries farthest from reaching the MDGs, 22 are in or emerging from conflict.[3] Environmental crises, which are increasing in frequency and severity, also disproportionately affect the poor. Almost two billion people were affected by natural disasters in the last decade of the 20th Century, 86 per cent of them by floods and droughts.[4]

The nature and scope of conflict has changed, with more armed conflicts taking place within, rather than between, countries. During the 1990s, of the 118 armed conflicts, the majority were internal.[5] These tend to last longer than wars between countries and take a huge toll on civilians, including abduction, rape, mutilation, torture and massacre. Many civilians are forced to flee their homes and communities, and sexual violence is often widespread. During conflict and its aftermath, women and young people are particularly vulnerable; 80 per cent of the world's 35 million refugees and internally displaced persons are women and children.[6]

Recovery from armed conflict is a decades-long process, and the ensuing peace may be fragile. Roughly half of all countries that emerge from war lapse back into violence within five years.[7] Strategic investments in women and young people during and after crises can contribute to reducing poverty and enhancing prospects for sustainable development and lasting peace.

Largely due to the efforts of civil society organizations, the international community increasingly recognizes the needs and rights of young people and women in humanitarian crises. Closer attention is now being paid to how these groups can be empowered to participate in the peace-building process and repair and transform their shattered societies.

## After a Crisis: Opportunities for Equity and Peace

When conflict or natural disaster strikes, women survivors usually bear the heaviest burden of relief and reconstruction. They become primary caretakers for other survivors—including children, the injured or sick, and the elderly. The vulnerability and responsibilities of women are further increased by the loss of husbands and livelihoods and the need to procure essentials for family survival.[8]

Gender-specific needs have often been overlooked when it comes to relief and recovery planning. The vulnerability of girls and women to exploitation, trafficking and abuse has largely been ignored, as have their needs for pregnancy-related care, sanitary supplies and locally appropriate clothing. The distribution of emergency assistance has often been managed by, and delivered to, men, without attention to whether women and their dependents will benefit.

The post-crisis transition period offers a prime opportunity to establish policies and processes to accelerate recovery, as well as formulate sound action plans to meet the MDGs and the broader development and security agenda. But when peace negotiations are underway, women have frequently been excluded. And when a new government takes control, makes decisions and prepares budgets, women are often left out of the process.

Women and girls in conflict and post-conflict settings are one of three key groups for whom support is critical, according to the UN Millennium Project.[9] Domestic policies and external assistance that provide such support enable communities to reconcile, break the cycle of conflict and speed the transition to sustainable development. They can take full advantage of women's skills in reweaving the social fabric and rebuilding the economic life of destroyed communities.

> "Women must be full and equal participants in the building of peace, in the development of post-conflict legislative, judicial and constitutional structures. Because it is only in this way that these structures will be fully representative of the post-conflict society and therefore fully able to meet the needs and demands of all. This is sustainable peace."
>
> — Sir Emyr Jones Parry, President of the United Nations Security Council

## An Evolving Human Rights Framework

In 2000, the United Nations Security Council passed Resolution 1325—a landmark decision mandating the inclusion of women in peace processes. It calls upon all parties to protect women in armed conflict and to integrate gender perspectives into peacekeeping operations, UN reporting systems and peacebuilding programmes.[10]

The resolution builds on earlier gains for women's rights during armed conflict. The 1998 Rome Statute of the International Criminal Court, the first permanent court charged with prosecuting individuals for crimes against humanity, specifically defines "rape, sexual slavery, enforced prostitution, forced pregnancy, enforced sterilization, or any other form of sexual violence" as crimes against humanity.[11] Prior to the advent of the International Criminal Court, the special tribunals set up to prosecute crimes against humanity in Rwanda and the former Yugoslavia broke new legal ground in prosecuting perpetrators of rape during wartime.[12] The Special Court of Sierra Leone, for the first time in international law, established forced marriage as an "inhumane act" and a crime against humanity.[13]

In December 2004, the report of the UN Secretary-General's High-Level Panel on Threats, Challenges, and Change reiterated the importance of ending sexual violence against women during war and recommended that Member States and UN agencies fully implement Resolution 1325.[14] If brought to fruition, the Peacebuilding Commission proposed by the panel and endorsed in the UN Secretary-General's Report *In Larger Freedom*,[15] would provide another opportunity to implement these recommendations.

The 1949 Geneva Conventions and Optional Protocols protect civilians during wartime and prohibit attacks, rape, deportation and the use of children as soldiers. The 1989 Convention on the Rights of the Child and its Optional Protocols protect children and adolescents during armed conflict and forbid recruitment of children under the age of 18. Four UN Security Council resolutions passed between 1999 and 2003 affirmed the importance of protecting children and adolescents during and directly after conflicts. They also urged their inclusion in peace processes, noted the specific needs and vulnerabilities of girls, and condemned sexual violence during peacekeeping operations.[16]

The international legal framework for protecting women and children during conflicts has proven inadequate to the task, especially for the world's 25 million internally displaced persons. The majority are women and children, often from indigenous and ethnic minorities.[17] Forced to flee their homes by conflict or natural disasters, displaced persons are vulnerable to impoverishment, disease, violence and "disappearance", and may also be persecuted during flight by armed groups. Their living conditions can test the limits of human endurance. They may have to do without food, water, sanitation, housing, privacy or access to education and health services. With no land to cultivate, no employment options and their properties seized, internally displaced persons can quickly

> ### 33 | GAINS FOR GENDER EQUALITY IN CAMBODIA
>
> The aftermath of conflict can provide an opportunity to promote the participation of women as an integral part of national reconstruction and development. In Cambodia, a country that has emerged from 30 years of conflict, women and war widows head more than one in four households, which are also among the poorest. Today, 80 per cent of the country's female population are of working age and economically active—the highest female labour force participation of any country in the region. Ignoring their contributions would result in missed opportunities for poverty reduction.
>
> The Ministry of Women's Affairs and a number of international and non-governmental organizations have been staunch advocates of gender equality. The 1993 Constitution enshrines equality between men and women. The Royal Government of Cambodia has supported an evolving legal framework that safeguards gender equality in marriage, family, employment and land ownership. The Government has also mainstreamed gender across all major policy initiatives, including the 2002 National Poverty Reduction Strategy, the 2003 Cambodian Millennium Development Goals, the 2003 National Population Policy, and the 2004 Rectangular Strategy for Growth, Employment, Efficiency and Equity. The latter recognizes that "women are the backbone of our economy and society", and calls for "ensuring the rights of women to actively and equally participate in nation building". The 2005 National Strategic Development Plan clearly defines gender mainstreaming and a human rights approach as strategic to all sectors. Plans are underway to prioritize married women in policy development in recognition of their high vulnerability to HIV infection. The development of draft laws on domestic violence and trafficking were included as 2005 targets in the national MDG plan—making Cambodia the first country in the world to do so.
>
> The Ministry of Women's Affairs mobilized alliances with other ministries, civil society and international donors to develop a comprehensive gender mainstreaming strategy. Five-year plans are now in place, with staff at central, provincial and communal levels and gender focal points and technical working groups stationed in all government ministries. The ministry has initiated gender training for its officers and promoted gender-sensitive policies for civil servants. Gender-sensitive budgeting has resulted in increased funding to provide scholarships for girls, eliminate costs to families and make schools more girl-friendly. Efforts to strengthen gender-sensitive data analysis for the national MDG plan resulted in the addition of new indicators to track progress on women's political participation, education, health and employment, and on violence against women.
>
> Such measures have enabled Cambodia to advance gender equality and progress toward realization of other MDGs as well. Maternal mortality, fertility and HIV prevalence have dropped among certain groups. In rural and remote areas, primary and secondary school enrolment has risen, and the number of women studying in colleges and universities has increased. Women leaders are contributing to good governance and poverty reduction through the establishment of government-civil society partnerships, the promotion of peaceful resolution of local disputes and cross-party cooperation. Though many challenges remain, Cambodia offers a prime example of how comprehensive and sustained gender mainstreaming can improve the lives of citizens.

descend into dire poverty. In camps, they may be targets of attacks. Children and adolescents may be recruited as soldiers or forced into sexual slavery. The needs of the elderly or disabled are often disregarded.[18]

Internally displaced persons, who comprise more than two thirds of all those uprooted by crises, lack the international legal protections granted to refugees who have crossed a national border.[19] Because they fall under national sovereignty and jurisdiction, the plight of the internally displaced is considered a domestic issue, limiting possibilities for intervention by the international community.

This issue has gradually gained greater attention from the international community. In 1992, the UN Secretary-General appointed his first Representative on the Human Rights of Internally Displaced Persons[20] and in 1998 the Commission on Human Rights adopted guiding principles, which establish standards for the protection of the rights of displaced populations.[21] The Representative's 2005 report to the Commission highlighted the "disproportionate burden from displacement" suffered by women and girls and emphasized their vulnerability to rape and domestic violence. Discriminatory inheritance laws and practices make it difficult for women to reclaim the land and property of deceased husbands when they return home.[22] Securing employment is another major obstacle. The UN Secretary-General, in his major report, *In Larger Freedom*, urged governments to adopt the guiding principles and step up efforts to meet the needs of internally displaced persons. As he stated: "[I]f national authorities are unable or unwilling to protect their citizens, then the responsibility shifts to the international community to use diplomatic,

> **34  RWANDA: POWER THROUGH THE BALLOT BOX**
>
> In the 2003 parliamentary elections, women won 49 per cent of seats in the lower house and 34 per cent in the upper house. Rwanda now has the highest proportion of female parliamentarians in the world. A "triple-balloting" technique was instituted by the Government in the 2001 district-level elections: Every voter chose a general candidate, a female candidate and a youth candidate. "Not only did this system set aside seats for women and youth," one expert noted, "it also required that the entire electorate vote for women." The Forum of Women Parliamentarians, composed of ethnic Hutu and Tutsi women, was the first cross-party caucus in the Rwandan Parliament. Women leaders have implemented national and local reconciliation programmes, drafted a new Constitution and actively promoted transparency and accountability at all levels of government.

humanitarian and other methods to help protect the human rights and well-being of civilian populations."[23]

## Participation of Women and Gender Equality: The Path to Recovery

In the aftermath of conflict, the full political participation of women can improve security and governance and foster reconciliation and socio-economic development. As the Cambodia model demonstrates (see Box 33), women politicians, working together with government ministries and women's groups, can effectively call attention to gender equality and development issues and advance poverty reduction strategies. In South Africa, for example, women parliamentarians and civil society leaders contributed to the reform of the post-apartheid military.[24] The Government appointed women to senior positions within the Ministry of Defence, provided gender training for all of ministry personnel and instituted equitable personnel policies, including maternity leave. The United Nations Development Fund for Women (UNIFEM) has worked in post-conflict countries to build the skills of women leaders and encourage women voters to involve themselves in the political process. In Afghanistan, in the run-up to the 2004 elections, UNIFEM facilitated the first public forum of its kind on women's rights, bringing together women's rights activists, journalists and presidential candidates.[25] UNFPA supported the effort through training of women leaders on gender issues.[26]

Women also have a strong role to play in promoting justice and reconciliation. At the international level, the appointment of women judges has led to significant advances. For example, in every case tried by the International Criminal Tribunal for the former Yugoslavia that resulted in significant retribution for sex crimes (against men as well as women), a woman judge was on the bench.[27] In Sierra Leone, a women's task force participated in the design of the Truth and Reconciliation Commission and a special unit to investigate war crimes.[28] In Rwanda, at the local level, UNIFEM supports the post-genocide *gacaca* system of community justice and has trained 100 judges in the concepts of gender, justice, reconciliation and peacebuilding.[29]

Many international organizations recognize that supporting women is an effective way to help their communities recover from crises. In war- and disaster-affected areas of the Islamic Republic of Iran, the Government established, with UNFPA technical support, a broad programme to help women who head households. It includes support to begin income-generating projects and training in literacy, life skills and reproductive health.[30] In Sierra Leone, the Women in Crisis Movement assists young women who are sexually exploited or at risk of engaging in "survival sex" in exchange for basic necessities. It provides occupational training, psychosocial counselling, health care and services to prevent sexually transmitted infections.[31]

## Empowering Young People in the Aftermath of Crises

Although peacebuilding processes often overlook them, young survivors of violent conflict are an important constituency for peace and reconstruction. The sheer numbers of young people make them a force to be reckoned with: About two thirds of the populations of Rwanda and Cambodia are under the age of 25.[32] Countries that do not invest in the skills and productive capacities of young people in the struggle to recover from war miss important opportunities to reduce poverty and forge a lasting peace.

But young survivors may first need help. Former child combatants are likely to need rehabilitation and family reunification services; psychological and physical health care; education and training; and opportunities to earn income. Young women who have been sexually abused and enslaved require gender-sensitive counselling and care. Those forcibly impregnated during a conflict need added supports to protect them and their children from stigma, impoverishment and further sexual exploitation when they return to their communities.

Former child soldiers have historically been left out of formal disarmament, demobilization and reintegration programmes, even though their numbers are significant. In Liberia, for instance, an estimated 15,000 children served in the war.[33] In Sierra Leone, children constituted nearly 37 per cent of the fighting forces in some armed factions.[34] Though the role of girls in conflict is often overlooked, they make up nearly half of all children involved with armed groups.[35] Girls—over 12,000 of them—comprised 25 per cent of soldiers in Sierra Leone.[36] Girls are recruited as soldiers, cooks, cleaners and, often, forced sexual partners, otherwise known as "bush wives". When they return to their communities, their families may reject them.[37] In their rehabilitation work with former child soldiers, UNICEF and other agencies have developed gender-sensitive demobilization programmes for girls such as those in the Democratic Republic of the Congo and Liberia.[38] In Sri Lanka, UNICEF's work with the Liberation Tigers of Tamil Eelam led to a significant decrease in child recruitment.[39]

Whether they are former combatants or victims of war, young people are important to post-conflict justice and reconciliation. In South Africa, special hearings and workshops were set up so that children could testify before the Truth and Reconciliation Commission.[40] In many countries, local community and religious leaders conduct traditional healing processes for children and adolescents as a means to reintegrate them into society.[41]

The emerging recognition of the neglect of young people's needs and rights, and of their crucial roles in post-crisis situations, is prompting countries to respond. Some have appointed special representatives for children or created ministries for youth. The Sierra Leone National Youth Policy, developed in partnership with young people, outlined their rights and responsibilities and set plans for a youth ministry, youth focal points in other ministries, and district youth committees.[42]

As the World Bank notes, young people are an "under-utilized voice" in addressing post-conflict concerns, who "can be resilient, resourceful, and responsive. . . . in addressing corruption and consequently improving governance in their countries." The Youth for Good Governance Distance Learning Programme was designed by the World Bank to train youth—in Uganda, the Ukraine and the former Yugoslavia, among other countries—on good governance. In Bosnia and Herzegovina, youth groups organized successful anti-corruption campaigns and formed a youth party to demand better education and accountability.[43] In 2003, the Democratic Republic of the Congo formed a 36-member National Children's Parliament, with UNICEF support, charged with promoting children's rights and finding solutions to their problems.[44]

**GETTING ON TRACK FOR THE MDGS: EDUCATION, HEALTH AND LIVELIHOODS.** Young people need education, health care and counselling, vocational training and jobs in order to rebuild their lives following crises. If they cannot earn a living, they may be forced into survival sex, trafficking or other forms of exploitation. This undermines their own prospects for a better life and their country's chances for reaching MDG targets on education, HIV/AIDS and decent and productive work for youth.

Education is vital, both to give young people a sense of structure and ordinary life and to build a foundation on which their societies can grow. Half of the world's out-of-school children live in conflict or post-conflict countries. Girls may be kept home to care for siblings while their impoverished or widowed mothers seek the means to provide for the family. Girls may also be discouraged from attending school for fear of rape or abduction.[45] In Sierra Leone, participatory research with adolescents found that education was their top priority.[46]

UN agencies and civil society organizations have taken note and jointly developed minimum standards for education in emergencies.[47] Burundi's Education for Repatriation policy, supported by UNICEF and other international organizations, directs schools in refugee camps to follow a curriculum recognized by children's home countries.[48] In Sierra Leone, women's groups provide education and vocational training for young people, primarily ex-combatant girls.[49]

## Safeguarding Reproductive Health and Rights in Humanitarian Emergencies

War, natural disaster and forced displacement take a heavy toll on the reproductive health of adolescent girls and women. Sudanese women fleeing combat had to give birth without even the barest essentials for clean delivery, such as a fresh razor blade and soap. This condemned many to fatal infections,[50] and their children to a life without a mother's love and support. One in nine of these women were estimated to die in pregnancy or childbirth in 2003.[51] The death of a widow also deprives her children of their primary provider of food, shelter and health care.

Safeguarding reproductive health and rights in humanitarian emergencies is fundamental to saving lives and laying the foundation for gender equality and sustainable development when stability returns. Until fairly recently, however, reproductive health care was seldom available during emergencies. In 1995, a coalition of UN agencies, governments and non-governmental organizations formed the Inter-Agency Working Group on Reproductive Health in Refugee Situations. This group produced a field manual for humanitarian operations that outlined a package of critical interventions to prevent maternal mortality and HIV infection and guarantee access to family planning.[52] The Reproductive Health Response in Conflict Consortium, a network of international humanitarian non-governmental organizations, also works to improve reproductive health care during emergencies.[53]

Protecting maternal and infant health is now becoming a critical element of relief efforts. In the past five years, UNFPA and its partners have provided clean delivery kits in more than 30 countries, from Liberia to Timor-Leste. Since 2003, UNFPA has worked to strengthen primary health centres and has made emergency reproductive health supplies available in Iraq.[54] In 2005, UNFPA distributed clean delivery and personal hygiene kits to displaced women in parts of Indonesia, the Maldives and Sri Lanka that were hardest hit by the tsunami. Support was also provided to re-establish obstetric care in hospitals throughout the region.[55]

Humanitarian crises disrupt women's access to family planning services and expose them to unintended pregnancies, unsafe abortion and sexually transmitted infections, including HIV. In emergency settings, relief organizations increasingly supply free condoms as the first line of defence against unintended pregnancies and the spread of sexually transmitted infections, including HIV. In 22 war-affected countries, UNFPA and the Office of the United Nations High Commissioner for Refugees (UNHCR) are working together to provide male and female condoms in displacement camps.

After an acute emergency winds down, UNFPA and its partners continue to support governments to sustain reproductive health care programmes. In Burundi, for example, the Ministry of Health developed standards for reproductive health services, including for emergency obstetric care. Support was provided to train midwives and physicians, equip hospitals serving displaced people and educate communities on the need for skilled care during deliveries.[56] Following earthquakes in Turkey (1999) and Bam, in the Islamic Republic of Iran (2003), mobile medical teams were deployed to deliver reproductive health care.

The particular challenges that Palestinian women face in Gaza and the West Bank face has been a top priority for UNFPA. Since even before the escalation of conflict in 2000, an estimated one fifth of pregnant women could not receive prenatal care because of the difficulty of travelling through checkpoints to health facilities. Delays at checkpoints have resulted in unattended roadside births and even the deaths of some women and infants. UNFPA is working to provide access to life-saving emergency care.[57] As part of a larger effort to improve the well-being of women in underserved areas, UNFPA has been involved in establishing women's health centres that offer reproductive health care as well as other needed services, including psychosocial counselling, legal aid on reproductive rights, and support for women's rights within the family.

**MENDING LIVES, ADDRESSING SEXUAL VIOLENCE.** Millions of women have been raped and sexually tortured during conflicts. Rape camps, sexual slavery, and forced impregnation or intentional infection with HIV have all occurred in recent conflicts.[58] In Rwanda, sexual violence during the genocide triggered the country's HIV/AIDS epidemic: It is estimated that a half million girls and women were raped and that 67 per cent of them became infected with HIV.[59] During the 1991-2001 conflict in Sierra Leone, young girls were specifically singled out for rape. Many, particularly the very young, did not survive.[60] In the same country, an estimated 70 to 90 per cent of rape victims contracted sexually transmitted infections.[61]

Even when women fleeing conflict find their way to refugee camps, they are not necessarily safe. In one Tanzanian camp, 26 per cent of women refugees from Burundi were raped.[62] It is not uncommon for family members and the community at large to ostracize the victims of rape, at times forcing them out of the home and leaving them to fend for themselves. Survivors of rape often face severe life-long problems, including persistent post-traumatic stress and debilitating depression.[63]

Humanitarian organizations are supporting educational campaigns to reduce violence against women, including installing safety measures; training community leaders, police and judges; and improving law enforcement. The importance of reaching men is also recognized: The International Rescue Committee (IRC) now routinely forms men's committees to raise awareness and support survivors of violence.[64] Despite initial

> *"At my parents' house, seven men raped a widow who was staying with the family. The men said, 'At least one of us must be HIV positive.' The widow contracted AIDS, and she has already died."*
>
> — A survivor of the Rwandan genocide

| 35 | **MOBILIZING TO STOP VIOLENCE AGAINST WOMEN IN TIMOR-LESTE** |

Since gaining independence in 2002, Timor-Leste, though still one of the poorest countries in Asia, is taking a stand for gender equality. Women leaders, who had been active during the struggle for independence, pressed for policy attention and equal participation in political institutions established since independence. Now women hold 27 per cent of parliamentary seats, and an Advisory Office to the Prime Minister for the Promotion of Equality has been created.

The women's movement identified gender-based violence as a top priority. UNFPA sponsored the country's first reliable study, which revealed that 50 per cent of women had experienced some form of abuse. A National Police report indicates that violence against women constitutes 68 per cent of all cases received. The police are being trained to protect and support victims. Mass awareness-raising efforts and campaigns using drama, radio programmes and a television soap opera have opened widespread discussion on a formerly taboo subject, and a new domestic violence law has raised the issue's public profile.

With UNFPA support, Timor-Leste set up its first legal support services for abused women, and the first hospital "safe room", where women receive medical care and counselling in private. The Association of Men Against Violence has held social education workshops with men living in remote and rural areas and has provided anger-management training for male offenders in the national prison.

community resistance, an IRC initiative in Burundian refugee camps in the United Republic of Tanzania led to the use of mobile courts to enforce laws on gender-based violence. The programme is now sustained by community support and also offers awareness training, a reporting and referral system, counselling and health services and a 24-hour drop-in centre.[65] In the Darfur region of Sudan, UNFPA supports women's organizations that assist survivors, supply medical equipment, work to make refugee settlements safe, and train medical professionals to manage cases of sexual violence.[66] Reports of abuse and exploitation of girls and women, such as in the Democratic Republic of the Congo and Liberia,[67] have furthermore led the UN Department for Peacekeeping Operations to develop new guidelines to reduce the possibility of sexual violence and exploitation by peacekeepers and uniformed personnel working in humanitarian relief settings.[68]

**HALTING THE SPREAD OF HIV.** Conflict, displacement and the resulting loss of access to health services and information can increase the possibility of HIV transmission. In the Democratic Republic of the Congo, for example, 5 per cent of the population was HIV-positive before the war erupted in 1997. In 2002, that estimate spiked to 20 per cent in the eastern area of the country where the conflict began.[69] The near-total collapse of security and social protection systems, the high incidence of rape and lack of safe blood supplies undoubtedly contributed to these increases. Situations in which a major military or militia presence routinely mingles with the civilian population can create additional risks because military forces tend to have higher rates of sexually transmitted infections, including HIV, than civilian populations.[70] If HIV prevalence is already rising, conflict can be the spark that ignites a full blown epidemic. The end of conflict does not mean the end of risk. Conflicts bring in their wake lasting social disruption, loss of familial and community protection from sexual exploitation and abuse, and the collapse of preventive services. Many women and girls are forced into transactional sex simply to survive.

With rising international awareness about the impact of armed conflict on the AIDS epidemic, humanitarian relief efforts are integrating prevention and treatment earlier in their work. UN system and reproductive health networks operating in emergencies are issuing guidelines for humanitarian workers.[71] Many organizations are specifically targeting men, particularly within disarmament, demobilization and reintegration programmes. In Eritrea and Ethiopia, for example, UNFPA supported the training of demobilized soldiers on HIV prevention and counselling, so that when they returned home, they could educate others in their communities.[72]

In Liberia, UNFPA helps a broad coalition of non-governmental organizations undertake massive awareness-raising campaigns aimed at displaced populations living in refugee camps—particularly where large numbers of women and girls have turned to commercial sex to survive. Community-based organizations operating along the borders with Sierra Leone and Guinea have now educated 60,000 displaced persons and returnees on the prevention and treatment of sex-

> **36  THE HEALING POWER OF THE ARTS: WORKING WITH DISPLACED ADOLESCENTS IN COLOMBIA**
>
> In Colombia, where at least two million people have been displaced by the 30-year internal conflict, UNFPA, with assistance from Belgium, has supported an innovative approach: artistic expression as a release and remedy for the violence in adolescents' lives. Since 2003, the project has worked with displaced adolescents in cities on the Caribbean coast, where sexual violence is rampant and impunity is the norm. Displaced girls there are three times more likely than their peers to become pregnant before age 15. Drawing on adolescents' creative energy, the programme uses drama, role-playing, music and dance to encourage them to recount the trauma they have experienced. Health providers visit twice a week to talk about reproductive health and prevention and offer services. Participants in the programme acquire the tools to challenge harmful aspects of gender relations, resist peer pressure, address sexual violence and raise their self-esteem.

ually transmitted infections including HIV, and 3.2 million male condoms have been distributed. Some 5,000 peer educators have reached schools, camps and communities with HIV-prevention education. People living with HIV and AIDS are also being recruited as "Prevention Ambassadors". There are weekly training sessions for UN peacekeepers on sexual violence and the prevention of sexually transmitted infections and HIV. These intensive efforts have broken the silence, denial and stigma surrounding the AIDS epidemic. More people are seeking counselling and treatment.

Peacekeeping operations can also help to educate recovering societies about risks and play a positive role in HIV prevention. The UN Department of Peacekeeping Operations (DPKO) now works hand in hand with UNAIDS to include HIV prevention advisers in each mission and has set up an HIV/AIDS Trust Fund to support its programmes.[73] In Sierra Leone and the Democratic Republic of the Congo, DPKO, UNAIDS, UNIFEM and UNFPA work together on HIV prevention and gender awareness for peacekeepers and the newly established army and police forces.[74] Recognizing the increase in regional peacekeeping operations, the US Department of Defense allocated $14 million in 2002 for HIV prevention programmes specifically for African armed forces.[75]

**INITIATIVES FOR YOUNG PEOPLE.** Following a crisis, involving young people in reproductive health programmes is essential in order to slow the spread of HIV and reduce unwanted pregnancies. The Women's Commission for Refugee Women and Children supports youth-led programmes in areas affected by conflict.[76] In the United Republic of Tanzania, UNHCR established youth-friendly centres in refugee camps, run by youth-led committees, in order to address reproductive health issues and provide services, produce media campaigns and offer vocational skills training and information on how to care for HIV-affected relatives.[77]

UNFPA, with Belgian support, is working with local partners to provide reproductive health services to young people in selected countries (see Box 36). In Rwanda, UNFPA has supported the establishment of youth-friendly health centres where young people learn about HIV prevention and other reproductive health issues. The centres also offer training on income-generating skills such as producing soap, handicrafts and embroidery, and opportunities for participation in cultural and sports activities.[78]

In Egypt, Uganda and Zambia, the Health of Adolescent Refugees Project worked in partnership with Girl Guides who served as peer educators to advise health providers on adolescents' needs. Providers are trained by medical personnel on key aspects of reproductive health. The initiative has increased young people's self-confidence and sense of solidarity.[79]

Initiatives such as these are mostly incipient and rare. But they hold the promise of empowering young people to contribute to their countries' road to recovery, peace and prosperity, to the MDGs and beyond.

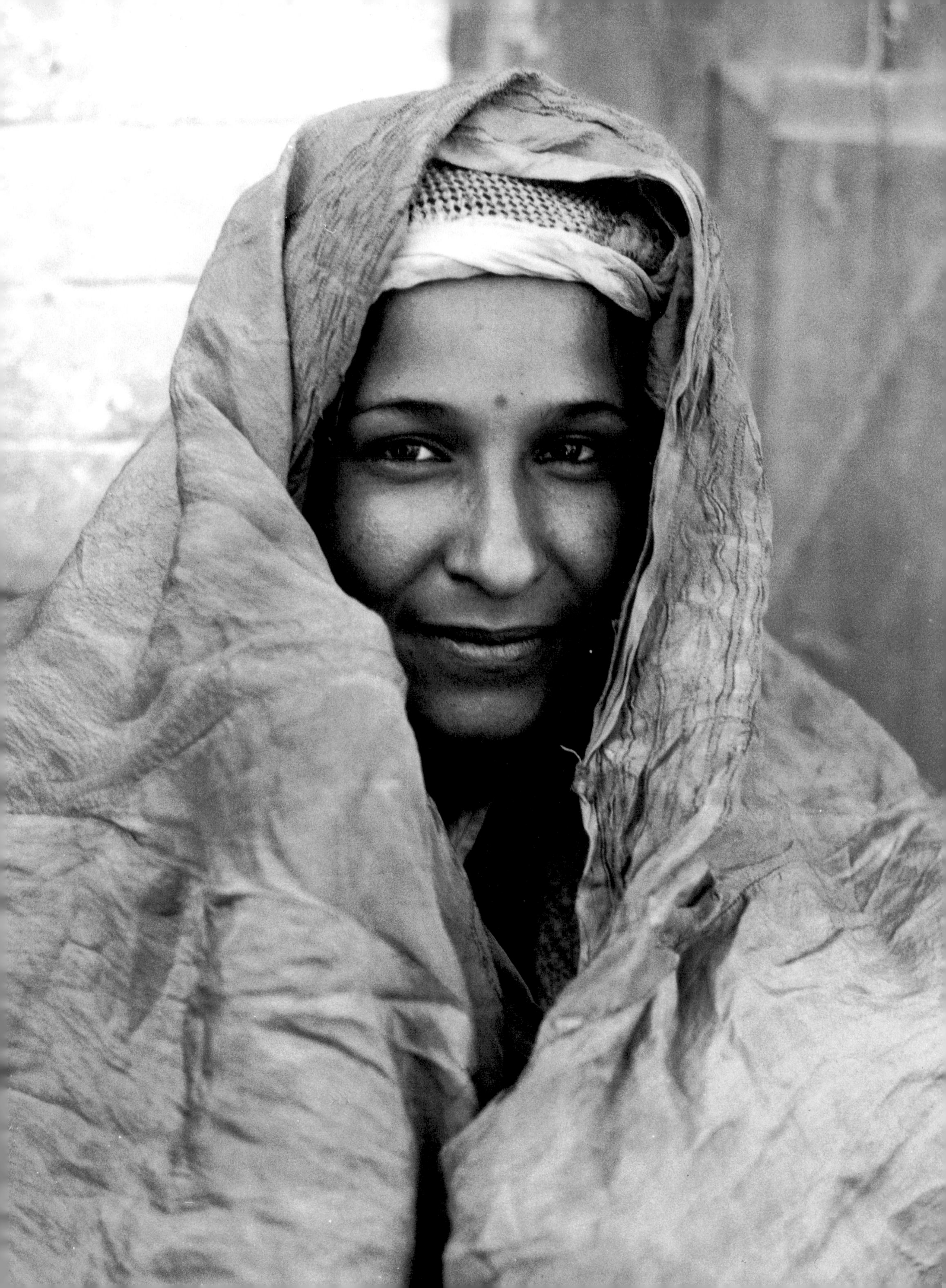

# 9 Road Map to the Millennium Development Goals and Beyond

*"Empowered women can be some of the most effective drivers of development."*

— UN Secretary-General Kofi Annan, *In Larger Freedom*

The Millennium Development Goals (MDGs) can only be achieved by putting gender equality and reproductive health at the forefront of political and budgetary agendas. Power imbalances and inequities—between rich and poor, men and women, young and old, mainstream society and marginalized groups—squander human capital and limit opportunities to overcome poverty. Women and young people represent a tremendous reservoir of human potential, but they lack power and they lack voice.

Freeing impoverished families and countries from the grip of gender inequality and poor reproductive health is not only an end in itself, but also an ethical imperative. Equality unleashes the full potential of all human beings. This was the vision of the 1994 International Conference on Population and Development (ICPD) and the 1995 Fourth World Conference on Women (Beijing).

This chapter offers a reminder of strategic opportunities available to countries and the international community as the MDG deadline approaches. Taken together, they can move the global community forward towards the broader agenda of "development, security and human rights for all", as called for in the 2005 UN Secretary-General's report, *In Larger Freedom*.

## Women's Empowerment:
### Lifting Families and Nations Out of Poverty

There is ample evidence of the multiplier effects of investing in gender equality and women's empowerment. More than 1.7 billion women worldwide are in their productive and reproductive years, between the ages of 15 and 49.[1] They already contribute enormously to their families, communities and countries. In most families, women are either primary or contributory breadwinners. They are the guardians of their countries' precious human capital—their children. Targeted investments—in the education, reproductive health, economic and political rights of women—can catalyse progress on poverty reduction, sustainable development and lasting peace.

Gender equality benefits families, communities and countries as well as women themselves. Stronger partnerships between women and men, and shared rights and responsibilities, hold the answer to many of the challenges that thwart human development. Some of the projects documented in this report prove that it is possible to transform harmful gender stereotypes and behaviours. But implementing such projects on the scale needed to achieve the MDGs will require concerted political and community leadership at all levels and resources to promote gender equality through policies and budgets.

## Empowering Young People:
### The MDGs and Beyond

Investing in adolescents and youth is a matter of human rights. It can also provide the "greatest poverty-pay off".[2] Investing wisely in young people now will contribute to the transition to educated and healthy adults—agents of change prepared to take the vision of equitable development forward. This will demand stepped up efforts by policymakers and donors. It will require granting young people access to a fair share of resources for education, reproductive health, skills development, work and life opportunities. And it will require doing so in ways that break down gender stereotypes and expand the prospects of young women.

## Universal Reproductive Health:
### Fulfilling Cairo to Reach the MDGs

The UN Millennium Project has unambiguously established that reproductive health is a central and cost-effective strategy for meeting the MDGs.[3]

Reproductive health is a human right, affirmed and reaffirmed as a development priority in international agreements since 1994, including at the ICPD and Beijing ten-year anniversary commemorations. Overwhelming support for the ICPD agenda, and recognition of the strong links between reproductive health and development, were reiterated in 2005 at several high-level meetings on the MDGs with ministers of health, finance and planning, as well as representatives from development banks, civil society and UN agencies.[4]

Most reproductive health problems are preventable through proven interventions. Reproductive health and rights are an integral aspect of poverty reduction, gender equality and women's empowerment, and of efforts to lower maternal and infant mortality and combat HIV/AIDS. Better reproductive health improves families' quality of life. The ability of individuals and couples to choose family size and space births, and a trend towards smaller families overall, can help low-income countries escape the "demographic poverty trap".[5]

Reproductive health programmes can provide convenient access—"one-stop shopping"—to a constellation of services for the poor. Reproductive health services include family planning, prevention and management of sexually transmitted infections, including HIV, and maternal and child health care.[6] They can also cover nutritional education, vitamin supplementation, immunization and malaria prevention. Ideally, as some projects have demonstrated, reproductive health services can also provide information and referrals to other programmes, such as those that address female literacy, gender-based violence, legal rights, access to micro-credit, and training in marketable skills. Linking reproductive health programmes to additional opportunities for women and young people can help them overcome other constraints that compromise reproductive choices and fuel the AIDS epidemic.

**LINKING REPRODUCTIVE HEALTH AND HIV/AIDS PROGRAMMES.** Addressing HIV is a component of reproductive health. However, as resources to combat the epidemic have poured in, parallel services have evolved, with their own personnel, administrative structures and funding. The continuing influx of resources presents an opportunity to gain efficiencies, advance the MDG health goals, and make the ICPD vision of universal reproductive health care a reality for the millions of people living in poverty whose quality of life and very survival depend on them.

If these programmes lead to a proliferation of specialized clinics, however, funds earmarked for HIV/AIDS have the potential to pull staff and resources away from other priority health needs of the poor—and from other MDG health goals.[7] This could undercut efforts to strengthen and streamline health systems. It would also be a grave disservice to users. The poor typically receive only piecemeal information and services—even though they may have pressing concerns regarding both HIV *and* other reproductive health issues. Moreover, sexually transmitted HIV and many other reproductive health problems are rooted in the same attitudes and behaviours.

Linking and integrating HIV prevention and care with general reproductive health services can strengthen both. Both types of services face the same health system challenges—shortages of trained staff, essential supplies and equipment, adequate facilities, and management skills. Both face similar obstacles in building demand for available services and in overcoming the stigmatization that prevents

---

**37  GLOBAL CAMPAIGN ON YOUNG PEOPLE AND THE MDGS**

In recognition of the role young people play in achieving the Millennium Development Goals (MDGs), UNFPA has taken the lead in launching the Faces of Young People and the MDGs campaign in collaboration with other UN agencies, the World Bank and regional economic commissions. The effort aims to raise awareness and garner policy attention. Its message is simple: Invest in young people.

In 2005, the initiative included a photographic exhibit at the United Nations headquarters in New York that documents the lives of youth from Africa, the Arab States, Asia, Eastern Europe and Latin America and the Caribbean. Each photographic series tells a tale of a young person's life that relates to the MDGs. Other activities include the development of strategic guidance for policymakers, brochures, a website and a planned fundraising concert in 2006 with musical celebrities and young artists focused on young people, AIDS and poverty.

clients from using them, an area in which the reproductive health field has considerable experience. They both require similar supplies and the same types of health provider skills. In some regions, integration is a moral obligation: In sub-Saharan Africa, where the AIDS epidemic is widespread, 63 per cent of women have an unmet need for effective contraception[8] and, consequently, a high proportion of unintended pregnancies. Many women do not know their HIV status and risk passing the virus to their children. Under these circumstances, access to even a minimal integrated package of family planning, HIV, and maternal health services can enable women to protect themselves from both unintended pregnancies and HIV and also prevent HIV transmission to their children.

Integrating a minimum package of reproductive health and HIV/AIDS services can be cost-effective. For example, one study found that integrating services for family planning and sexually transmitted infections into primary health care cost 31 per cent less than if separate services were provided, with savings in staff costs, supplies and administrative overhead.[9] Other pilot studies undertaken by the International Planned Parenthood Federation (IPPF) and UNFPA showed considerable savings and increased demand for services when voluntary HIV testing and counselling was integrated into existing sexual and reproductive health services.[10]

The international community is taking note: A number of agreements and UN resolutions have called for an essential and comprehensive package of reproductive health *and* HIV/AIDS services to be made available to all service users.[11] This recommendation was echoed by the UN Millennium Project Task Force on Combating AIDS.[12] Providing an essential integrated package is both equitable and ethical. It is also a strategic way to ensure that health systems are strengthened rather than weakened by fragmented approaches and competing priorities.

**STRENGTHENING HEALTH SYSTEMS.** Experts agree that achieving the three MDGs related to health will depend on whether investments can shore up health systems and extend their reach to underserved groups, especially in rural areas and urban slums.[13] Both the ICPD and the UN Millennium Project call for an approach that focuses on prevention and primary health care—the first point of contact for people living in poor communities.

Most countries have undertaken reforms intended to improve the quality, efficiency and equity of their health care systems. But the result, many experts conclude, is less equity in access and more expensive health care for the poor.[14] In various countries, macroeconomic factors, such as debt servicing and spending caps on health care, have transferred many health costs to families. Subsidies and user fee exemptions are not always well targeted and sometimes benefit higher-income groups rather than the poorest people who need them most.[15]

The cost of health care continues to be a significant barrier to service access and use. For example, country studies have found that user fees introduced by health sector reforms cause steep drops in the use of maternal health services.[16] The intended beneficiaries of fee exemptions are not necessarily aware of them, nor are the exemptions consistently applied. Some health systems are so underfunded that under-the-table payments for services are common, and clients are obliged to purchase their own basic medical supplies. The UN Millennium Project has called for the elimination of user fees for basic health services as a "quick win"[17] that can diminish health inequities related to poverty and gender discrimination.

Despite the challenges, sector-wide health reforms provide excellent opportunities for setting priorities and addressing bottlenecks in the delivery of quality services. Investing more in hospitals and less on prevention has left basic health care out of reach and out of touch with the urgent needs of the poorest of the poor. In sub-Saharan Africa and Asia, 75 per cent of the poor live in rural areas.[18] Well-functioning preventive services could help ward off millions of cases of HIV, infant and maternal deaths, and fatalities from malaria and other maladies unheard of in industrialized countries.

The shortage of skilled professionals is a paramount concern. In African countries, a ratio of one doctor for every 10,000 people is not uncommon. This compares to 1 doctor per 500 people in the United States.[19] Reforming laws and policies to devolve authority to midwives and nurses wherever medically safe and feasible is one solution, as successful efforts to lower maternal mortality have proven.[20] The UN Millennium Project has called for immediate training of community health workers so that they can make essential information and services available at local levels.[21]

Stemming the "brain drain" of qualified medical personnel seeking better salaries and working conditions abroad is another priority. This will need to be a collaborative undertaking by governments of the North and South, with attention paid to the rights and working conditions of health workers.[22] Researchers estimate that in 1999 as many midwives emigrated from Ghana as were trained in that country that same year.[23] Similar losses are occurring throughout the developing world. Only about half of developing countries have midwifery training centres, though this is a health sector priority for meeting the MDGs.[24] Sub-Saharan Africa will need an estimated one million more health workers in order to reach the health-related MDGs.[25] Filling this gap can be achieved by providing better incentives, training and recruitment, including of those who left the health field to work in other occupations in their own countries.[26] Skilled managers are also urgently needed.[27]

**TRANSFORMING AND ENGENDERING HEALTH SYSTEMS.** Quality of care remains one of the key challenges to improving health systems and achieving the MDGs. Quality of care goes beyond meeting medical and scientific standards, offering safe and continuous supplies of essential medicines and other commodities, and practising proper procedures. It also encompasses the personal interactions that take place when a person visits a health centre. It thus requires transformations in the attitudes and communication skills of health providers and managers with particular attention to ensuring non-discriminatory, gender and culturally-sensitive care. All of these dimensions of care suffer when health services are underfunded or overwhelmed. Health providers can be valuable assets to their communities, but often lack the backup support to provide the best possible care for their clients. Weak management, ineffectual policies and lack of essential medical supplies and equipment add to the challenges.

Poor people often report feeling mistreated or disrespected by health providers.[28] As a result, many women, men and adolescents turn instead to trusted members of the community. These traditional birth attendants and healers, however, lack the medical training to resolve serious health problems. Integrating gender and culturally sensitive curricula in health-provider training institutions, especially in reproductive health, HIV/AIDS and adolescent health, is a medium-term investment with long-term returns. It is central to sustained improvements in quality of care and can maximize the efficiency and efficacy of health sector investments.

As the UN Millennium Project Task Force on Maternal and Child Health emphasizes, health systems are an integral part of the social fabric. Their success relies on the trust of the communities they serve. This trust, in turn, can be built on a platform of rights-based, participatory, gender-responsive and youth-friendly approaches that encourage ongoing dialogue between clients and health managers. Human rights, and the duties implied by them, can serve as guideposts for health system performance, and can help governments and managers address the factors hampering progress towards the MDG health goals. For instance, the primacy of a woman's right to life carries with it a legal obligation for health systems to provide skilled attendance during delivery and prompt emergency obstetric care 24 hours a day.[29] The fundamental rights to control one's own fertility and to protect oneself from HIV must be guiding principles for any policy and health provider. Discrimination based on gender, ethnicity, age or other biases may have severe and irreversible consequences for clients.

## Rights and Equality: Guiding Poverty Reduction Policies

The UN Millennium Project recommends an immediate review of national poverty reduction strategies and policies. Identifying groups with the least power and ability to exercise their rights is a key step. Their effective participation in identifying solutions to their own problems is both a human right and a principle of sound and sustainable programming. Infusing policy development with the principles of human rights and gender equality can help produce effective strategies for the progressive realization of the rights of the poorest of the poor.[30]

However, even though applying a human rights framework to policy development is "an essential prerequisite to achieving all the goals", according to the UN Millennium Project, in practice "there has been no systematic effort" to do so.[31] This is confirmed through reviews of Poverty Reduction Strategy Papers (PRSPs), which have been required of heavily indebted countries seeking debt relief since 1999. Civil society, including women's and youth groups, have had only limited or ineffective involvement in the development of these frameworks,[32] even though participatory processes form the very essence of a rights-based approach and have been found to be the most important element in arriving at "pro-poor" PRSPs that address gender issues.[33] National and regional policy frameworks, such as the New Partnership for Africa's Development, afford additional opportunities to integrate gender equality, youth development and reproductive health in poverty reduction strategies. But these frameworks have often ignored gender factors in macroeconomic and labour policies.[34]

The World Bank's 2002 assessment found the quality of gender analysis in most PRSPs to be generally weak,[35] although improving. UNFPA's own review of PRSPs confirms the inconsistent and often limited attention to gender, youth, reproductive health and human rights issues.[36] Half did not address the relationship between poverty and human rights, and few countries gave it more than superficial attention.[37] Although the scope and depth varies,[38] countries are now giving these issues greater priority in their poverty reduction strategies, with positive implications for the 2005 World Summit follow-up.

The UN Millennium Project recommends that national human rights institutions prepare "human rights assessments" on MDG follow up.[39] It also recommends training community development agents to promote local participation, gender equality and minority rights.[40] Using their local knowledge, these agents could also help refine and implement culturally sensitive approaches. Rwanda's PRSP, considered a leading example in integrating gender equality, engaged women's groups as active participants from the outset.[41] The success of this strategy is now acknowledged: One of the UN Millennium Project's "quick wins" calls for "empowering women to play a central role in formulating and monitoring MDG-based poverty reduction strategies and other critical policy reform processes, particularly at the level of local governments".[42]

Lacking political or economic power, young people often get short shrift from policymakers. Although they comprise a sizeable proportion of the population in all developing countries—and more so in the poorest—resources earmarked for them are often limited and ad hoc. Policies rarely address young people as a specific group living in poverty. Even in cases where Poverty Reduction Strategy Papers have included youth as a specific group, few countries link those strategies to budgets.[43]

Just as gender-responsive budgeting can inform national policymaking for the MDGs, efforts to analyze budgets from the added perspective of youth needs *and* gender equality can shed light on neglected priorities and strategic investments. Costa Rica provides a model: It monitors the percentage of GNP spent on children and adolescents in education, health, water, shelter, nutrition, protection and recreation.[44] The Ministry of Education, Youth and Sports in Cambodia provides another good example of institutional scommitment to gender issues. The Ministry uses sex-disaggregated data to address gender inequities in its budget, particularly for girls' education. It has developed a gender mainstreaming strategy and works to implement it with a committee representing provincial, district and commune levels.[45]

> *"A [health system] should also be understood and addressed as a core social institution. When characterized by neglect, abuse, or exclusion of certain individuals or groups, the health system is a major contributor to social injustice. Conversely, the strengthening of health systems increases social capital within the community and fulfils the rights of individuals."*
>
> — UN Millennium Project

## Resources: A Modest Price Tag for Human Dignity and Equity

Global military spending is about one trillion dollars a year.[46] Development aid in 2003 was $69 billion.[47] Given this disparity, the MDGs' price tag is clearly a matter of global political will and commitment. The cost of meeting the MDGs—estimated at $135 billion in 2006 and reaching $195 billion by 2015[48]—seems a modest and feasible sum, considering what it could accomplish. Thousands of lives could be saved each day. Millions of the world's people could escape the grip of poverty. Every girl and boy could be educated. The spread of AIDS could be curtailed. These are also fundamentals of a more secure world. All could be accomplished with a fraction of what the world spends for military purposes.

Various proposals, including by the European Commission and European heads of state, have been put forth since the 2000 UN Millennium Summit to make additional resources available for MDG implementation. Proposed revenue streams include the creation of an International Finance Facility[49] and taxes on airline fuel, financial transactions and carbon emissions.[50] The 2005 Commission for Africa Report lays out a plan on how best to end poverty in the region. It calls for a doubling of development aid to the continent within the next three to five years, debt cancellation, elimination of agricultural protection and trade subsidies by industrialized countries (which amount to $350 billion a year, or 16 times current aid flows to Africa), and the return of billions of dollars from corruption in bank accounts abroad.[51] It also calls for African countries to strengthen governance, ensure the inclusion of women and youth, and keep to the pledge made in 2001 to allocate 15 per cent of annual budgets to health care and expand access to reproductive health services.[52] The United States established the Millennium Challenge Account in 2002, which places selected countries with good governance records on a preferential list of aid recipients.[53]

Fulfilling the longstanding international commitment on development aid is the single most important step. Thirty-five years ago at the UN General Assembly, donor countries agreed to assign 0.7 per cent of their gross national income to official development assistance. Despite numerous and repeated calls, including at the 2002 high-level International Conference on Financing for Development held in Monterrey, Mexico,[54] only five donor countries have fulfilled their commitment: Denmark, Luxembourg, the Netherlands, Norway and Sweden.[55] Six others have set timetables to reach the goal.[56] Promising developments were unfolding just as this report was going to press: The European Union, as a bloc of its 25 members, made a unanimous, landmark decision in May 2005 to almost double aid in the next five years—with half of it for Africa—and set benchmarks towards the achievement of the 0.7 per cent target.[57] In the same month, Japan announced a doubling of aid for Africa in three years.[58]

The international community can reflect on the costs of failure to meet resource commitments by considering the case of the ICPD and its aftermath. The 1994 Programme of Action was one of the few international agreements that provided cost estimates for meeting the goal it set forth on universal access to reproductive health services by 2015. The international community, both donors and developing countries, did not meet the 2000 target of $17 billion. They were

---

### 38 THE RETURNS ON MAINSTREAMING GENDER

Sceptics have long underrated the value of gender mainstreaming. The "So What?" report looked at 400 reproductive health and HIV/AIDS projects from around the world. Its findings debunk the common perception that gender mainstreaming is peripheral. The report shows that integrating gender improves outcomes for both reproductive health and gender equity, and offers evidence of what gender mainstreaming can bring to MDG follow up. The projects that incorporated a gender perspective obtained these results, all of which are relevant to the MDGs:

- Positive changes in gender relations and more respectful societal attitudes towards women;
- More decision-making and political participation by women in the community;
- Women's increased knowledge of their legal rights;
- Greater likelihood that girls would stay in school;
- Reduced violence against women;
- Improved communication and mutual support between men and women on family planning, HIV and other sexually transmitted infections;
- Increased knowledge by men of women's health care issues;
- Shifts in attitudes about shared roles and responsibilities between men and women in childrearing, labour, and reproductive health issues.

still lagging behind in 2003 and it is still uncertain whether the target of $18.5 billion for 2005 will be reached. Preliminary data for 2003 show that donors have mobilized $4.7 billion, or 77 per cent of their one-third share of the target agreed for 2005. Developing countries mobilized approximately $11 billion, or 88 per cent of their corresponding share.[59] Narrower funding gaps could have saved and improved millions of lives in the past ten years.

One of the priorities singled out as an immediate "quick win" by the UN Millennium Project is ensuring adequate funding for sexual and reproductive health supplies and logistics, including contraceptives. Donor support for family planning has decreased since 1995, when family planning received 55 per cent of all global population assistance. This share dropped to only 11 per cent in 2003.[60] Meanwhile, demand is growing, especially as the largest generation of adolescents in history enters their reproductive years.

Parliamentarians committed to the ICPD continue to play a key role in maintaining policy attention and influencing budgetary appropriations. In Paraguay, UNFPA's support to the Senate's Commission on Equity, Gender and Social Development resulted in a 300 per cent increase in 2005 funding for family planning supplies. Parliamentarians can also use their power to raise additional funds: In Guatemala, the Parliament approved a 2004 law that allocates 15 per cent of taxes on alcoholic beverages and tobacco products to reproductive health programmes.

The ICPD agenda remains highly relevant for both developed and developing countries. UNFPA, the largest multilateral provider of population and reproductive health assistance, received a record high in voluntary contributions for its core resources from 166 countries in 2004. Some European donors, the United States and Japan have been leaders in the provision of international population assistance.[61]

International development cooperation is not a matter of charity, but a collective responsibility of the global community. This principle is enshrined in the UN Charter, the Universal Declaration of Human Rights, and international treaties such as the Convention on the Rights of the Child.[62] The fulfilment of human rights underpins the 2000 UN Millennium Declaration—a global development compact to end poverty.[63] It calls on donor governments and international financial institutions, the private sector and multinational corporations[64] to set rights-based standards for poverty reduction through fair trade, credit and debt facilities, and not least, migration flows and workers' rights. Shocking levels of corruption, estimated at one trillion dollars each year[65]—a cost borne largely by the poor who are left without basic services—underscore the importance of improved governance and the rule of law. Inconsistencies between debt repayment and the macroeconomic policies of international financial institutions with the MDGs need to be reconsidered. Such policies have often resulted in cutbacks to the social sectors. Adjusting them could restore funding to education and health sectors.[66] Some African countries, for instance, have used resources released by debt relief to assign health workers to where they are needed most. Mauritania used these to provide incentives to midwives in order to increase coverage in remote rural areas.[67]

The urgency of the AIDS epidemic has led to a rapid mobilization of commitments and resources, though these still fall short of need. Two major recent funding initiatives include the Global Fund to Fight AIDS, Tuberculosis and Malaria, and the United States President's Emergency Plan for AIDS Relief. The World Bank has also increased support for expanded access to AIDS treatment.[68] As the long overdue support for treatment is increasing, however, resources for HIV prevention—the front-line strategy to avert the epidemic's consequences and costs—still need to be stepped up.[69]

**'KNOW HOW' AND PARTNERSHIPS.** Specialized knowledge of what works best to attain the goals is a valuable resource. As highlighted by the UN Millennium Project, accelerated transfer of knowledge

> *"Development policies and actions that fail to take gender inequality into account or that fail to enable women to be actors in those policies and actions will have limited effectiveness and serious costs to societies."*
> 
> — UN Millennium Project Task Force on Education and Gender Equality

through cooperation among developed and developing countries is needed to ensure that investments in the MDGs are sound. This includes exchanges among government and non-governmental partners, civil society networks, women's and youth groups, research and training institutes. It calls for the transfer of medical advances and drugs, of knowledge sharing on simple means and proven strategies that can save lives.

Civil society, with its vast global networks and service infrastructure, its considerable flexibility, knowledge and experience, and connections to the on-the-ground realities of specific groups, will be essential to meeting the MDG challenge.[70] Strengthened collaboration and partnership between governments and civil society in national poverty reduction and development strategies, as well as in the direct delivery of services, will be required to implement the larger-scale programmes the MDGs require. Community ownership is one of the "requirements for success" rightly pointed out by the UN Millennium Project,[71] key to the design, accountability and sustainability of interventions. Communities are the best informants on what is working or faltering as MDG-related programmes are developed for their benefit.

Strengthened public-private sector partnership can bring in additional resources. The private sector can contribute both financial and in-kind support. Businesses can provide health information and services to their employees, and transfer skills and training to the communities in which they operate. The International Labour Organization's Code of Practice on HIV/AIDS and the World of Work has led to an increased number of firms adopting helpful policies to address the disease. Nonetheless, a survey of business leaders in 104 countries found that 71 per cent of the companies have no HIV/AIDS policies in place. Some companies in sub-Saharan Africa have set the example for others to follow, by providing services to their employees.[72] Multinational companies and large public employers who recognize the link between the productivity and reproductive health of their employees offer natural entry points to extend education and services.

Ever-expanding coalitions and networks are also forging ahead with focused campaigns on issues that are critical to meeting the MDGs. The "3 by 5" campaign of WHO and UNAIDS to provide 3 million HIV-positive people with access to treatment by 2005 is a prime example. Several others in the health arena have mobilized to address infant mortality, safe motherhood, youth, gender equality and HIV/AIDS.

Additional tools include the expanded use of the media and incentives, such as tax reductions. These can increase public commitment to MDG causes and philanthropic donations by private individuals and foundations, who are major contributors in the United States and some developed countries. Bill Gates and Ted Turner are leading examples of individuals who have made enormous contributions by establishing global foundations that provide MDG-related grants. Donations and in-kind contributions small and large can make a difference in saving and improving lives. The 34 Million Friends of UNFPA, for instance, has raised more than $2.6 million in support of the Fund, mostly in small contributions from more than 100,000 individuals, primarily from the United States. The media and parliamentarians can take advantage of their power to keep the MDGs high on public and policymakers' agendas and to press for accountability in the countdown to 2015.

**TIME TO ACT.** The world has an unprecedented opportunity to "make poverty history".[73] With nearly 3 billion people[74] struggling to live on less than $2 a day; one woman dying needlessly every minute in childbirth; 6,000 young people acquiring HIV daily; and millions of women and girls living in fear of violence, the ethically-acceptable response is self-evident: to fulfil the promises for global action on poverty, equality and equity espoused at the UN conferences of the 1990s and the 2000 UN Millennium Summit. Under international law, these agreements are more than rhetoric: They are collective obligations. They embody the principles that led to the formation of the community of countries known as the United Nations. They assert that the right to live in dignity, free of fear and shame, free of oppression and violence and free from want are the minimal rights and entitlements of every human being.

The world has an unprecedented opportunity to enable disenfranchised people to prevail over the circumstances that hold them back and claim their full rights. The strategies are clear. A plan is in place. The needed resources are attainable. The time to act is now.

# Notes and Indicators

## CHAPTER 1

1. UN Millennium Project. 2005a. *Investing in Development: A Practical Plan to Achieve the Millennium Development Goals: Overview*. Report to the Secretary-General. London and Sterling, Virginia: Earthscan.

2. The World Bank. 2001. *Engendering Development: Through Gender Equality in Rights, Resources, and Voice*, pp. 33, 35, 74, and 99. New York and Washington, D.C.: Oxford University Press and the World Bank.

3. Malhotra, A., and R. Mehra. 1999. *Fulfilling the Cairo Commitment: Enhancing Women's Economic and Social Options for Better Reproductive Health*. Washington, D.C.: International Center for Research on Women.

4. Based on calculations of disability-adjusted life years (DALYs). See: WHO. 2002. "Estimates of DALYs by Sex, Cause and WHO Mortality Sub-region: Estimates for 2001." Geneva: WHO. Web site: www3.who.int/whosis/menu.cfm?path=evidence,burden, burden_estimates,burden_estimates_2001,burden_estimates_2001_subregion&language=english, accessed 9 July 2003. Cited in: Singh, S., et al. 2004. *Adding It Up: The Benefits of Investing in Sexual and Reproductive Health Care*. New York: The Alan Guttmacher Institute and UNFPA.

5. The Alan Guttmacher Institute. 2004. "The Benefits of Investing in Sexual and Reproductive Health." *Issues in Brief*. 2004 Series. No. 4. New York: The Alan Guttmacher Institute.

6. The World Bank 2001.

7. UN Millennium Project. 2005a. *Taking Action: Achieving Gender Equality and Empowering Women*, p. 77. Task Force on Education and Gender Equality. London and Sterling, Virginia: Earthscan.

8. The World Bank. 2003a. *Gender Equality and the Millennium Development Goals*. Washington, D.C.: The World Bank; The World Bank 2001, p. 11; and The World Bank. 2003b. "Poverty Reduction through Gender-disaggregated Analysis of Public Expenditures: The Case of Cambodia." Promising Approaches to Engendering Development. Washington, D.C.: The World Bank.

9. UN Millennium Project. 2005b. *Investing in Development: A Practical Plan to Achieve the Millennium Development Goals*, p. 120. Report to the UN Secretary-General. London and Sterling, Virginia: Earthscan.

10. Ibid., p. 120; and Shenker, S., and E. Shields. 22 December 2004. "Mixed Views on UN Indigenous Decade." BBC News Online, accessed 18 April 2005.

11. United Nations. 2005a. *2004 World Survey on the Role of Women in Development: Women and International Migration* (A/59/287/Add.1, ST/ESA/294). New York: Division for the Advancement of Women, Department of Economic and Social Affairs, United Nations.

12. UN Millennium Project 2005b.

13. UN Millennium Project. 2005c. *Who's Got the Power: Transforming Health Systems for Women and Children*. Task Force on Child Health and Maternal Health. London and Sterling, Virginia: Earthscan.

14. Starrs, A., and P. Ten Hoope-Bender. 2004. "Dying for Life." Pp. 78-81 in: *Countdown 2015: Sexual and Reproductive Health and Rights for All: Special Report: ICPD at Ten: Where are We Now*, by Countdown 2015. 2004. New York, London, and Washington, D.C.: Family Care International, International Planned Parenthood Federation, and Population Action International; and Sein, T., and U. M. Rafei. 2002. "No More Cradles in the Graveyards." *Regional Health Forum* 6(2). New Delhi: WHO South-East Asia Region.

15. UN Millennium Project 2005c.

16. United Nations. 2004. *World Youth Report 2005: Report of the Secretary-General* (A/60/61 – E/2005/7), p. 1. New York: United Nations.

17. ILO. 2004. *Global Employment Trends for Youth*. Geneva: ILO.

18. The Population Council. n.d. "Transitions to Adulthood: Married Adolescents/First-Time Parents: Child Marriage." New York: The Population Council. Web site: www.popcouncil.org/ta/childmar.html#2, accessed 1 July 2005.

19. UNFPA. 2004. *The State of World Population 2004: The Cairo Consensus at Ten: Population, Reproductive Health and the Global Effort to End Poverty*, p. 76. New York: UNFPA.

20. United Nations. 2001. *We the Children: End-decade Review of the Follow-up to the World Summit for Children: Report of the Secretary-General* (A/S-27/3). New York: United Nations.

21. UNICEF. 2004. *The State of the World's Children 2005: Childhood under Threat*. New York: UNICEF.

22. UNFPA. 2005. *The Case for Investing in Young People as Part of a National Poverty Reduction Strategy*. New York: UNFPA.

23. "A Role for Men in Gender Equality Fight." 13 September 2004. *IPS UN Journal* 11(165): 6.

24. Heise, L., M. Ellsberg, and M.Gottemoeller. 1999. "Ending Violence against Women." *Population Reports*. Series L. No. 11. Baltimore, Maryland: Population Information Program, Johns Hopkins University School of Public Health.

25. UN Millennium Project 2005a, pp. 15 and 110.

26. The figure represents the estimated costs of intimate partner violence. See: Waters, H., et al. 2004. *The Economic Dimensions of Interpersonal Violence*. Geneva: Department of Injuries and Violence Prevention, WHO.

27. UNFPA. n.d. "Population Issues: Culture: India: Restoring the Sex Ratio Balance." New York: UNFPA. Web site: www.unfpa.org/culture/case_studies/india_study.htm, accessed 18 June 2005.

28. United States Department of State. 2005. *Trafficking in Persons Report: June 2005*. Washington, D.C.: United States Department of State.

29. United Nations 2005b

30. United Nations. 2005c. *Summary of the Economic and Social Survey of Asia and the Pacific: 2005* (E/2005/18). New York: United Nations

31. UN Millennium Project 2005b.

32. United Nations 2005b, para 8.

33. UN Millennium Project. n.d. "Fast Facts. Faces of Poverty." Web site: www.unmillenniumproject.org/facts/index.htm, accessed 3 June 2005.

34. UN Millennium Project. 2005b.

35. While nearly one trillion dollars are spent on military expenditures every year, total development assistance for 2003 was $69 billion. See: Skoens, E., C. Perdomo, and P. Stalenheim. 2004. "Military Expenditure." Ch. 10 in: *SIPRI Yearbook 2004: Armaments, Disarmament and International Security*, by Stockholm International Peace Research Institute. 2004. Oxford: Oxford University Press. Also see: Organization for Economic Co-operation and Development. 11 April 2005. "Official Development Assistance Increases Further: But 2006 Targets Still a Challenge." Paris: Organization for Economic Co-operation and Development. Web site: www.oecd.org/document/3/0,2340,en_2649_201185_34700611_1_1_1_1,00.html, last accessed 5 July 2005.

36. Maathai, W. 10 December 2004. Nobel Lecture, Nobel Foundation, Oslo, Norway.

## CHAPTER 2

1. The UN Millennium Project is a two-year project that brought together over 250 leading development experts from around the world to serve as an independent advisory board to the UN Secretary-General in order to identify strategic, proven and cost-effective strategies to achieve the MDGs. See web site: www.unmillenniumproject.org.

2. United Nations. 2005a. *Review of the Implementation of the Beijing Platform for Action and the Outcome Documents of the Special Session of the General Assembly Entitled "Women 2000: Gender Equality, Development and Peace for the Twenty-first Century": Report of the Secretary-General* (E/CN.6/2005/2), paras. 47, 50, and 93. New York: United Nations; and The World Bank. 2001. *Engendering Development: Through Gender Equality in Rights, Resources, and Voice*, p. 7. New York and Washington, D.C.: Oxford University Press and the World Bank.

3. This section relies on: The World Bank 2001.

4. Ibid., pp. 14, 19, 37, and 99.

5. Malhotra, A., and R. Mehra. 1999. *Fulfilling the Cairo Commitment: Enhancing Women's Economic and Social Options for Better Reproductive Health*. Washington, D.C.: International Center for Research on Women; and The World Bank 2001, p. 83.

6. UNFPA. 2003a. *Population and Poverty: Achieving Equity, Equality and Sustainability*, p. 46. Population and Development Strategies Series. No. 8. New York: UNFPA.

7. UN Millennium Project. 2005a. *Investing in Development: A Practical Plan to Achieve the Millennium Development Goals: Overview*, Box 5, p. 32. Report to the Secretary-General. London and Sterling, Virginia: Earthscan.

8. Ibid., Box 3, p. 13.

9. UNESCO Institute for Statistics. 2004. *Global Education Digest 2004: Comparing Education Statistics Across the World*. Montreal, Canada: UNESCO Institute for Statistics. Data refer to 2001/2002.

10. Of the 104 million children currently out of school, it is estimated that 54 to 57 per cent are girls. See: UN Millennium Project. 2005b. *Taking Action: Achieving Gender Equality and Empowering Women*, p. 42. Task Force on Education and Gender Equality. London and Sterling, Virginia: Earthscan.

11. United Nations. 27 April 2005. "Millennium Indicators Database." New York: Statistics Division, Department of Economic and Social Affairs, United Nations. Web site: http://millenniumindicators.un.org, last accessed 14 June 2005.

12. UN Millennium Project 2005b, p. 44.

13. UNFPA. 2005a. *Beijing at Ten: UNFPA's Commitment to the Platform for Action*, p. 5. New York: UNFPA.

14. UN Millennium Project 2005b, p. 5.

15. Schultz, T .P. 1993. "Returns to Women's Schooling." Ch. 2 in: *Women's Education in Developing Countries: Barriers, Benefits, and Policy*, edited by E. King and M. A. Hill. 1993. A World Bank Book. Baltimore, Maryland: Johns Hopkins University Press; and UN Millennium Project 2005b, p. 38.

16. UN Millennium Project 2005b, pp. 39, 40 and 41.

17. Grown, C., G. R. Gupta , and R. Pande. 2005. "Taking Action to Improve Women's Health through Gender Equality and Women's Empowerment." *The Lancet* 365(9458): 541-543.

18. Abu-Ghaida, D., and S. Klasen. 2004. "The Costs of Missing the Millennium Development Goal on Gender Equity." *World Development* 32(7): 1075-1107.

19. Klasen, S. 1999. "Does Gender Inequality Reduce Growth and Development: Evidence from Cross-Country Regressions." Policy Research Report on Gender and Development. Working Paper Series. No. 7. Washington, D.C.: The World Bank. Also in: The World Bank 2001, p. 11.

20. Filmer, D. 2004. "If You Build It, Will They Come: School Availability and School Enrollment in 21 Poor Countries." World Bank Policy Research Working Paper. No. 3340. Washington, D.C.: The World Bank; Lloyd, C. B., and A. K. Blanc. 1996. "Children's Schooling in Sub-Saharan Africa: The Role of Fathers, Mothers, and Others." *Population and Development Review* 22(2): 265-298; and Thomas, D., et al. 1996. "Parental Investments in Schooling: The Roles of Gender and Resources in Urban Brazil." RAND Labor and Population Program Working Papers. No. 96-02. Santa Monica, California: RAND Corporation; and UN Millennium Project 2005b, p. 41.

21. The World Bank 2001; Smith, L. C., and L. Haddad. 2000. *Explaining Child Malnutrition in Developing Countries: A Cross Country Analysis*. Research Report. No. 111. Washington, D.C.: International Food Policy Research Institute; and Schultz 1993

22. Quisumbing, A. 1996. "Male-female Differences in Agricultural Productivity: Methodological Issues and Empirical Evidence." *World Development*. 24(10): 1579-1595.

23. The World Bank 2001, p. 83.

24. Toure, Aminata. 2004. "Strengthening Families Through the Implementation of ICPD Programme of Action: UNFPA's Perspective." Presentation at the panel held to Observe the 10th Anniversary of the International Year of the Family, United Nations, 6 December 2004. Web site: www.unicef.ch/childfamily/files/Strengthening_families_through_the_implementation_of_ICPD_PA.doc, last accessed 29 June 2005; and Seligman, B., et al. 1997. *Reproductive Health and Human Capital: A Framework for Expanding Policy Dialogue*. POLICY Occasional Paper Series. No. 1. Washington, D.C.: POLICY Project, the Futures Group International.

25. UN Millennium Project 2005b, pp. 4, 5, 42, and 44.

26. See: MDG Target 4; and UN Millennium Project 2005a, p. 10.

27. UNFPA 2005a.

28. Teicher, S. A. 4 May 2005. "Gains for Girls, but Many Still Shut Out." *The Christian Science Monitor*; Herz, B., and G. B. Sperling. 2004. *What Works in Girls' Education: Evidence and Policies from the Developing World*. New York: Council on Foreign Relations; and UN Millennium Project 2005b, pp. 48-49.

29. UN Millennium Project 2005b, p. 51; Grown, Gupta, and Pande 2005; and Commission for Africa. 2005. *Our Common Interest: Report of the Commission for Africa*. London: Commission for Africa.

30. United Nations 2005a, para. 603.

31. UNFPA. 2003b. *Achieving the Millennium Development Goals: Population and Reproductive Health as Critical Determinants*. Population and Development Strategies Series. No. 10. New York: UNFPA.

32. Narayan, D., et al. 1999. *Can Anyone Hear Us? Voices From 47 Countries*. Voices of the Poor: Volume 1. New York: Oxford University Press for the World Bank.

33. McCauley, A. P., et al. 1994. "Opportunities for Women Through Reproductive Choice." *Population Reports*. Series M. No. 12. Baltimore, Maryland: Population Information Program, Johns Hopkins School of Public Health.

34. Seligman, et al. 1997.

35. UN Millennium Project 2005c.

36. McCauley, et al. 1994.

37. The Alan Guttmacher Institute. 2004. "The Benefits of Investing in Sexual and Reproductive Health." *Issues in Brief*. 2004 Series. No.4. New York: The Alan Guttmacher Institute.

38. United Nations. 2005b. *World Population Prospects: The 2004 Revision: Highlights* (ESA/P/WP.193). New York: Population Division, Department of Economic and Social Affairs, United Nations.

39. Bloom, D. E., et al. 2002. *The Demographic Dividend: A New Perspective on the Economic Consequences of Population Change*. Santa Monica, California: RAND; and Birdsall, N., et al. (eds.). 2001. *Population Matters: Demographic Change, Economic Growth, and Poverty in the Developing World*. New York: Oxford University Press; and Singh, S., et al. 2004. *Adding It Up: The Benefits of Investing in Sexual and Reproductive Health Care*. New York: The Alan Guttmacher Institute and UNFPA.

40. Bloom, D., and D. Canning. 2004. "Population, Poverty Reduction, and the Cairo Agenda." Paper prepared for the Seminar on the Relevance of Population Aspects for the Achievement of the Millennium Development Goals, New York, 17-19 November 2004. New York: Population Division, Department of Economic and Social Affairs, United Nations.

41. Mason, A., and S. H. Lee. 2004. "The Demographic Dividend and Poverty Reduction." Paper prepared for the Seminar on the Relevance of Population Aspects for the Achievement of the Millennium Development Goals, New York, 17-19 November 2004. New York: Population Division, Department of Economic and Social Affairs, United Nations.

42. Singh, et al. 2004.

43. For example, see: World Bank. n.d. "Why Invest in Children and Youth?" Geneva: WHO. Web site: http://web.worldbank.org/WBSITE/EXTERNAL/TOPICS/EXTCY/0,,contentMDK:20243901~menuPK:565261~pagePK:148956~piPK:216618~theSitePK:396445,00.htm, accessed 28 June 2005; UNFPA. 2005b. *The Case for Investing in Young People as Part of a National Poverty Reduction Strategy*. New York: UNFPA; and Knowles, J., and J. Behrman. 2003, *Assessing the Economic Returns to Investing in Youth in Developing Countries*. Health, Nutrition and Population (HNP) Discussion Paper. Washington, D.C.: World Bank.

44. The World Bank 2001, p. 66.

45. UN Millennium Project 2005a, p. 87.

46. UN Millennium Project 2005b, p. 7.

47. Ibid., p. 7.; The World Bank 2001, pp. 24-25; and Grown, Gupta, and Pande 2005.

48. UN Millennium Project 2005b, p. 77; and The World Bank 2001.

49. United Nations. 2005c. *Progress Made in the Implementation of the Declaration of Commitment on HIV/AIDS: Report of the Secretary-General* (A/59/765), para. 61. New York: United Nations; and United Nations 2005a, para. 375.

50. UN Millennium Project 2005b, p. 87.

51. The World Bank 2001. See also: The World Bank. 2004. "Poverty Reduction through Gender-disaggregated Analysis of Public Expenditures: The Case of Cambodia." Promising Approaches to Engendering Development. Washington, D.C.: The World Bank.

52. Blackden, M. C., and C. Bhanu. 1999. "Gender, Growth, and Poverty Reduction: Special Program of Assistance for Africa: 1998 Status Report on Poverty in Sub-Saharan Africa." Technical Paper. No. 428. Poverty Reduction and Social Development, Africa Region. Washington, D.C.: The World Bank.

53. The World Bank. 2003. *Gender Equality and the Millennium Development Goals*. Washington, D.C.: The World Bank; The World Bank 2001, p. 11; and The World Bank 2004.

54. Bruce, J., C. Lloyd, and A. Leonard. 1995. *Families in Focus: New Perspectives on Mothers, Fathers and Children*. New York: The Population Council.

55. The World Bank 2001.

56. An extensive literature reports that women are more likely to spend their incomes on food, education and healthcare that enhance the welfare of their children as well as their own. See: The World Bank 2001, p. 18; Grown, Gupta, and Pande 2005; and UN Millennium Project 2005b.

57. UN Millennium Project 2005b.

58. United Nations 2005a, para. 315.

59. UNIFEM. 2002a. *Progress of the World's Women 2002: Gender Equality and the Millennium Development Goals*. New York: UNIFEM.

60. UN Millennium Project 2005c, p. 138.

61. United Nations 2005a, paras. 288, 294, and 295.

62. The World Bank 2001.

63. See: ILO. n.d. "C111 Discrimination (Employment and Occupation) Convention, 1958"; "C100 Equal Remuneration Convention, 1951"; "C156 Workers with Family Responsibilities Convention, 1981;" and "C183 Maternity Protection Convention, 2000." All available on ILO, "Gender: Equality Between Men and Women," web site: www.ilo.org/public/english/gender.htm, accessed 29 June 2005; and United Nations 2005a, para. 283.

64. Hein, C. 2005. *Reconciling Work and Family Responsibilities: Practical Ideas from Global Experience*. Geneva: ILO; and O'Brien, M. 2004. *Shared Caring: Bringing Fathers into the Frame*. EOC Working Paper Series. No. 18. Manchester, United Kingdom: Equal Opportunities Commission.

65. The World Bank 2001, p. 24.

66. United Nations 2005a, para. 298.

67. James, B. 2002. *European, Australian and Canadian Policies to Reconcile Paid Work and Family Life*. Report prepared for the Ministry of Women's Affairs of New Zealand, Wellington, New Zealand. Web site: www.mwa.govt.nz/pub/InternationalPolicies.doc, last accessed 1 July 2005.

68. Ibid.

69. United Nations 2005a, para. 316.

70. James 2002.

71. Malhotra and Mehra 1999.

72. Lloyd, C. B. (ed.) 2005. *Growing Up Global: The Changing Transitions to Adulthood in Developing Countries*. Washington, D.C.: The National Academies Press.

73. United Nations 2005a, para. 303.

74. Business for Social Responsibility. 2002. *Addressing the General and Reproductive Health of Women in Global Supply Chains*. San Francisco, California: Business for Social Responsibility.

75. Lovenduski, J., and A. Karam 2002. "Women in Parliament: Making a Difference." Ch. 6 in: *Women in Parliament: Beyond Numbers*, by International IDEA. Stockholm, Sweden: International IDEA. Web site: http://archive.idea.int/women/parl/, last accessed 11 July 2005.

76. See, for example: Swamy, A., et al. 2001 "Gender and Corruption." *Journal of Development Economics* 64(1): 25-55; and The World Bank 2001, pp. 8, 12, and 95. See also: UN Millennium Project 2005b.

77. UN Millennium Project 2005b.

78. United Nations 2005a, p. 348; and UNFPA 2005a.

79. United Nations. n.d. "Millennium Indicators Database: World and Regional Trends." New York: Statistics Division, United Nations. Web site: http://millenniumindicators.un.org/unsd/mi/mi_worldregn.asp, last accessed 7 July 2005. In 1990, the UN Economic and Social Council recommended a target for increasing the proportion of women in leadership positions to "at least 30% by 1995". See: UN Economic and Social Council Resolution E/RES/1990/15, Recommendation VI, para, 2.

80. UN Millennium Project 2005b, p. 109.

81. United Nations 2005a, para. 333.

82. Vyasulu, P., and V. Vyasulu. 2000. "Women in the Panchayati Raj: Grassroots Democracy in India." Ch. 5 in: UNDP. 2000. *Women's Political Participation and Good Governance: 21st Century Challenges*. New York: UNDP.

83. United Nations 2005a, paras. 333 and 338.

84. Inter-Parliamentary Union. 2005. "Women in National Parliaments: World Classification." Situation as of 30 April 2005. Web site: www.ipu.org/wmn-e/classif.htm, acessed 3 July 2005. Data reported relate to lower house parliamentary seats.

85. United Nations. 17 March 2005. "10 Stories the World Should Hear About: Women as Peacemakers: From Victims to Re-Builders of Society." New York: United Nations. Web site: www.un.org/events/tenstories/story.asp?storyID=700, accessed 29 June 2005.

86. United Nations 2005a, para 731; and United Nations. 2002. *Gender Mainstreaming: An Overview*. New York: Office of the Special Advisor on Gender Issues and Advancement of Women, United Nations.

87. Waldorf, L. 2004. *Pathway to Equality: CEDAW, Beijing and the MDGs*. New York: UNIFEM. Also see: Corner, L. n.d. "Gender-sensitive and Pro-poor Indicators of Good Governance." Paper prepared for the UNDP Governance Indicators Project, Oslo Governance Centre. New York: UNDP. Web site: www.undp.org/oslocentre/docs05/cross/2/Gender-sensitive%20and%20pro-poor%20indicators%20for%20Democratic%20Governance.pdf, last accessed 5 July 2005; and Neimanis, A., and A. Tortisyn. 2003. *Gender Thematic Guidance Note*. NHDR Guidance Note on Gender. No. 2. New York: UNDP.

88. For example, see the Demographic and Health Survey (DHS) module on women's status; UNDP's Gender-related Development Index and Gender Empowerment Measure; and measurements under development by the UN Regional Commissions, such as the Africa Gender and Development Index, Western Asia efforts to improve data availability, and indicators to monitor the proportions of men and women living in poverty in Latin America and the Caribbean. UN agencies, including UNFPA and UNIFEM, support countries

89  UNDP. 2003. *Millennium Development Goals: National Reports: A Look Through a Gender Lens.* New York: UNDP.

90  Valdes, T. 2002. "Index of Fulfilled Commitments 1995-2000: A *Social Watch* Instrument for Women." International Seminar: Latin America and the Caribbean: Challenges before the Millennium Development Goals, Washington, D.C., 10-11 June 2002. Washington, D.C.: Inter-American Development Bank. Web site: http://www.iadb.org/sds/doc/SOCSes4 GeneroTeresaValdes1.pdf, accessed 22 June 2005. See also: FLACSO Chile. "Area de Estudios de Genero, Grupo Iniciativa Mujeres." Santiago, Chile: FLACSO. Web site: http://www.flacso.cl/, accessed 22 June 2005.

91  United Nations 2005a, para. 737. See also: United Nations. 2003. *Indicators for Monitoring the Millennium Development Goals: Definitions, Rationale, Concepts, and Sources* (ST/ESA/STAT/SER.F/95). New York: United Nations Development Group, United Nations.

92  United Nations 2002.

93  United Nations 2003.

94  Grown, C., and G. R. Gupta. 2004. "An Agenda for Engendering: the Millennium Project Task Force on Education and Gender Equality." In: *Seeking Accountability on Women's Human Rights: Women Debate the Millennium Development Goals,* by the Women's International Coalition for Economic Justice. 2004. New York: Women's International Coalition for Economic Justice.

95  United Nations. 2001. "Aide-Memoire: Regional Meeting to Discuss a Needs Assessment on: National Machineries for Gender Equality in African Countries." Addis Ababa, Ethiopia: Department of Economic and Social Affairs, United Nations.

96  United Nations 2005a, para. 725. See also: Norwegian Ministry of Foreign Affairs. 2002. "Strategies for Gender Equality: Is Mainstreaming a Dead End?" Report from an Informal Consultation of Gender Focal Points in Multilateral Development Organizations, Oslo, Norway, November 2002.

97  United Nations 2005a, paras. 724, 726, and 736; and UNDP. 2003. "From Recovery to Transition: Women, the Untapped Resource." *Essentials.* No. 11. New York: Evaluation Office, UNDP.

98  UN Millennium Project 2005b.

99  United Nations 2005a, para. 703.

100 Center of Arab Women, Training and Research. n.d. Training Session on "Gender Institutionalization through Planning and Budgeting," Tunis, December 2003. Web site: www.cawtar.org.tn, accessed 22 May 2005. See also: UNDP, Government of Tunisia, and AGFUND. 2002. "Support to the Center for Arab Women's Training and Research: CAWTAR" (RAB/02/001/A/01/31). Project document. New York: UNDP.

101 Sharp, R. 2003. *Budgeting for Equity: Gender Budget Initiatives within a Framework of Performance Oriented Budgeting.* UNIFEM: New York; and Elson, D. 2005. "Monitoring Government Budgets for Compliance with CEDAW: Report Highlights and Key Conclusions." New York: UNIFEM. Web site: www.gender-budgets.org/en/ev-72845-201-1-DO_TOPIC.html, accessed 22 May 2005.

102 United Nations. 2005d. *United Nations Development Fund for Women: Implementing the Multi-Year Funding Framework: 2004* (DP/2005/24). New York: United Nations.

103 UN Millennium Project 2005b, pp. 25, 149, and 150.

104 UNIFEM. 2005. *Gender Responsive Budgets: Program Results (2001-2004).* Brochure. New York: UNIFEM.

105 UN Millennium Project 2005b, p. 147.

106 United Nations 2005a, para. 690.

107 UNIFEM 2005; and UNIFEM. May-June 2004. "Gender Budgets: Tracking Gender Equality." *Currents.* Electronic Newsletter. Web site: http://www.unifem.org/news/currents/currents200406.html, accessed 3 July 2005.

108 United Nations 2005d; and UNIFEM May-June 2004.

109 United Nations. 2000. *Resolution Adopted by the General Assembly: S-23/3 Further Actions and Initiatives to Implement the Beijing Declaration and Platform for Action* (A/RES/S-23/3). New York: United Nations.

## CHAPTER 3

1  There are seven core international human rights conventions: the International Covenant on Civil and Political Rights (1966); the International Covenant on Economic, Social and Cultural Rights (1966); the International Convention on the Elimination of all forms of Racial Discrimination (1965); the Convention on the Elimination of All Forms of Discrimination Against Women (1979); the Convention on the Rights of the Child (1989); the Convention Against Torture and other Cruel, Inhuman and Degrading Treatment or Punishment (1984); and the International Convention on the Protection of the Rights of All Migrant Workers and Members of their Families (1990). Years shown indicate adoption of a convention, not date of entry into force.

2  Of the various relevant protocols adopted, particularly relevant in the context of women's rights is the Optional Protocol to the CEDAW entered into force in 2000. See: United Nations. 1999a. *Resolution Adopted by the General Assembly: 54/4: Optional Protocol to the Convention on All Forms of Discrimination against Women* (A/RES/54/4). New York: United Nations.

3  UNDP. 2000. *Human Development Report 2000: Human Rights and Human Development.* New York: Oxford University Press.

4  Ibid.

5  United Nations. 2005a. *In Larger Freedom: Towards Development, Security and Human Rights for All: Report of the Secretary-General* (A/59/2005). New York: United Nations; and UN Millennium Project. 2005a. *Investing in Development: A Practical Plan to Achieve the Millennium Development Goals.* Report to the UN Secretary-General. London and Sterling, Virginia: Earthscan.

6  United Nations. 2002a. "Draft Guidelines: A Human Rights Approach to Poverty Reduction Strategies." Geneva: Office of the High Commissioner for Human Rights, United Nations. Web site: www.ohchr.org/english/issues/docs/guidelinesfinal-poverty.doc, last accessed 30 June 2005.

7  Ibid.

8  Ibid, pp. 1 and 5.

9  UN Millennium Project 2005a.

10 United Nations 2002a.

11 Ibid.

12 United Nations 2005a.

13 United Nations. 2005b. *Economic, Social and Cultural Rights: Draft Resolution: 2005: Human Rights and Extreme Poverty* (E/CN.4/2005/L.18). New York: United Nations.

14 United Nations. 2005c. *Economic, Social and Cultural Rights. Human Rights and Extreme Poverty. Report of the Independent Expert on the Question of Human Rights and Extreme Poverty: Arjun Sengupta* (E/CN.4/2005/49.) New York: United Nations.

15 United Nations. 2005d. *Review of the Implementation of the Beijing Platform for Action and the Outcome Documents of the Special Session of the General Assembly Entitled "Women 2000: Gender Equality, Development and Peace for the Twenty-first Century": Report of the Secretary-General* (E/CN.6/2005/2), para. 374. New York: United Nations.

16 Ibid., para. 468.

17 Boland, R. 2004. "Legal Progress in Implementing the ICPD Programme of Action." Statement at the 2004 International Parliamentarians' Conference on the Implementation of the ICPD Programme of Action, Strasbourg, France, 18-19 October 2004. Web site: www.unfpa.org/parliamentarians/ipci/strasbourg/docs/boland.doc, last accessed 5 July 2005.

18 United Nations 2005d, paras. 383 and 386.

19 Ibid., para. 382.

20 The World Bank. 2001. *Engendering Development: Through Gender Equality in Rights, Resources, and Voice,* p. 4. New York and Washington, D.C.: Oxford University Press and the World Bank.

21 Equality Now. 2005. "Words and Deeds. Holding Governments Accountable in the Beijing + 10 Review Process." Women's Action 16.8: Update: May 2005. New York: Equality Now. Web site: www.equalitynow.org/english/wan/beijing10/beijing10_en.pdf, last accessed 11 July 2005.

22 United Nations 2005d, paras. 231 and 397.

23 Ibid., paras. 394 and 401; and The World Bank 2001.

24 United Nations 2005d, paras. 70 and 232.

25 UNIFEM. 2003. *Not a Minute More: Ending Violence against Women.* New York: UNIFEM.

26 The ICPD and Beijing articulated the international consensus based on the foundation established by earlier international human rights instruments and standards.

27 Equality Now 2005.

28 Organization of American States. 2003. "Third Biennial Report on Fulfillment of Resolution AG/RES. 1456 (XXVII-O/97): 'Promotion of the Inter-American Convention on the Prevention, Punishment and Eradication of Violence Against Women, 'Convention of Belem do Para'" (AG/RES. 1942 [XXXIII-O/03]). Washington, D.C.: Organization of American States.

29 African Union. 2003. "Protocol to the African Charter on Human and People's Rights on the Rights of Women in Africa." Adopted by the 2nd Ordinary Session of the Assembly of the Union, Maputo, Mozambique, 11 July 2003. Addis Ababa, Ethiopia: African Union. Web site: www.africa-union.org/Official_documents/Treaties_%20Conventions_%20Protocols/Protocol%20on%20the%20Rights%20of%20Women.pdf., accessed 5 July 2005.

30 International Center for Research on Women. 2004. *To Have and To Hold: Women's Property and Inheritance Rights in the Context of HIV/AIDS in Sub-Saharan Africa.* Information Brief. Washington, D.C.: International Center for Research on Women.

31 UNFPA. 2005. *Beijing at Ten: UNFPA's Commitment to the Platform for Action.* New York: UNFPA.

32 UN Millennium Project. 2005b. *Taking Action: Achieving Gender Equality and Empowering Women,* p. 144. Task Force on Education and Gender Equality. London and Sterling, Virginia: Earthscan.

33 UN Millennium Project 2005a, Box 1.3, p. 8.

34 United Nations. 1995. *Population and Development,* vol. 1: *Programme of Action adopted at the International Conference on Population and Development: Cairo: 5-13 September 1994,* Principle 2. New York: Department of Economic and Social Information and Policy Analysis, United Nations.

35 Defined in: United Nations. 1966. "International Covenant on Economic, Social and Cultural Rights: Adopted and Opened for Signature, Ratificaton and Accession by General Assembly Resolution 2000A(XXI) of 16 December," Article 12.1. Geneva: Office of the High Commissioner for Human Rights. Web site: www.unhchr.ch/html/menu3/b/a_cescr.htm, last accessed 11 July 2005; and reflected in various other human rights treaties.

36 WHO. 1948. *Constitution of the World Health Organization (1946),* Preamble. Geneva: WHO.

37 United Nations. n.d. "The International Covenant on Economic, Social and Cultural Rights: Adopted and Opened for Signature, Ratification and Accession by General Assembly Resolution 2200A (XXI) of 16 December 1966," Article 12. New York: United Nations; and United Nations. 2005e. *Economic, Social and Cultural Rights: Report of the Special Rapporteur on the Right of Everyone to the Enjoyment of the Highest Attainable Standard of Physical and Mental Health: Paul Hunt* (E/CN.4/2005/51), para. 46. New York: United Nations.

38 United Nations Office of the High Commissioner for Human Rights and UNAIDS. 1998. *HIV/AIDS and Human Rights: International Guidelines: Second International Consultation on HIV/AIDS and Human Rights, Geneva, 23-25 September 1996* (HR/PUB/98/1). New York and Geneva: United Nations. These guidelines are available at: http://www.unaids.org/en/in+focus/hiv_aids_human_rights/international_guidelines.asp, accessed 5 July 2005.

39 United Nations. 2005f. *Progress Made in the Implementation of the Declaration of Commitment on HIV/AIDS: Report of the*

Secretary-General (A/59/765), paras. 15 and 54. New York: United Nations.

40 United Nations 2005d, para. 544.

41 United Nations 1995, para. 7.3.

42 See, for example, General Recommendation 24 on Women and Health of CEDAW (1999); General Comment 14 on the Right to Health of the ICESCR (2000); General Comment 3 on HIV/AIDS and the Rights of the Child (2003); and General Comment 4 on Adolescent Health and Development (2003) of the CRC. Note also that the treaty bodies, such as the CEDAW Committee, issue recommendations to States Party submitting reports that often address reproductive health issues. See also the reports of the Special Rapporteurs on the Right to Health and on Violence Against Women, among others. Available on the web site of the Office of the High Commissioner for Human Rights: www.unhchr.org/, last accessed 12 July 2005.

43 UNFPA. 2004a. *Investing in People: National Progress in Implementing the ICPD Programme of Action: 1994-2004*. New York: UNFPA.

44 Boland 2004.

45 Ibid.; Boland, R. April 2005. Personal communications; and Center for Reproductive Rights. 2005. "Governments in Action: Legal and Policy Developments Affecting Reproductive Rights." Briefing Paper. New York: Center for Reproductive Rights.

46 Center for Reproductive Rights. 2003. "The Slovak Government's Response to Reproductive Rights Violations against Romani Women: Analysis and Recommendations." New York: Center for Reproductive Rights; and Republic of Peru. 2000. "Peru Resolution No. 03-DP-2000 of 28 January 2000 of the Public Defender." Lima, Peru: Republic of Peru.

47 Center for Reproductive Rights 2005.

48 The 2002 International Parliamentarians' Conference on the Implementation of the ICPD Programme of Action (IPCI/ICPD), Ottawa, Canada, 21-22 November 2002. See: *Report of the First International Parliamentarians' Conference on the Implementation of the ICPD Programme of Action*. Web site: www.unfpa.org/parliamentarians/ipci/ottawa/documents/ottawareport.pdf; accessed 5 July 2005; and the 2004 International Parliamentarians' Conference on the Implementation of the ICPD Programme of Action, Strasbourg. France, 18-19 October 2004. See: "Strasbourg Statement of Commitment." Web site: www.unfpa.org/parliamentarians/ipci/strasbourg/docs/comm.doc, accessed 5 July 2005.

49 Kols, A. 2003. "A Rights-Based Approach to Reproductive Health." *Outlook* 20(4): 1-8. Seattle, Washington: PATH.

50 The IPPF Charter on Sexual and Reproductive Rights is based on 12 rights, which are grounded in international human rights instruments and the additional rights implied by them. See: International Planned Parenthood Federation. 1996. *The IPPF Charter on Sexual and Reproductive Rights*. London: IPPF. Web site: http://content.ippf.org/output/ORG/files/6385.pdf, last accessed 8 July 2005.

51 See Articles 2(f,g) and 5(a) of CEDAW and Article 24.3 of CRC. In: United Nations. 1999b. *Integration of the Human Rights of Women and the Gender Perspective: Violence Against Women: Report of the Special Rapporteur on Violence Against Women, Its Causes and Consequences, Ms. Radhika Coomaraswamy: In Accordance with Commission on Human Rights resolution 1997/44: Addendum, Policies and Practices that Impact on Women's Reproductive Rights and Contribute to, Cause or Constitute Violence against Women* (E/CN.4/1999/68/Add.4). New York: United Nations. See also: United Nations. 1993. *48/104: Declaration on the Elimination of Violence Against Women* (A/RES/48/104), Article 4. New York United Nations.

52 United Nations 2003. *Integration of the Human Rights of Women and the Gender Perspective: Violence Against Women* (E/CN.4/2003/75). New York: United Nations.

53 UNFPA. 2004b. *Working from Within: Culturally Sensitive Approaches in UNFPA Programming*. New York: UNFPA; and UNDP. 2004. *Human Development Report: Cultural Liberty in Today's Diverse World*. New York: UNDP.

54 UNFPA 2004b; and UNFPA. 2004c. *Culture Matters: Working with Communities and Faith-based Organizations: Case Studies From Country Programmes*. New York: UNFPA.

55 UNFPA. 24 June 1998. "Reproductive Health Round Table Focuses on Violence Against Women, Including FGM." Press Release. New York: UNFPA.

56 United Nations. 2003a. *United Nations Common Country Assessment for the Islamic Republic of Iran*. Tehran: United Nations Country Team in Iran, United Nations; United Nations. 2003b. *Population and Development: Selected Issues*.(ST/ESCAP/2288). Asian Population Studies Series. No. 161. New York: Economic and Social Commission for Asia and the Pacific, United Nations; United Nations. n.d. "Views and Policies Concerning Population Growth and Fertility Among Governments in Intermediate-Fertility Countries." New York: Population Division, Department of Economic and Social Affairs, United Nations; and Mehryar, A. H. 2001. *Proceedings of the First International Workshop on Integrated Approach to Reproductive Health and Family Planning in the Islamic Republic of Iran*. Tehran: UNFPA and the Institute for Research on Planning and Development.

57 Dungus, A. 2000. "Iran's Other Revolution." *Populi* 27(2): 8-13.

58 UNFPA 2004b.

59 United Nations. n.d. "Disabilities." Geneva: Office of the United Nations High Commissioner for Human Rights, United Nations. Web site: www.ohchr.org/english/issues/disability/index.htm, accessed 21 June 2005.

60 UN Millennium Project 2005a, p.120; and United Nations. 2002b. *Report of the United Nations High Commissioner for Human Rights to the Economic and Social Council* (E/2002/68). New York: United Nations; and Shenker, S., and E. Shields. 22 December 2004. "Mixed Views on UN Indigenous Decade." BBC News Online, accessed 18 April 2005.

61 United Nations. 2005g. *2004 World Survey on the Role of Women in Development: Women and International Migration* (A/59/287/Add.1, ST/ESA/294). New York: Division for the Advancement of Women, Department of Economic and Social Affairs, United Nations.

62 Hall, G., and H. Patrinos (eds.). Forthcoming. "Indigenous People, Poverty, and Human Development in Latin America: 1994-2004." Washington, D.C.: The World Bank and Palgrave/MacMillan; and United Nations. 2004a. *Report of the Secretary-General on the Preliminary Review by the Coordinator of the International Decade of the World's Indigenous People on the Activities of the United Nations System in Relation to the Decade* (E/2004/82). New York: United Nations.

63 Quinn, G., and T. Degener. 2002. *Human Rights and Disability: The Current Use and Future Potential of United Nations Human Rights Instruments in the Context of Disability* (HR/PUB/02/1). New York and Geneva: United Nations. See also: CEDAW General Recommendation No. 18. Web site: www.un.org/womenwatch/daw/cedaw/recommendations/recomm.htm#recom18, last accessed 1 July 2005.

64 UNIFEM. 2004. "Securing Indigenous Women's Rights and Participation." *At-a-Glance*. New York, UNIFEM. Web site: www.unifem.org/filesconfirmed/2/355_at_a_glance_indigenous_women.pdf, last accessed 5 July 2005.

65 See para. 31, among others, in: United Nations 2004b. *Specific Groups and Individuals, Migrant Workers. Report of the Special Rapporteur, Ms. Gabriela Rodríguez Pizarro, Submitted Pursuant to Commission on Human Rights Resolution 2003/46* (E/CN.4/2004/76). New York: United Nations.

66 The 1990 International Convention on the Protection of the Rights of All Migrant Workers and Members of their Families, which came into force in 2003. Efforts are now underway to draft an international convention on the rights of persons with disabilities. See: United Nations. n.d. "Draft Article 12: Freedom from Violence and Abuse." New York: United Nations. Web site: www.un.org/esa/socdev/enable/rights/ahcwgreporta12.htm, last accessed 6 July 2005. The Convention Concerning the Protection and Integration of Indigenous and other Tribal and Semi-Tribal Populations and Independent Countries came into force in 1991 (ILO. n.d. "C107 Indigenous and Tribal Populations Convention." Web site: www.ilo.org/ilolex/cgi-lex/convde.pl?C107, last accessed 6 July 2005).

67 For example, the 1982 UN World Programme of Action concerning Disabled Persons and the 1995 Beijing Conference Declaration of Indigenous Women. The Durban Declaration and Programme of Action of the World Conference against Racism, Racial Discrimination, Xenophobia and Related Intolerance (2001) also addressed the rights of indigenous people. For the latter see web site: www.un.org/WCAR/durban.pdf, last accessed 13 July 2005.

68 See the reports of the Special Rapporteurs on indigenous people; on trafficking in persons, especially in women and children; on migrants; and on disability. See also the Representative of the Secretary-General on internally displaced persons; the ICESCR General Comment No. 5 on Persons with Disabilities; and CEDAW General Recommendation No. 18 on Disabled Women, among others.

69 United Nations. 2002c. *Recommended Principles and Guidelines on Human Rights and Trafficking* (E/2002/68/Add.1). New York: United Nations. See also the Standard Rules on the Equalization of Opportunities for Persons with Disabilities cited in: United Nations. 2003c. *Specific Groups and Individuals: Other Vulnerable Groups and Individuals: Report of the High Commissioner for Human Rights on Progress in the Implementation of the Recommendations Contained in the Study on the Human Rights of Persons with Disabilities* (E/CN.4/2003/88). New York: United Nations.

70 The Inter-American Convention on the Elimination of All Forms of Discrimination against Persons with Disabilities was adopted in 1999, and a draft declaration on indigenous rights is underway by the Organization of American States. The African Commission on Human and People's Rights established a working group on indigenous people. International human rights treaty bodies and special rapporteurs have issued recommendations on indigenous people's rights to food, health, housing and land, and on the rights of indigenous women and children, as well as on the equal rights of disabled persons to non-discrimination. (For the latter, see the regional forums on the rights of indigenous people cited in: United Nations 2005d, para. 579.). See also: United Nations. 2004a. *Report of the Secretary-General on the Preliminary Review by the Coordinator of the International Decade of the World's Indigenous People on the Activities of the United Nations System in Relation to the Decade* (E/2004/82). New York: United Nations; and United Nations 2003c.

71 United Nations 2005d, para. 579.

72 Ibid., paras. 580 and 582.

73 Ibid., para. 524.

74 UNIFEM. 2005. "Report to the Forty-fifth Session of the Consultative Committee." New York: UNIFEM; and United Nations. 2005h. *United Nations Development Fund for Women: Implementing the Multi-Year Funding Framework: 2004* (DP/2005/24). New York: United Nations.

75 United Nations 2004b.

76 United Nations. n.d. "Indigenous and Tribal Peoples Convention, 1989 (No. 169): Adopted on 27 June 1989 by the General Conference of the International Labour Organisation at Its Seventy-sixth Session." Geneva: Office of the United Nations High Commissioner for Human Rights. Web site: www.ohchr.org/english/law/indigenous.htm, accessed 5 July 2005.

77 United Nations 2004a.

78 United Nations. n.d. "International Convention on the Protection of the Rights of All Migrant Workers and Members of Their Families: Adopted by General Assembly Resolution 45/158 of 18 December 1990." New York: United Nations. Web site: www.ohchr.org/english/law/pdf/cmw.pdf, last accessed 8 July 2005.

79 United Nations. 2000. *Resolution Adopted by the General Assembly: 55/2: United Nations Millennium Declaration* (A/RES/55.2), para. 25. New York: United Nations.

# CHAPTER 4

1 Koblinsky, M. A. (ed.). 2003. *Reducing Maternal Mortality: Learning from Bolivia, China, Egypt, Honduras, Indonesia, Jamaica, and Zimbabwe*. Human Development Network Health, Nutrition, and Population Series. Washington, D.C.: The World Bank; and UNFPA. 2004a. *Saving Mothers' Lives: The Challenge*

*Continues*. New York: UNFPA. In the 1990s, Zimbabwe also made progress in reducing maternal mortality.

2. UN Millennium Project. 2005a. *Combating AIDS in the Developing World*, pp. 22 and 32. Working Group on HIV/AIDS, Task Force on HIV/AIDS, Malaria, TB, and Access to Essential Medicines. London and Sterling, Virginia: Earthscan.

3. United Nations. 1995. *Population and Development*, vol. 1: *Programme of Action adopted at the International Conference on Population and Development: Cairo: 5-13 September 1994*, para. 7.6. New York: Department of Economic and Social Information and Policy Analysis, United Nations.

4. UN Millennium Project. 2005b. *Investing in Development: A Practical Plan to Achieve the Millennium Development Goals*, pp. 13 and 20. London and Sterling, Virginia: Earthscan.

5. UNFPA and University of Aberdeen. 2005. *Maternal Mortality Update 2004: Delivering into Good Hands*. New York: UNFPA; and UN Millennium Project. 2005c. *Who's Got the Power: Transforming Health Systems for Women and Children*. Task Force on Child Health and Maternal Health. London and Sterling, Virginia: Earthscan.

6. The exact relation of levels of maternal morbidity in relation to mortality varies in different settings and data are limited, including according to age group. Estimates of annual global maternal morbidity range from a conservative 8 million to over 20 million. See, for example: UN Millennium Project 2005c; and for a reference on 15 million: UNFPA and University of Aberdeen 2005, p. 26.

7. UNFPA 2004a.

8. WHO, UNICEF, and UNFPA. 2004. *Maternal Mortality in 2000: Estimates Developed by WHO, UNICEF and UNFPA*. Geneva: Department of Reproductive Health and Research, WHO; and WHO. 2005. *World Health Report 2005: Make Every Mother and Child Count*. Geneva: WHO.

9. UNFPA and University of Aberdeen 2005.

10. WHO, UNICEF, and UNFPA 2004. Based on 2000 estimates of maternal deaths. See: Caro, D. A., S. F. Murray, and P. Putney. 2004. "Evaluation of the Averting Maternal Death and Disability Program." A Grant from the Bill and Melinda Gates Foundation To the Columbia University Mailman School of Public Health. Silver Spring, Maryland: Cultural Practice.

11. UN Millennium Project. 2005d. *Taking Action: Achieving Gender Equality and Empowering Women*, p. 6. Task Force on Education and Gender Equality. London and Sterling, Virginia: Earthscan.

12. UN Millennium Project 2005c.

13. Singh, S., et al. 2004. *Adding it Up: The Benefits of Investing in Sexual and Reproductive Health Care*. Washington, D.C., and New York: The Alan Guttmacher Institute and UNFPA.

14. Ibid.

15. WHO. 2004a. *Unsafe Abortion: Global and Regional Estimates of Unsafe Abortion and Associated Mortality in 2000*, 4th Edition. Geneva: World Health Organization.

16. Ibid.

17. WHO 2004a.

18. EngenderHealth. 2003. *Taking Postabortion Care Services Where They are Needed: An Operations Research Project Testing PAC Expansion in Rural Senegal: FRONTIERS Final Report*. Washington, D.C.: Frontiers in Reproductive Health Program, the Population Council.

19. See: United Nations 1995, para. 8.25: "In no case should abortion be promoted as a method of family planning. All Governments and relevant intergovernmental and non-governmental organizations are urged to strengthen their commitment to women's health, to deal with the health impact of unsafe abortion as a major public health concern and to reduce the recourse to abortion through expanded and improved family-planning services. Prevention of unwanted pregnancies must always be given the highest priority and every attempt should be made to eliminate the need for abortion. Women who have unwanted pregnancies should have ready access to reliable information and compassionate counselling. Any measures or changes related to abortion within the health system can only be determined at the national or local level according to the national legislative process. In circumstances where abortion is not against the law, such abortion should be safe. In all cases, women should have access to quality services for the management of complications arising from abortion. Post-abortion counselling, education and family-planning services should be offered promptly, which will also help to avoid repeat abortions."

20. UNFPA and WHO. 2000. *From Abortion to Contraception: Family Planning and Reproductive Health in Central and Eastern Europe and the Newly Independent States*, 3rd Edition. Copenhagen, Denmark: WHO.

21. Popov, A. 1999. "Family Planning and Induced Abortion in Post-Soviet Russia of the Early 1990s: Unmet Needs in Information Supply." In: *Russia's Demographic "Crisis,"* edited by J. Da Vanzo. 1999. Santa Monica, California: RAND. Cited in: United Nations. 2004a. *World Population Monitoring 2002: Reproductive Rights and Reproductive Health* (ST/ESA/SER), by the UN Population Division. New York: Population Division, Department of Economic and Social Affairs, United Nations.

22. United Nations 2004a.

23. Roth, D., and M. Mbizvo. 2001. "Promoting Safe Motherhood in the Community: The Case for Strategies That Include Men." *African Journal of Reproductive Health* 5(2): 10-21.

24. Nuwaha, F., and B. Amooti-Kaguna. 1999. "Predictors of Home Deliveries in Rakai District, Uganda." *African Journal of Reproductive Health* 3(2): 79-86.

25. Varkey, L. C., et al. 2004. "Involving Men in Maternity Care in India." *FRONTIERS Final Report*. Washington, D.C.: Frontiers in Reproductive Health Program, the Population Council.

26. Li, Jianghong. 2004. "Gender Inequality, Family Planning, and Maternal and Child Care in a Rural Chinese County." *Social Science and Medicine* 59(4): 695-708.

27. Cholil, A., M. B. Iskandar, and R. Sciortino. 1998. *The Life Saver: The Mother Friendly Movement in Indonesia*. Jakarta, Indonesia: The State Ministry for the Role of Women and the Ford Foundation.

28. It is estimated that the maternal mortality ratio has increased in some countries where HIV/AIDS and malaria are rising. See: UN Millennium Project 2005c; and The World Bank. 2003. *Gender Equality and the Millennium Development Goals*. Washington, D.C.: The World Bank.

29. Caro, Murray, and Putney 2004.

30. UNFPA. 2005. *Beijing at Ten: UNFPA's Commitment to the Platform for Action*. New York: UNFPA.

31. UNFPA. 2004b. *Into Good Hands: Progress Reports from the Field*, p. 6. New York: UNFPA.

32. UNFPA 2004a.

33. UNFPA. 2004c. "The New Route to Safer Childbirth in Rural Senegal." News Feature. New York: UNFPA. Web site: www.unfpa.org/news/news/news.cfm?ID=389&Language=1, accessed 17 January 2005; and UNFPA 2004b, p. 6.

34. UNFPA 2004b, p. 15.

35. UNFPA 2005.

36. London, S. 2004. "Midwife Care is as Safe as Physician-Led Care for Nepalese Women with Low-Risk Pregnancies." *International Family Planning Perspectives*.30(1): 47-48.

37. Koblinsky, M., et al. 2000. *Issues in Programming for Safe Motherhood*. p.43. Arlington, Virginia: MotherCare, John Snow, Inc.

38. UNFPA 2004c; and UNFPA 2004b.

39. Annan, K. 29 December 2002. " In Africa, AIDS has a Woman's Face." *The New York Times/International Herald Tribune*. Web site: www.un.org/News/ossg/sg/stories/sg-29dec-2002.htm, last accessed 20 April 2005.

40. UN Millennium Project 2005a.

41. Ibid., p.2; and UNAIDS, UNFPA, and UNIFEM. 2004. *Women and HIV/AIDS: Confronting the Crisis*. New York and Geneva: UNAIDS, UNFPA, and UNIFEM.

42. UNAIDS, UNFPA, and UNIFEM 2004.

43. UNAIDS. 2004a. "Fact Sheet: Women and AIDS: A Growing Challenge." Geneva: UNAIDS.

44. Ibid.

45. Based on the Policy Project of the Futures Group for USAID and UNAIDS. Cited in: UN Millennium Project 2005a, p. 23.

46. UNAIDS. 2004b. "A UNAIDS Initiative: The Global Coalition on Women and AIDS." Geneva: UNAIDS. Web site: womenandaids.unaids.org/, accessed 23 June 2005.

47. International Community of Women Living with HIV/AIDS. 2004. *Visibility, Voices and Visions: A Call for Action from HIV Positive Women to Policy Makers*. London: International Community of Women Living with HIV/AIDS; and Ogden, J., and L. Nyblade. 2005. *Common at Its Core: HIV-Related Stigma Across Contexts*. Washington, D.C.: International Center for Research on Women.

48. International Community of Women Living with HIV/AIDS 2004.

49. Bianco, M. 2003. "The Balance of 20 Years Fight against HIV/AIDS in Argentina." *Sexual Health Exchange* 2003/1. Amsterdam: Royal Tropical Institute. Web site: www.kit.nl/ils/exchange_content/assets/images/Exchange_2003-1_eng.pdf, last accessed 12 May 2005; and Ipas. 2003. "Bill of Rights Launched to Commemorate International Women's Day." Chapel Hill, North Carolina: Ipas. Web site: www.ipas.org/english/press_room/2003/releases/03072003.asp, accessed 12 May 2005.

50. International Relief Teams. n.d. "Mothers 2 Mothers 2 Be℠." San Diego, California: International Relief Teams. Web site: www.irteams.org/programs/M2M2B.htm, last accessed 22 April 2005.

51. USAID, UNAIDS, WHO, UNICEF, and the POLICY Project. 2004. *Coverage of Selected Services for HIV/AIDS Prevention, Care, and Support in Low and Middle Income Countries in 2003*. Washington, D.C.: POLICY Project, the Futures Group.

52. UN Millennium Project 2005a, p. 43.

53. Columbia University's Mailman School of Public Health's MTCT-Plus Initiative supports the provision of specialized care to HIV-infected women, their partners and their children identified in PMTCT programmes. It announced grants of more than $9 million to twelve hospitals, health centres and clinics in eight African countries and Thailand for treatment and support services such as counselling, education and community outreach, ARVs and drugs for AIDS complications, training, and other technical assistance.

54. United Nations. 2005a. *Progress Made in the Implementation of the Declaration of Commitment on HIV/AIDS: Report of the Secretary-General* (A/59/765), para. 14. New York: United Nations.

55. WHO and UNAIDS. 2004. "Ensuring Equitable Access to Antiretroviral Treatment for Women: WHO/UNAIDS Policy Statement," p. 6. Geneva: WHO. Web site: http://www.who.int/gender/violence/en/equitableaccess.pdf, accessed 1 January 2005.

56. Ogden and Nyblade 2005; and International Community of Women Living with HIV/AIDS 2004.

57. WHO and UNAIDS 2004, p. 5.

58. Nieuwboer, I. 2003. *Once You Know You can Never Not Know Again: The Effect of a Digital Guide in Persuading Students to go for VCT*, p. 10 Tilburg: Tilburg University Press.

59. Ogden and Nyblade 2005.

60. Painter, T., et al. 2004. "Women's Reasons for Not Participating in Follow Up Visits Before Starting Short Course Antiretroviral Prophylaxis for Prevention of Mother to Child Transmission of HIV: Qualitative Interview Study." *British Medical Journal* 329(7465): 543.

61. UNFPA 2005.

62. UNFPA. 2004d. *Sexually Transmitted Infections: Breaking the Cycle of Transmission*. New York: UNFPA.

63. UNFPA 2005.

64. UNFPA. 2004e. *The State of World Population 2004: The Cairo Consensus at Ten: Population, Reproductive Health and the Global Effort to End Poverty*. New York: UNFPA.

65. UNFPA 2004d.

66. Global HIV Prevention Working Group. 2003. *Access to HIV Prevention: Closing the Gap*. Menlo Park, California: Kaiser Family Foundation and the Bill & Melinda Gates Foundation.

67  Singh, et al. 2004.

68  Hobcraft, J. 2003. "Towards a Conceptual Framework on Population, Reproductive Health, Gender and Poverty Reduction," p. 135. Ch. 7 in: *Population and Poverty: Achieving Equity, Equality and Sustainability*, by UNFPA. 2003. Population and Development Strategies Series. No. 8. New York: UNFPA.

69  United Nations. 2005b. *World Population Prospects: The 2004 Revision: Highlights* (ESA/P/WP.193). New York: Population Division, Department of Economic and Social Affairs, United Nations.

70  Ibid., Table II.1.

71  UNFPA. 2002. *The State of World Population 2002: People, Poverty and Possibilities: Making Development Work for the Poor*, pp. 22-23. New York: UNFPA; and Bernstein, S., and E. White. 2005. "The Relevance of the ICPD Programme of Action for the Achievement of the MDGs: *and Vice Versa*: Shared Visions and Common Goals." Chapter 12 in: *Proceedings of the Seminar on the Relevance of Population Aspects for the Achievement of the Millennium Development Goals: New York: 17-19 November 2004* (ESA/P/WP.192), by the UN Population Division. New York: Population Division, Department of Economic and Social Affairs, United Nations.

72  United Nations. 2004b. *World Fertility Report: 2003* (ESA/P/WP.189). New York: Population Division, Department of Economic and Social Affairs, United Nations. Web site: www.un.org/esa/population/publications/worldfertility/World_Fertility_Report.htm, last accessed 23 February 2005.

73  See: Selected Indicators in annex of this report; and United Nations 2005b.

74  A worldwide analysis using data from 2000 found that an estimated 105 million married women and 8 million unmarried women in developing countries expressed an unmet need for family planning, that is, they wanted to delay or avoid another birth. When women using traditional family planning methods— such as periodic abstinence or withdrawal—are added, this figure reaches 201 million. These women run risks of unwanted pregnancies because traditional family planning methods are far less effective than modern methods such as sterilization, condoms, intra-uterine devices, hormonal pills and injectibles. See: Singh, et al. 2004. See also: Westoff, C. F. 2001. *Unmet Need at the End of the Century*. DHS Comparative Reports. No. 1. Calverton, Maryland: ORC Macro.

75  Barnett, B., and J. Stein. 1998. *Women's Voices and Women's Lives: The Impact of Family Planning: A Synthesis of Findings from the Women's Studies Project*, pp. 9-11, 15 and 83. Research Triangle Park, North Carolina: Family Health International.

76  Westoff 2001.

77  Becker, S. 1999. "Measuring Unmet Need: Wives, Husbands or Couples?" *International Family Planning Perspectives* 25(4): 172-180.

78  Ashford, L. 2001. "Securing Future Supplies for Family Planning and HIV/AIDS Prevention," pp. 2-3. Washington, D.C.: Population Reference Bureau.

79  Haub, C., 2002. "Family Planning Worldwide 2002." Data sheet. Washington, D.C.: Population Reference Bureau.

80  Nass, S. J., and J. F. Strauss, eds. 2004. *New Frontiers in Contraceptive Research: A Blueprint for Action*, pp. 20-23. Washington, D.C.: National Academy Press.

81  Agha, S. 2001. "Patterns of Use of the Female Condom After One Year of Mass Marketing." *AIDS Education and Prevention* 13(1): 55-64.

## CHAPTER 5

1  United Nations. 2004. *World Youth Report 2005: Report of the Secretary-General* (A/60/61 – E/2005/7), p. 1. New York: United Nations.

2  Ibid.

3  United Nations. 2005a. "World Population Prospects: The 2004 Revision: File 1: Total Population Both Sexes by Age Group, Major Area, Region and Country, Annually for 1950-2050 (in thousands) (Pop/DB/WPP/Rev.2004/4/F1)." Spreadsheet. New York: Population Division, Department of Economic and Social Affairs, United Nations.

4  Ibid.

5  Lloyd, C. B. (ed.). 2005. *Growing Up Global: The Changing Transitions to Adulthood in Developing Countries*. Washington, D.C.: The National Academies Press; and UNFPA. 2005a. *The Case for Investing in Young People as Part of a National Poverty Reduction Strategy*. New York: UNFPA.

6  Lloyd 2005.

7  BBC News. 20 June 2002. "Human Smuggling Eclipses Drugs Trade." Web site: http://news.bbc.co.uk/1/hi/world/2056662.stm, accessed 7 May 2005.

8  Lloyd 2005.

9  Ibid.

10  The Population Council. 2005. *Population Briefs: Reports on Population Council Research* 11(1). New York: The Population Council.

11  Bernstein, S., and E. White. 2005. "The Relevance of the ICPD Programme of Action for the Achievement of the MDGs: *and Vice Versa*: Shared Visions and Common Goals." Chapter 12 in: *Proceedings of the Seminar on the Relevance of Population Aspects for the Achievement of the Millennium Development Goals: New York: 17-19 November 2004* (ESA/P/WP.192), by the United Nations. 2005b. New York: Population Divison, Department of Economic and Social Affairs, United Nations.

12  UNESCO. 2004. *EFA Global Monitoring Report 2005: Education for All, the Quality Imperative*. Paris: UNESCO.

13  Lloyd 2005; and Grown, C., G. R. Gupta , and R. Pande. 2005. "Taking Action to Improve Women's Health through Gender Equality and Women's Empowerment." *The Lancet* 365(9458): 541-543.

14  UNFPA 2005a, p. 59.

15  United Nations 2004, p. 5.

16  United Nations. 2005c. *Review of the Implementation of the Beijing Platform for Action and the Outcome Documents of the Special Session of the General Assembly Entitled "Women 2000: Gender Equality, Development and Peace for the Twenty-first Century": Report of the Secretary-General* (E/CN.6/2005/2), para. 496. New York: United Nations; and United Nations 2004, para. 18.

17  UNFPA. 2005b. *Policy Development Supporting Adolescent and Youth Sexual and Reproductive Health: Nine Countries' Experiences and Collaboration with UNFPA*. New York: UNFPA.

18  Ad Hoc Working Group for *Youth and the MDGs*. 2005. *Youth and the Millennium Development Goals: Challenges and Opportunities for Implementation: Final Report of the Ad Hoc Working Group for Youth and the MDGs: April 2005*. Web site: http://tig.phpwebhosting.com/themes/mdg/YouthMDG.pdf, last accessed 27 June 2005.

19  International Planned Parenthood Federation. 2003. *Youth Participation: Youth in Decision Making Processes*. IPPF/WHR Spotlight on Youth. No. 7. Informational Sheet. New York: Western Hemisphere Region, International Planned Parenthood Federation.

20  UNFPA. 2003a. *UNFPA and Young People: Imagine*. New York: UNFPA; and UNFPA. 2005c. *Beijing at Ten: UNFPA's Commitment to the Platform for Action*. New York: UNFPA.

21  UNFPA 2005b.

22  Ibid.

23  The project is part of a multi-country programme supported by a grant of the European Union.

24  UNFPA. 2 May 2005. "Laotian Youth Teach Peers to Protect their Health." News Feature. New York: UNFPA. Web site: www.unfpa.org/news/news.cfm?ID=609&Language=1, accessed 6 July 2005; and UNFPA 2005b.

25  UNFPA 2005b.

26  Ibid.

27  Ibid.

28  UNFPA 2005a; and United Nations 2005a.

29  UNFPA 2005a.

30  Ibid., p 16.

31  United Nations. 2005d. *World Population Prospects: The 2004 Revision: Highlights* (ESA/P/WP.193), pp. vii and 1. New York: Population Division, Department of Economic and Social Affairs, United Nations.

32  UNFPA 2005a.

33  Ibid., p. 44.

34  Cincotta, R., R. Engelman, and D. Anastasion. 2003. *The Security Demographic: Population and Civil Conflict after the Cold War*. Washington, D.C.: Population Action International. Cited in: UNFPA 2005a, p. 46. See also: Urdal, H. 2004. *The Devil in the Demographics: The Effect of Youth Bulges on Domestic Armed Conflict, 1950-2000*. Social Development Papers: Conflict Prevention and Reconstruction. No. 14. Washington, D.C.: The World Bank.

35  UNFPA 2005a.

36  The World Bank. n.d. "Why Invest in Children and Youth?" Web site: http://web.worldbank.org/WBSITE/EXTERNAL/TOPICS/EXTCY/0,,contentMDK:20243901-menuPK:565261-pagePK:148956-piPK:216618-theSitePK:396445,00.htm, accessed 28 June 2005.

37  See, for example, the Committee on the Elimination of All Forms of Discrimination Against Women (CEDAW); the Committee on Economic, Social and Cultural Rights; and the UN Special Rapporteur on the Right to Health. All can be found on: Office of the UN High Commissioner for Human Rights. n.d. "Human Rights Bodies: Mechanisms for the Protection and the Promotion of Human Rights." Web site: www.ohchr.org/english/bodies/, last accessed 7 July 2005.

38  Center for Reproductive Rights. 2005. "Governments in Action: Legal and Policy Developments Affecting Reproductive Rights." Briefing Paper. New York: Center for Reproductive Rights.

39  The recently passed Law of the Kyrgyz Republic on Reproductive Rights was the first of its kind in countries of the Commonwealth of Independent States. See: UNFPA. 2003b. *Preventing HIV Infection: Promoting Reproductive Health*. New York: UNFPA. See also: WHO. n.d. "Law [of 2001] on Reproductive Rights of the Kyrgyz Republic." *International Digest of Health Legislation* 54. Geneva: WHO. Web site: http://www3.who.int/idhl/001Kyrg.pdf, accessed 3 March 2005.

40  Center for Reproductive Rights 2005.

41  National Assembly of Panama. n.d. "Que Garantiza la Salud y la Educacion de la Adolescente Embarazada." Law No. 29 of 13 June 2002. Web site: http://www.asamblea.gob.pa/NORMAS/2000/2002/2002_522_1581.PDF, accessed 3 March 2005.

42  Center for Reproductive Rights 2005.

43  United Nations. n.d. "Convention on Consent to Marriage, Minmum Age for Marriage and Registration of Marriages." Geneva: Office of the United Nations High Commissioner for Human Rights, United Nations Web site: www.ohchr.org/english/law/convention.htm, last accessed 21 June 2005.

44  Center for Reproductive Rights 2005.

45  UNFPA. n.d. "Intermediate Report to the European Commission, Sexual and Reproductive Health Programme 2003-2006: April 2003-2004" (EC/ACP/UNFPA). New York: UNFPA.

46  For more on Laos and UNFPA-supported initiatives, see: UNFPA 2 May 2005.

47  Lloyd 2005.

48  UNFPA 2005b.

49  UNFPA. 2005d. "Y-Peer at a Glance." Briefing Package. New York: UNFPA.

50  UNFPA. n.d. "Strategic Partnership with the Arab Scout Organization for Youth Reproductive Health." Web site: http://www.cstamman.org.jo/news/01_news.htm, last accessed 21 June 2005.

51  Lloyd 2005.

52  UNFPA. 2004. *The State of World Population 2004: The Cairo Consensus at Ten: Population, Reproductive Health and the Global Effort to End Poverty*, p. 76. New York: UNFPA.

53  UNFPA. 2003c. *The State of World Population 2003: Making 1 Billion Count: Investing in Adolescents' Health and Rights*. New York: UNFPA. Cited in: UN Millennium Project 2005a.

54  UN Millennium Project 2005a, p. 58.

55  The World Bank. 2004. "Round II Country Reports on Health, Nutrition, and Population Conditions Among the Poor and the Better-Off in 56 Countries." Washington, D.C.: The World Bank. Web site: www1.worldbank.org/prem/poverty/health/data/round2.htm, last accessed 12 July 2005; and Rani, M., and E. Lule. 2004. "Exploring the Socioeconomic Dimensions of Adolescent Reproductive Health: A Multicountry Analysis." *International Family Planning Perspectives* (30(3): 112.

56  Lloyd, C. B. (ed.). 2005. *Growing Up Global: The Changing Transitions to Adulthood in Developing Countries*. Washington, D.C.: The National Academies Press.

57  United Nations. 2001a. *We the Children: End-decade Review of the Follow-up to the World Summit for Children: Report of the Secretary-General* (A/S-27/3). New York: United Nations.

58  UNICEF. 2001. *Early Marriage: Child Spouses*, p. 11. Innocenti Digest. No. 7. Florence, Italy: UNICEF. Innocenti Research Centre.

59  de Bruyn, M., and S. Packer. 2004. *Adolescents, Unwanted Pregnancy and Abortion: Policies, Counseling and Clinical Care*. Chapel Hill, North Carolina: Ipas.

60  UNFPA 2003a.

61  Holschneider, S. 1998. *Investing in Young Lives: The Role of Reproductive Health: Why Invest in Young People?* Washington, D.C.: The World Bank. Cited in: de Bruyn and Packer 2004, p. 10; and UN Millennium Project. 2005b. *Who's Got the Power: Transforming Health Systems for Women and Children*. Task Force on Child Health and Maternal Health. London and Sterling, Virginia: Earthscan.

62  Raufu, A. 2002. "Unsafe Abortions Cause 20,000 Deaths a Year in Nigeria." *British Medical Journal* 325(7371): 988. Cited in: de Bruyn and Packer 2004, p. 10.

63  de Bruyn and Packer 2004, p. 11.

64  UN Millennium Project 2005a, p. 3.

65  UNAIDS Inter-agency Task Team on Young People. 2004. *At the Crossroads: Accelerating Youth Access to HIV/AIDS Interventions*. New York: UNAIDS. Web site: www.unfpa.org/upload/lib_pub_file/316_filename_UNFPA_Crossroads.pdf, accessed 24 February 2005.

66  UNAIDS. 2004. *2004 Report on the Global AIDS Epidemic*. Geneva: UNAIDS.

67  UNAIDS Inter-agency Task Team on Young People 2004.

68  Ibid., p. 48.

69  UNFPA 2003a.

70  United Nations. 2005e. *Progress Made in the Implementation of the Declaration of Commitment on HIV/AIDS: Report of the Secretary-General* (A/59/765), para. 8. New York: United Nations.

71  UNAIDS Inter-agency Task Team on Young People 2004.

72  UNAIDS 2004.

73  The Alan Guttmacher Institute. 2003. *In Their Own Right: Addressing the Sexual and Reproductive Health Needs of Men Worldwide*. New York: The Alan Guttmacher Institute. Based on Demographic and Health Surveys in 39 developing countries conducted between 1996 and 2003. See also: The Alan Guttmacher Institute. 1998. *Into a New World: Young Women's Sexual and Reproductive Lives*. New York: The Alan Guttmacher Institute.

74  UNAIDS Inter-agency Task Team on Young People 2004.

75  United Nations 2005e.

76  United Nations. 2001b. *Resolution Adopted by the General Assembly: S-26.2: Declaration of Commitment on HIV/AIDS* (A/RES/S-26/2), paras. 47 and 53. New York: United Nations.

77  See: Global Youth Coalition on HIV/AIDS web site: www.youthaidscoalition.org, last accessed 11 May 2005.

78  UNFPA. 2004. *Global Youth Partners: Preventing HIV*. Brochure. New York: UNFPA; and UNFPA. n.d. "Global Youth Partners: Advocating for Increased Access by Young People to Information, Education and Services in the Area of HIV Prevention." New York: UNFPA. Web site: www.unfpa.org/hiv/gyp/index.htm, accessed 9 July 2005.

79  The Population Council and UNFPA. 2002. *Adolescent and Youth Sexual and Reproductive Health: Charting Directions for a Second Generation of Programming*. A Report on a Workshop of the UNFPA in Collaboration with the Population Council, New York, 1–3 May 2002. New York: The Population Council.

80  Fundación Puntos de Encuentro. 2002. *We're Different, We're Equal: A Project to Promote Young People's Rights: Results and Notes about Impact 2001-2002*. Managua: Nicaragua: Fundación Puntos de Encuentro.

81  UNFPA 2005c.

82  UNFPA. 2005e. *The Livelihoods Approach to Adolescent Programming: Expanding the Response to Adolescent Sexual and Reproductive Health: What, Why, How*. New York: UNFPA.

83  UNFPA 2005c.

84  UNFPA. n.d. "Case Studies: Reaching Out: Reaching the 'Busy Generation' in Mozambique." New York: UNFPA. Web site: www.unfpa.org/adolescents/casestudies/reachingout.htm, accessed 13 July 2005.

85  UNESCO. n.d. "Breaking the Poverty Cycle of Women: Empowering Adolescent Girls to Become Agents of Social Transformation in South Asia." Project relating to Cross-cutting Themes. Paris: UNESCO.

86  UNICEF 2001.

87  Based on girls aged 10 to 19 in developing countries, excluding China, projected to marry before their eighteenth birthday. See: Bruce, J., and S. Clark. 2004. *The Implications of Early Marriage for HIV/AIDS Policy*. Brief based on background paper prepared for the WHO/UNFPA/Population Council Technical Consultation on Married Adolescents, Geneva, 9-12 December 2003. New York: The Population Council.

88  Lloyd 2005; and The Population Council and UNFPA 2002

89  UN Millennium Project 2005a, p. 57; and Lloyd 2005.

90  The Population Council and UNFPA 2002; and UNFPA 2003a.

91  UNICEF 2001.

92  Grown, Gupta and Pande 2005.

93  Jejeebhoy, S. 1996. "Adolescent Sexual and Reproductive Behavior: A Review of the Evidence from India." ICRW Working Paper. No. 3. Washington, D.C.: International Center for Research on Women. Cited in: Mensch, B., J. Bruce, and M. E. Greene. 1998. *The Uncharted Passage: Girls' Adolescence in the Developing World*, p. 46. New York: The Population Council.

94  Clark, S. 2004. "Early Marriage and HIV Risks in sub-Saharan Africa." *Studies in Family Planning* 35(3): 149-160; and UN Millennium Project 2005c.

95  UN Millennium Project 2005a, p. 35.

96  "Decent work" is defined by the International Labour Organization (ILO) as work under conditions of freedom, equity, security and dignity. See: ILO. 1999. *Report of the Director-General: Decent Work*. International Labour Conference Report. Geneva: ILO. Web site: www.ilo.org/public/english/standards/relm/ilc/ilc87/rep-i.htm, last accessed 12 May 2005.

97  ILO. 2004a. *Improving Prospects for Young Women and Men in the World of Work: A Guide to Youth Employment*. Geneva: ILO; and ILO. 2004b. *Global Employment Trends for Youth*. Geneva: ILO.

98  Lloyd 2005.

99  ILO 2004b.

100  ILO. 2002a. "International Labour Conference: 90th Session 2002: Report VI. Decent Work and the Informal Economy." Geneva: ILO. Web site: www-ilo-mirror.cornell.edu/public/english/standards/relm/ilc/ilc90/pdf/rep-vi.pdf, last accessed 6 July 2005; and ILO 2004b.

101  Ibid.

102  ILO. 1973. "R146 Minimum Age Recommendation, 1973." Geneva: ILO. Web site: www.ilo.org/public/english/standards/ipec/publ/law/ilc/r1461973/#0, last accessed 13 May 2005.

103  ILO. 2003. *Guide Book II: Time-Bound Programmes for Eliminating the Worst Forms of Child Labour: An Introduction*. Geneva: ILO; and ILO. 2002b. *Every Child Counts: New Global Estimates on Child Labour*. Geneva: International Programme on the Elimination of Child Labour (IPEC), Statistical Information and Monitoring Programme on Child Labour (SIMPOC), International Labour Office, ILO.

104  UNFPA 2005e.

105  ILO. 2002c. *Report of the Director-General: A Future without Child Labour: Global Report under the Follow-up to the ILO Declaration on Fundamental Principles and Rights at Work: International Labour Conference: 90th Session 2002*. Geneva: International Labour Office, ILO.

106  ILO. 2005. "Report of the Director-General: A Global Alliance Against Forced Labour: Global Report under the Follow-up to the ILO Declaration on Fundamental Principles and Rights at Work: 2005." Report 1(B). International Labour Conference. 93rd Session. Geneva: ILO. Web site: www.ilo.org/dyn/declaris/DECLARATIONWEB.DOWNLOAD_BLOB?Var_DocumentID=5059, last accessed 7 July 2005.

107  UNICEF. 11 June 2004. "Children Used as Domestic Servants One of the Most Hidden Forms of Child Labour." Sydney, Australia: UNICEF. Web site: www.unicef.org.au/mediaCentre-Detail.asp?ReleaseID=534, accessed 13 January 2005.

108  Ad Hoc Working Group for Youth and the MDGs 2005.

## CHAPTER 6

1  Boserup, E. 1970. *Woman's Role in Economic Development*. London and New York: Earthscan.

2  Naciones Unidas. 2002. *Paternidad Responsable en el istmo centroamericano* (LC/MEX/L.475/Rev.1). Santiago, Chile: Comisión Económica para América Latina y el Caribe (CEPAL), Naciones Unidas; Abdalla, J. 2001. "The Absent Father." Pp. 214-246 in: *The New Arab Family: Cairo Papers in Social Science* 24(1/2), edited by N. Hopkins. 2001. Cairo: The American University in Cairo Press; and Nosseir, N. 2003. "Family in the New Millennium: Major Trends Affecting Families in North Africa." In: *Major Trends Affecting Families: A Background Document*, by United Nations. 2003. New York: Division for Social Policy and Development, United Nations.

3  Naciones Unidas. 2002.

4  For example, this is supported by research from countries in East and South East Asia. Women who are single mothers with limited marketable skills or employment prospects may be obliged to bring their children along to help them with their small businesses and sale of goods. See: Quah, S. R. 2003. "Major Trends Affecting Families in East and Southeast Asia: Final Report," p. 30. New York: Division for Social Policy and Development, Department of Social and Economic Affairs, United Nations.

5  United States Department of Health and Human Services. 1993. Survey on Child Health. Washington, D.C.: National Center for Health Statistics, United States Department of Health and Human Services; Centro de Análisis Sociocultural - Universidad Centroamericana, CEPAL and UNFPA. 2005. "Estudio Masculinidad y factores socioculturales asociados al comportamiento de los hombres frente a la paternidad en Centroamerica: Caso Nicaragua." Draft; Naciones Unidas. 2002; and UNICEF. 1997. *Role of Men in the Lives of Children: A Study of How Improving Knowledge About Men in Families Helps Strengthen Programming for Children and Women*. New York: UNICEF.

6  Naciones Unidas. 2002.

7  Baker, G., et al. 2003. "Men's Participation as Fathers in the Latin American and Caribbean Region: A Critical Literature Review with Policy Considerations." Final draft. Document prepared for the World Bank; and Naciones Unidas 2002.

8  UNFPA. n.d. "It Takes 2: Partnering with Men in Reproductive & Sexual Health," p. 15. Programme Advisory Note. New York: UNFPA. See also a study in Nicaragua: Organización Panamericana de la Salud, Fondo de Población de las Naciones Unidas, Cooperación Alemana-GTZ, Ministerio de Salud. 2003. "Promoción de la Participación de los Hombres en los Programas de Salud Sexual y Reproductiva. Versión Resumen del Informe Final." Managua, Nicaragua.

9  UNFPA. 2000. *Partnering: A New Approach to Sexual and Reproductive Health*. Technical Paper. No.3. New York: UNFPA; and UNFPA n.d.

10  UNFPA 2000; and Scalway, T. 2001. *Young Men and HIV: Culture, Poverty and Sexual Risk*. London: Panos and UNAIDS.

11  UNFPA 2000.

12. The World Bank. 2001. *Engendering Development: Through Gender Equality in Rights, Resources, and Voice*, pp. 9 and 77. New York and Washington, D.C.: Oxford University Press and the World Bank.

13. The World Bank. n.d. "Latin America and the Caribbean: Crime and Violence Prevention." Washington, D.C.: The World Bank Group. Web site: http://lnweb18.worldbank.org/LAC/LAC.nsf/ECADocByUnid/65A4BF3B8D10247D85256CFD007A5D62?Opendocument, last accessed 16 May 2005.

14. Ajuwon, A. 2003. "Research in Sexual Coercion among Young Persons: The Experiences and Lessons Learned from Ibadan, Nigeria." Presentation at Non-consensual Sexual Experiences of Young People in Developing Countries: A Consultative Meeting, New Delhi, India, 22-25 September 2003; Caceres, C. "The Complexity of Young People's Experiences of Sexual Coercion: Lessons Learned from Studies in Peru." Presentation at Non-consensual Sexual Experiences of Young People in Developing Countries: A Consultative Meeting, New Delhi, India, 22-25 September 2003; Jewkes, R. "Non-consensual Sex among South African Youth: Prevalence of Coerced Sex and Discourses of Control and Desire." Presentation at Non-consensual Sexual Experiences of Young People in Developing Countries: A Consultative Meeting, New Delhi, India, 22-25 September 2003; and Wilkinson, J. W., L. S. Bearup, and T. Soprach. "Youth Gang-rape in Phom Penh." Presentation at Non-consensual Sexual Experiences of Young People in Developing Countries: A Consultative Meeting, New Delhi, India, 22-25 September 2003. All cited in: The Population Council, WHO and YouthNet. 2004. *Sexual Coercion: Young Men's Experience as Victims and Perpetrators*. New Delhi: The Population Council.

15. Greene, M. E., and A. E. Biddlecom. 2000. "Absent and Problematic Men: Demographic Accounts of Male Reproductive Roles." *Population and Development Review* 26(1): 81-115; and Jacobson, J. 2000. "Transforming Family Planning Programmes: Towards a Framework for Advancing the Reproductive Rights Agenda." *Reproductive Health Matters* 8(15): 21-32.

16. The Alan Guttmacher Institute. 2003. *In Their Own Right: Addressing the Sexual and Reproductive Health Needs of Men Worldwide*. New York: The Alan Guttmacher Institute. Based on Demographic and Health Surveys in 39 developing countries conducted between 1996 and 2003.

17. The data do not include all groups in all regions, leaving out some key groups such as boys under 15, unmarried men, and men in prison, the military, migrants or refugees, many of whom are sexually active.

18. The Alan Guttmacher Institute 2003.

19. The Alan Guttmacher Institute. 2004. *Risk and Protection: Youth and HIV/AIDS in Sub-Saharan Africa*, p. 34. New York and Washington, D.C.: The Alan Guttmacher Institute.

20. The Alan Guttmacher Institute 2004, Appendix Table 5, p. 36.

21. The Alan Guttmacher Institute 2004, Appendix Table 4, p. 35.

22. United Nations. 2005a. *Review of the Implementation of the Beijing Platform for Action and the Outcome Documents of the Special Session of the General Assembly Entitled "Women 2000: Gender Equality, Development and Peace for the Twenty-first Century": Report of the Secretary-General* (E/CN.6/2005/2), para. 658. New York: United Nations.

23. Chattopadhay, T. 2004. *Role of Men and Boys in Promoting Gender Equality: An Advocacy Brief*. Bangkok: UNESCO; PLANetWiRE Clips. 13 April 2005. "Saudi Clerics Rule Against Forced Marriage;" and Barker, G. 2002. "Instituto PROMUNDO: Engaging Young Men in Gender-Based Violence Prevention and Sexual and Reproductive Health Promotion: Rio de Janeiro, Brazil." Presentation at the Oxfam workshop, Gender Is Everyone's Business: Programming with Men to Achieve Gender Equality, Oxford, United Kingdom, 10-12 June 2002. Web site: www.oxfam.org.uk/what_we_do/issues/gender/gem/downloads/Promcase.pdf, last accessed 5 May 2005.

24. UNFPA 2005 "Regional Conference of African Islamic Faith-Based Organizations, Abuja, Nigeria, 14-18 March 2005." Conference Report. New York: UNFPA.

25. Greene, M. E. 2002. "Involving Men in Reproductive Health: Implications for Reproductive Health and Rights." Pp. 129-138 in: *Reproductive Health and Rights: Reaching the Hardly Reached*, edited by E. Murphy and A. Hendrix-Jenkins. Washington, D.C.: PATH. Web site: www.path.org/publications/pub.php?id=516, last accessed 22 June 2005.

26. Ndong, I., et al. 1999. "Men's Reproductive Health: Defining, Designing and Delivering Services." *International Family Planning Perspectives* 25(Supplement): S53-S55; Bergstrom, G. 1999. "Men's Voices, Men's Choices: How Can Men Gain From Improved Gender Equality?" A Sweden/Africa Regional Seminar, Lusaka, Zambia, 11-13 January 1999. Stockholm, Sweden: Ministry for Foreign Affairs; Johansson, A., et al. 1998. "Husbands' Involvement in Abortion in Vietnam." *Studies in Family Planning* 29(4): 400-413; Basu, A. M. 1996. "Women's Education, Marriage and Fertility: Do Men Really Not Matter?" Population and Development Program Working Paper Series. No. 96.03. Ithaca, New York: Cornell University; Laudari, Carlos. 1998. "Gender Equity in Reproductive and Sexual Health." Paper presented at the FAO/WHO/UNFPA Thematic Workshop on Male Involvement in Sexual and Reproductive Health Programmes, Rome, 9-13 November 1998; Hull, T. H. 1999. "Men and Family Planning: How Attractive is the Programme of Action?" Paper presented at the Psychosocial Meeting preceding the Annual Meeting of the Population Association of America, New York, New York, 23-24 March.1999; Hawkes, S. 1998. "Providing Sexual Health Services for Men in Bangladesh." *Sexual Health Exchange* 3: 14-15; and Collumbien, M., and S. Hawkes. 2000. "Missing Men's Messages: Does the Reproductive Health Approach Respond to Men's Sexual Health Needs?" *Culture, Health and Sexuality* 2(2): 135-150.

27. UNFPA 2000. The theme of "shame" in men (in seeking condoms, services, discussing reproductive health issues, sharing household responsibilities) was a salient finding in a study in Nicaragua. See: Organización Panamericana de la Salud, Fondo de Población de las Naciones Unidas, Cooperación Alemana-GTZ, Ministerio de Salud 2003.

28. Cates, W., Jr. 1996. "The Dual Goals of Reproductive Health." *Network* 16(3); Loaiza, E. 1998. "Male Fertility, Contraceptive Use, and Reproductive Preferences in Latin America: The DHS Experience." Paper prepared for the seminar, "Men, Family Formation and Reproduction," the Committee on Gender and Population of the International Union for the Scientific Study of Population (IUSSP) and the Centro de Estudios de Poblacion (CENEP), Buenos Aires, Argentina 13-15 May 1998. Liege, Belgium: International Union for the Scientific Study of Population; and Lamptey, P., et al. 1978. "An Evaluation of Male Contraceptive Acceptance in Rural Ghana." *Studies in Family Planning* 9(8): 222-226; Fapohunda, B. M., and N. Rutenberg. 1998. "Enhancing the Role of Men in Family Planning and Reproductive Health." Unpublished paper.

29. UNFPA 2000; and Nzioka, C. 2001. "Perspectives of Adolescent Boys on the Risks of Unwanted Pregnancy and Sexually Transmitted Infections: Kenya," *Reproductive Health Matters* 9(17): 108-117.

30. UNFPA 2000.

31. Scalway 2001.

32. Blanc, A. 2001. "The Effect of Power in Sexual Relationships on Sexual and Reproductive Health: An Examination of the Evidence." *Studies in Family Planning* 32(3): 189-213.

33. De Keijzer, B. 2004. "Masculinities: Resistance and Change." Pp. 28-49 in: *Gender Equality and Men: Learning from Practice*, edited by S. Ruxton. 2004. Oxford: Oxfam GB.

34. UNFPA. 2004. *Working from Within: Culturally Sensitive Approaches in UNFPA Programming*, p. 12. New York: UNFPA.

35. Sayages, M. 13 June 2003. "Africa's Men Meet Challenge of Fighting HIV/AIDS." Reuters AlertNet. Web site: www.alertnet.org/thefacts/reliefresources/aidsfeature.htm, last accessed 9 July 2005.

36. United Nations 2005a, para. 388; and "A Role for Men in Gender Equality." 13 September 2004. *IPS UN Journal*.11(165): 6.

37. The Population Council. 2000. "Alone You Are Nobody, Together We Float: The Manuela Ramos Movement." *Quality/Calidad/Qualite*, No. 10. New York: The Population Council.

38. Siegfried, K. 3 March 2005. "Changing Men's Attitudes to Reduce AIDS in Africa." *The Christian Science Monitor*.

39. United Nations. 2004. "The Role of Men and Boys in Achieving Gender Equality." Panel II of the Forty-eighth Session of the Commission on Status of Women, New York, 2 March 2004. New York: Division for the Advancement of Women, United Nations.

40. Scalway 2001.

41. Raju, S., and A. Leonard (eds.). 2000. *Men as Supportive Partners in Reproductive Health: Moving from Rhetoric to Reality*, p. 57. New Delhi: The Population Council; Laack, S. 1995. "Thoughts about Male Involvement: Swedish Experiences." Paper presented at the Youth Sexuality Conference, Arusha, Tanzania, 13-18 August 1995; and Laack, S., et al. 1997. *Report on the RFSU Young Men's Clinic*. Stockholm, Sweden: Swedish Association of Sex Education.

42. Grant, E., et al. 2003. "Seizing the Day: Right Time, Right Place, Right Message for Adolescent Reproductive and Sexual Health (Kenya)." Presentation at the Conference on Reaching Men to Improve the Reproductive Health of All, Interagency Gender Working Group, USAID, Washington D.C., September 2003.

43. Pan-American Health Organization. 2003. "Improving the Lives of Adolescent Girls and Boys By Involving Adolescent Boys: A New Approach to Health Promotion and Prevention Through Soccer." Adolescent project. Washington, D.C.: Pan-American Health Organization.

44. The Population Council. 2003. "My Father Didn't Think This Way: Nigerian Boys Contemplate Gender Equality." 2003. *Quality/Calidad/Qualite*. No. 14. New York: The Population Council.

45. Mishra, A. 2003. "Enlightening Adolescent Boys in India on Gender and Reproductive and Sexual Health." Presentation at the Conference on Reaching Men to Improve the Reproductive Health of All, Interagency Gender Working Group, USAID, Washington D.C., September 2003.

46. Barker, G., et al. 2004. "How Do We Know if Men Have Changed?: Promoting and Measuring Attitude Change with Young Men: Lessons Learned from Program H in Latin America," Pp. 147-161 in: Ruxton 2004.

47. UNFPA. 2003a. *Enlisting the Armed Forces to Protect Reproductive Health and Rights: Lessons from Nine Countries*. Technical Report. New York: UNFPA

48. Ibid.

49. UNFPA. 2003b. *Salud Sexual y Reproductiva, Prevención del VIH/SIDA y Equidad de Género en Fuerzas Armadas en América Latina, Estudios de Caso de Ecuador, Nicaragua, Paraguay y Perú*. Bogota, Colombia: UNFPA.

50. Pathfinder International. 1998. "Reaching Young Men with Reproductive Health Programs." Watertown, Massachusetts: Pathfinder International. Web site: www.pathfind.org/pf/pubs/focus/IN%20FOCUS/ReachingYoungMen.doc, accessed 25 March 2005.

51. Rob, U., et al. 2004. "Integration of Reproductive Health Services for Men in Health and Family Welfare Centers in Bangladesh." FRONTIERS Final Report. Washington, D.C.: The Population Council.

52. United Nations 2005a, paras. 193, 239, 406, and 571; and United Nations. 2005b. *Progress Made in the Implementation of the Declaration of Commitment on HIV/AIDS: Report of the Secretary-General* (A/59/765), para. 63b. New York: United Nations.

# CHAPTER 7

1. UN Millennium Project. 2005a. *Taking Action: Achieving Gender Equality and Empowering Women*. Task Force on Education and Gender Equality. London and Sterling, Virginia: Earthscan.

2. Heise, L., M. Ellsberg, and M.Gottemoeller. 1999. "Ending Violence against Women." *Population Reports*. Series L. No. 11. Baltimore, Maryland: Population Information Program, Johns Hopkins University School of Public Health.

3. UN Millennium Project 2005a, pp. 15 and 110.

4. Heise, Ellsberg, and Gottemoeller 1999.

5 Krug, E., et al. (eds.). 2002. *World Report on Violence and Health*. Geneva: WHO.

6 Ibid.

7 Morrison, A. R., and M. B. Orlando. 1999. "Social and Economic Costs of Domestic Violence: Chile and Nicaragua." Ch. 3 in: Morrison, A., and L. Biehl (eds). 1999. *Too Close to Home: Domestic Violence in Latin America*. Washington, D.C.: Inter-American Development Bank. Cited in: UN Millennium Project 2005a.

8 International Center for Research on Women. 2000. *A Summary Report for a Multi-Site Household Survey*. Domestic Violence in India. No. 3. Washington, D.C.: International Center for Research on Women. Cited in: UN Millennium Project 2005a, p. 115.

9 Australian Government. 2004. *The Cost of Domestic Violence to the Australian Economy: Part I*. Report prepared by Access Economics Pty. for the Office of Women, Commonwealth of Australia; and Phillips, J., and M. Park. 6 December 2004. "Measuring Violence against Women: A Review of the Literature and Statistics." Canberra, Australia: Parliament of Australia. Online E-Brief. Web site: www.aph.gov.au/library/intguide/SP/ViolenceAgainstWomen.htm, last accessed 27 June 2005.

10 Waters, H., et al. 2004. *The Economic Dimensions of Interpersonal Violence*. Geneva: Department of Injuries and Violence Prevention, WHO.

11 UN Millennium Project 2005a, p. 119.

12 Heise, Ellsberg, and Gottemoeller 1999. Cited in: UN Millennium Project 2005a, p. 113. Another estimate, based on findings from 48 population-based surveys, placed this figure at between 16 and 50 per cent. See: Krug, et al. 2002

13 Krug, et al. 2002.

14 Solano, P., and M. Velzeboer. 2003. "Componentes clave para leyes y políticas contra la violencia contras las mujere," p. 13. Draft discussion document. Washington, D.C.: Pan-American Health Organization.

15 Krug, et al. 2002.

16 BBC News. 20 June 2002. "Human Smuggling Eclipses Drugs Trade." Web site: http://news.bbc.co.uk/1/hi/world/2056662.stm, accessed 7 May 2005.

17 United States Department of State. 2005. *Trafficking in Persons Report: June 2005*. Washington, D.C.: United States Department of State.

18 United States Department of State. 2004. *Trafficking in Persons Report: June 2004*. Publication No. 1150. Washington, D.C.: United States Department of State.

19 Martens, J. 2004. "Seduced, Imported, Sold: Trafficking in Women and Children in Africa." Paper prepared for the Seventh Regional Conference on Women (Beijing +10), Addis Ababa, 12-14 October 2004. Addis Ababa, Ethiopia: UN Economic Commission for Africa; and Miko, F. 2004. "Trafficking in Persons: The U.S. and International Response: Congressional Research Service." CRS Report for Congress. Washington, D.C.: Congressional Research Service, the Library of Congress.

20 United Nations. 2002. "Protocol to Prevent, Suppress and Punish Trafficking in Persons Especially Women and Children, Supplementing the United Nations Convention Against Transnational Organized Crime: Adopted and opened for signature, ratification and accession by General Assembly Resolution 55/25 of 15 November 2000." Geneva: Office of the United Nations High Commissioner for Human Rights. Web site: www.ohchr.org/english/law/protocoltraffic.htm, last accessed 11 July 2005.

21 Council of Europe. n.d. "Action against Trafficking in Human Beings: News." Web site: www.coe.int/T/E/human_rights/trafficking, accessed 26 May 2005.

22 Boland, R. 2004. "Legal Progress in Implementing the ICPD Programme of Action." Statement at the 2004 International Parliamentarians' Conference on the Implementation of the ICPD Programme of Action, Strasbourg, France, 18-19 October 2004. Web site: www.unfpa.org/parliamentarians/ipci/strasbourg/docs/boland.doc, last accessed 5 July 2005; and Boland, R. April 2005. Personal communications.

23 UNFPA. 2003. *UNFPA and Young People: Imagine*. New York: UNFPA

24 Krug, et al. 2002.

25 UN Millennium Project. 2005a, p. 114.

26 Jejeebhoy, S. 1996. "Adolescent Sexual and Reproductive Behavior: A Review of the Evidence from India." ICRW Working Paper. No. 3. Washington, D.C.: International Center for Research on Women. Cited in: Mensch, B., J. Bruce, and M. E. Greene. 1998. *The Uncharted Passage: Girls' Adolescence in the Developing World*, p. 46. New York: The Population Council.

27 UNICEF. 2001. *Early Marriage: Child Spouses*, p. 11. Innocenti Digest. No. 7. Florence, Italy: UNICEF. Innocenti Research Centre.

28 Im-em, W., K. Archvanitkul, and C. Kanchanachitra. 2004. "Sexual Coercion among Women in Thailand: Results from the WHO Multi-country Study on Women's Health and Life Experiences." Paper presented at the Annual Meeting of the Population Association of America, Boston, Massachusetts, 3-5 August 2004.

29 The Population Council. 2004a. *The Adverse Health and Social Outcomes of Sexual Coercion: Experiences of Young Women in Developing Countries*. New York: The Population Council; Jejeebhoy, S. J., and S. Bott. 2003. *Non-consensual Sexual Experiences of Young People: A Review of the Evidence from Developing Countries*. South and East Asia Regional Working Paper. No. 16. New Delhi: Population Council. See also: Im-em, Archvanitkul, and Kanchanachitra 2004.

30 de Bruyn, M., and S. Packer. 2004. *Adolescents, Unwanted Pregnancy and Abortion: Policies, Counseling and Clinical Care*. Chapel Hill, North Carolina: Ipas.

31 Amnesty International. 2004. *It's in Our Hands: Stop Violence against Women*. London: Amnesty International.

32 Krug, et al. 2002.

33 Amoakohene, M. A. 2004. "Violence Against Women in Ghana: A Look at Women's Perceptions and Review of Policy and Social Responses." *Social Science and Medicine* 59(2004): 2373-2385; Manh Loi, V., V. Tuan Huy, N. Huu Minh and C. Clement. 1999. "Gender Based Violence: The Case of Vietnam." Washington, D.C.: The World Bank; Garcia-Moreno, C. 2002. "Violence against Women: Consolidating a Public Health Agenda." Pp. 111-142 in: *Engendering International Health: The Challenge of Equity*, edited by G. Sen, A. George, and P. Ostlin. 2002. Cambridge, Massachusetts: MIT Press; and Koenig, M., et al. 2003. "Domestic Violence in Rural Uganda: Evidence From a Community-based Study." *Bulletin of the World Health Organization* 81(1): 53-60.

34 The Population Council. 2004b. *Sexual Coercion: Young Men's Experiences as Victims and Perpetrators*. New York: The Population Council.

35 Solano and Velzeboer 2003.

36 As recognized, for example, in the 1993 UN Declaration on the Elimination of Violence Against Women, Article 4(f) and the Beijing Platform for Action, para. 124(g). See: United Nations. 1993. *48/104: Declaration on the Elimination of Violence Against Women* (A/RES/48/104), Article 4. New York United Nations; and United Nations. 1996. *The Beijing Declaration and the Platform for Action: Fourth World Conference on Women: Beijing, China: 4-15 September 1995*. New York: Department of Public Information, United Nations.

37 Luciano, D., S. Esim, and N. Duvvury. 2003. "How to Make the Law Work: Budgetary Implications of Domestic Violence Laws in Latin America, Central America and the Caribbean." Paper presented at "Women Working to Make a Difference," Seventh International Women's Policy Research Conference, Washington, D.C., 22-24 June 2003.

38 UN Millennium Project. 2005b. *Investing in Development: A Practical Plan to Achieve the Millennium Development Goals: Overview*, p. 13. Report to the Secretary-General. London and Sterling, Virginia: Earthscan.

39 WHO. n.d. "Schools and Youth Health: Resources and Tools for Advocacy." Geneva: WHO. Web site: www.who.int/school_youth_health/resources/en/, last accessed 10 July 2005; UNESCO. 2004. "Making the Case for Violence Prevention through Schools." *FRESH Tools for Effective School Health*, 1st Edition. Geneva: UNESCO; and Larraín, S., J. Vega, and I. Delgado. 1997. *Relaciones familiares y maltrato infantil*. Santiago: UNICEF. Cited in: UN Millennium Project 2005a.

40 UN Millennium Project 2005a, p. 119.

41 Watts, C., and S. Mayhew. 2004. "Reproductive Health Services and Intimate Partner Violence: Shaping a Programmatic Response in Sub-Saharan Africa." *International Family Planning Perpectives* 30(4): 207-213; and UN Millennium Project. 2005c. *Who's Got the Power: Transforming Health Systems for Women and Children*. Task Force on Child Health and Maternal Health. London and Sterling, Virginia: Earthscan.

42 de Bruyn and Packer 2004.

43 UN Millennium Project 2005a, p. 111.

44 The Global Coalition on Women and AIDS and WHO. n.d. *Violence against Women: Critical Intersections: Intimate Partner Violence and HIV/AIDS*. Information Bulletin Series. No. 1. Geneva: WHO.

45 Human Rights Watch. 2002. *The War within the War: Sexual Violence against Women and Girls in the Eastern Congo*. New York: Human Rights Watch.

46 WHO. 2000. "Female Genital Mutilation." Fact Sheet. No. 241. Geneva: WHO. Web site: www.who.int/mediacentre/factsheets/fs241/en, accessed 3 March 2005.

47 Heise, Ellsberg, and Gottemoeller 1999.

48 Ganatra, B. R., K. J. Coyaji, and V. N. Rao. 1996. *Community cum Hospital Based Case-Control Study on Maternal Mortality: A Final Report*. Pune, India: KEM Hospital Research Centre. Worldwide, studies have identified a trend in the rationale for why violence occurs during pregnancy; reasons include disobeying one's husband, expressing suspicions of infidelity, refusing sex, or failing to adequately care for the children or home. According to a report of the Population Council, globally, one woman in every four is physically or sexually abused during pregnancy, usually by her partner. See: Jejeebhoy, S. J. 1998. "Association between Wife-beating and Fetal and Infant Death: Impressions from a Survey in Rural India." *Studies in Family Planning* 29(3): 300-308; Visaria, L. 1999. "Violence Against Women in India: Evidence from Rural Gujarat." Pp. 14-25 in: *Domestic Violence in India: A Summary Report of Three Studies*, by the International Center for Research on Women. 1999. Washington, D.C.: International Center for Research on Women; and Heise, Ellsberg, and Gottemoeller 1999.

49 UN Millennium Project 2005a, p. 16.

50 UN Millennium Project 2005c.

51 Leung, T. W., et al. 2002. "A Comparison of the Prevalence of Domestic Violence Between Patients Seeking Termination of Pregnancy and Other Gynecology Patients." *International Journal of Gynecology and Obstetrics* 77(1): 47-54. A 1999 case control study in a hospital in Hong Kong of 501 women (245 seeking abortion and 256 other ob/gyn patients) found that "the lifetime prevalence of abuse in the group seeking abortion was 27.3% compared to 8.2% in the ob/gyn group". The study also found that "among those with recent history of abuse, 27% (9/33) admitted that their decision for termination of pregnancy had been affected by their experience of abuse".

52 Kaye, D. 2001. "Domestic Violence Among Women Seeking Post-abortion Care." *International Journal of Gynecology and Obstetrics* 75(3(: 323-325. A 2000 study of 311 women seeking PAC at a national referral hospital in Uganda found that 70 women (23.2 per cent) had induced abortions and 28 of those (38.9 per cent) "gave domestic violence-related issues as the main reason for inducing the abortion".

53 Watts and Mayhew 2004.

54 United Nations 1996, para. 106(q).

55 Krug, et al. 2002.

56 Bott, S., et al. 2004. *Improving the Health Sector Response to Gender-based Violence: A Resource Manual for Health Care Professionals in Developing Countries*. New York: IPPF/Western Hemisphere Region.

57 UNFPA and AIDOS. 2003. *Addressing Violence against Women: Piloting and Programming: Rome, Italy, 15-19 September 2003*. New York and Rome: UNFPA and AIDOS.

58 UN Millennium Project 2005a, p. 40; and Global Campaign for Education. 2005. "Girls Can't Wait: Why Girls' Education Matters, and How to Make It Happen Now: Briefing Paper for the UN Beijing + 10 Review and Appraisal." Brussels, Belgium: Global Campaign for Education.

59 UNFPA. 2005. *Beijing at Ten: UNFPA's Commitment to the Platform for Action*. New York: UNFPA.

60 UN-HABITAT (United Nations Human Settlement Programme). 2001. *Cities in a Globalizing World: Global Report on Human Settlements 2001*. London: Earthscan.

61 UN Millennium Project 2005a, p. 76.

62 UNFPA 2005, Area 6.

63 The UN Millennium Project Task Force on Education and Gender Equality identified women's inheritance and property rights, and combating violence against women, as two of seven strategic priorities for achieving gender equality.

64 United Nations. 2005. *Review of the Implementation of the Beijing Platform for Action and the Outcome Documents of the Special Session of the General Assembly Entitled "Women 2000: Gender Equality, Development and Peace for the Twenty-first Century": Report of the Secretary-General* (E/CN.6/2005/2), para. 214. New York: United Nations.

65 Center for Reproductive Rights. 2005. "Governments in Action: Legal and Policy Developments Affecting Reproductive Rights." Briefing Paper. New York: Center for Reproductive Rights.

66 United Nations 2005, para. 207, 208 and 211.

67 Bendre, U., and T. Khorakiwala,. 2004. "Assessment of Family Counselling Centers in Madhya Pradesh." Report submitted to UNFPA.

68 UNFPA. 13 March 2003. "The Santa Maria/Sal Commitment: By African Women Ministers and Parliamentarians on Gender and HIV/AIDS: Reinforcing National Action." News Feature. New York: UNFPA.

69 UNFPA 2005, p. 6.

70 United Nations 2005, para. 223.

71 UN Millennium Project. 2005d. *Investing in Development: A Practical Plan to Achieve the Millennium Development Goals*, p. 68. Report to the UN Secretary-General. London and Sterling, Virginia: Earthscan.

72 UNFPA 2005, p. 6.

73 Garcia-Moreno, C. 2003. "Responding to Violence against Women: WHO's Multicountry Study on Women's Health and Domestic Violence." *Health and Human Rights: An International Journal* 6(2): 112-127.

74 The White Ribbon Campaign. n.d. " Men Working to End Men's Violence Against Women." Toronto, Canada: White Ribbon Campaign. Web site: www.whiteribbon.ca/about_us/, last accessed 5 May 2005.

75 Crossette, B. 2004. "Priorities Across Borders: For Many Women, Violence Shuts Out Hope." Media Center, UN Foundation. See web site: www.stopvaw.org/October_2004.html#25Oct200424, accessed 9 July 2005.

76 Ramos-Jimenez, P. 1996. "Philippine Strategies to Combat Domestic Violence Against Women." Task Force on Social Science and Reproductive Health. Manila, the Philippines: Social Development Research Center and De La Salle University.

77 Royal Government of Cambodia. 2004. *Nation Religion King: The Progress Report on Implementation of the Beijing Platform for Action on Women's Issues 1995-2005*, p. 10. Phnom Penh: Ministry of Women's Affairs, Royal Government of Cambodia; and "A Role for Men in Gender Equality." 13 September 2004. *IPS UN Journal* 11(165): 6.

78 United Nations 2005, para. 234.

79 Based on a costing exercise on gender-specific interventions that include training and awareness campaigns, interventions to combat violence against women, and capacity development of the women's ministry. See: UN Millennium Project 2005a, p. 36.

80 Waters, H., et al. 2004.

81 United Nations. 2000. *Resolution adopted by the General Assembly: 55/2: United Nations Millennium Declaration* (A/RES/55/2), para. 12. New York: United Nations.

## CHAPTER 8

1 United Nations. 2005a. *In Larger Freedom: Towards Development, Security and Human Rights for All: Report of the Secretary-General* (A/59/2005). New York: United Nations.

2 The earthquake and tsunami disaster of 26 December 2004 took over 280,000 lives and devastated coastal areas and communities around the Indian Ocean. See: United Nations. 2005b. *Summary of the Economic and Social Survey of Asia and the Pacific, 2005* (E/2005/18). New York: United Nations; and United States Agency for International Development. 2005. "Indian Ocean: Earthquake and Tsunamis." United States Agency for International Development Fact Sheet. No. 36. Washington, D.C.: Office of US Foreign Disaster Assistance, Bureau for Democracy, Conflict, and Humanitarian Assistance, United States Agency for International Development. Web site: www.usaid.gov/our_work/humanitarian_assistance/disaster_assistance/countries/indian_ocean/fy2005/indianocean_et_fs36_02-22-2005.pdf, accessed 25 March 2005.

3 UN Millennium Project. 2005a. *Investing in Development: A Practical Plan to Achieve the Millennium Development Goals*, ch. 12. Report to the UN Secretary-General. London and Sterling, Virginia: Earthscan,

4 UN Millennium Project. 2005b. *Health, Dignity and Development: What Will it Take?* Task Force on Water and Sanitation. London and Sterling, Virginia: Earthscan.

5 Smith, D. 2001. "Trends and Causes of Armed Conflict" In: *Berghof Handbook for Conflict Transformation: Trends and Causes of Armed Conflicts*, edited by D. Bloomfield, M. Fischer, and A. Schmerlze. Berlin, Germany: Berghof Research Centre for Constructive Conflict Management; and Dwan, R., and M. Gustavsson. 2004. "Major Armed Conflicts." Ch. 3 in: *SIPRI Yearbook 2004: Armaments, Disarmament and International Security*, by Stockholm International Peace Research Institute. 2004. Oxford: Oxford University Press.

6 Women's Commission for Refugee Women and Children. 2004. *Women's Commission Fact Sheet*. New York: Women's Commission for Refugee Women and Children. Web site: www.womenscommission.org/pdf/fctsht.pdf, accessed 25 March 2005.

7 United Nations 2005a, para. 114.

8 United Nations. 2005c. *Review of the Implementation of the Beijing Platform for Action and the Outcome Documents of the Special Session of the General Assembly Entitled "Women 2000: Gender Equality, Development and Peace for the Twenty-first Century": Report of the Secretary-General* (E/CN.6/2005/2), para. 76. New York: United Nations.

9 UN Millennium Project. 2005c. *Taking Action: Achieving Gender Equality and Empowering Women*. Task Force on Education and Gender Equality. London and Sterling, Virginia: Earthscan.

10 United Nations. 2000. *UN Security Council Resolution 1325 (2000): Adopted by the Security Council at Its 4213th Meeting on 31 October 2000* (S/RES/1325 [2000]). New York: United Nations.

11 Article 7.1 of the Rome Statute. Cited in: *Reproductive Rights are Human Rights*, by the Center for Reproductive Rights. 2005. New York: Center for Reproductive Rights; and United Nations. 2003a. *Integration of the Human Rights of Women and the Gender Perspective: Violence Against Women* (E/CN.4/2003/75). New York: United Nations.

12 United Nations 2003a.

13 United Nations 2005c, para. 248.

14 United Nations. 2004a. *A More Secure World: Our Shared Responsibility: Report of the Secretary-General's High-Level Panel on Threats, Challenges, and Change* (A/59/565), para. 238. New York: United Nations.

15 United Nations 2005a, para. 114.

16 These commitments are made in UN Security Council Resolutions 1261 (1999), 1314 (2000), 1379 (2001), and 1460 (2003).

17 United Nations 2005a.

18 United Nations. 2004b. *Specific Groups and Individuals: Mass Exoduses and Displaced Persons: Report of the Representative of the Secretary-General on the Human Rights of Internally Displaced Persons, Walter Kälin: Submitted Pursuant to Commission on Human Rights Resolution 2004/55* (E/CN.4/2005/84). New York: United Nations.

19 Globally, 25 million are internally displaced persons, and an additional 11 to 12 million are refugees. See: United Nations 2005a, p. 4.

20 See: Office of the United Nations High Commissioner for Human Rights. n.d. "Special Procedures of the Commission on Human Rights: Representative of the Secretary-General on Internally Displaced Persons." Geneva: Office of the United Nations High Commissioner for Human Rights. Web site: www.unhchr.ch/html/menu2/7/b/interndisp/, accessed 9 July 2005.

21 The Guiding Principles on Internal Displacement restate and compile human rights and humanitarian law relevant to internally displaced persons. See: United Nations. 1998a. *Report of the Representative of the Secretary-General, Mr. Francis M. Deng, submitted pursuant to Commission Resolution 1997/39: Addendum: Guiding Principles on Internal Displacement* (E/CN.4/1998/53/Add.2). New York: United Nations.

22 United Nations 2004b.

23 United Nations 2005a, paras. 209 and 210.

24 Anderlini, S. N. 2004. *Negotiating the Transition to Democracy and Reforming the Security Sector: Vital Contributions of South African Women*. Washington, D.C.: Hunt Alternatives Fund.

25 UNIFEM. 2005a. Report to the Forty-fifth Session of the Consultative Committee. New York: UNIFEM.

26 UNFPA. 2004a. *Dispatches*. No. 62.

27 Mertus, J. 2004. "Women's Participation in the International Criminal Tribunal for the Former Yugoslavia (ICTY): Transitional Justice for Bosnia and Herzegovina." Policy Commission Case Study. Washington, D.C.: Hunt Alternatives Fund.

28 Anderlini, S. N., C. P. Conaway, and L. Kays. 2004. "Transitional Justice and Reconciliation." In: *Inclusive Security, Sustainable Peace: A Toolkit for Advocacy and Action*, by International Alert and Women Waging Peace. 2004. Washington and London: Hunt Alternatives Fund and International Alert. Web site: www.womenwagingpeace.net/content/toolkit/chapters/Transitional_Justice.pdf, accessed 25 March 2005.

29 UNIFEM. 2005b. "Women, War, Peace, and Justice." New York: UNIFEM. Web site: www.womenwarpeace.org/issues/justice/justice.htm, accessed 25 March 2005.

30 UNFPA. 2004b. *Beijing at Ten: UNFPA's Commitment to the Platform for Action*. New York: UNFPA.

31 United Nations. n.d. "The UN Works for Women: Rescued from Horror." New York: United Nations. Web site: www.un.org/works/women/women5.html, accessed 9 July 2005.

32 The figures are 67 per cent in Rwanda and 64 per cent in Cambodia. For Rwanda, see: UNFPA. 2004c; and for Cambodia, see: Royal Government of Cambodia. 2004. *Nation Religion King: The Progress Report on Implementation of the Beijing Platform for Action on Women's Issues 1995-2005*. Phnom Penh: Ministry of Women's Affairs, Royal Government of Cambodia.

33 Global Information Networks in Education. n.d. "Child Soldier Projects: The Case of Liberia." Web site: www.ginie.org/ginie-crises-links/childsoldiers/liberia1.html, accessed 9 June 2005.

34 Mazurana, D., and K. Carlson. 2004. *From Combat to Community: Women and Girls of Sierra Leone*. Washington, D.C.: Hunt Alternatives Fund.

35 Save the Children. 2005. *Forgotten Casualties of War: Girls in Armed Conflict*. London: Save the Children.

36 Mazurana and Carlson 2004.

37 Save the Children 2005.

38 Verhey, B. 2003. *Going Home: Demobilising and Reintegrating Child Soldiers in the Democratic Republic of Congo*. London: Save the Children; and UNIFEM. 2004. *Getting It Right, Doing It Right: Gender and Disarmament, Demobilization, and Reintegration*. New York: UNIFEM.

39 UNICEF. 2005. *Factsheet: Child Soldiers*. New York: UNICEF. Web site: www.unicef.org/protection/childsoldiers.pdf, accessed 25 March 2005.

40 Chubb, K. 2001. *Between Anger and Hope: South Africa's Youth and the TRC*. Witwatersrand: Witwatersrand University Press.

41 Clark, C. 2003. "Juvenile Justice and Child Soldiering: Trends, Challenges, and Dilemmas." *Child Soldier Newsletter* 7: 6-8. Web site: www.child-soldiers.org/document_get.php?id=681, accessed 25 March 2005.

42 Republic of Sierra Leone. 2003. *Sierra Leone National Youth Policy*. Freetown: Republic of Sierra Leone. Web site:

www.statehouse-sl.org/policies/youth.html, accessed 25 March 2005.

43 The World Bank. 2005a. *Youth for Good Governance Distance Learning Program.* Washington, D.C.: The World Bank. Web site: http://info.worldbank.org/etools/docs/library/35958/overview.pdf, accessed 25 March 2005; and The World Bank. 2005b. "Module IX: The Role of Youth: The Significance of Coalition-Building." *Youth for Good Governance Distance Learning Program.* Washington, D.C.: The World Bank. Web site: http://info.worldbank.org/etools/docs/library/35976/mod09.pdf, accessed 25 March 2005.

44 "Congo: Children's Parliament Launched by Government and UNICEF." 30 September 2005. *IRINnews.* Web site: www.irin.asp?ReportID=36903&SelectRegion=Great_Lake, accessed 25 March 2005.

45 Save the Children 2005; and UNESCO. 2004. *EFA Global Monitoring Report 2003/4.* Paris: UNESCO.

46 Women's Commission for Refugee Women and Children. 2002. *Precious Resources: Participatory Research Study with Adolescents and Youth in Sierra Leone: April-July 2002.* New York: Women's Commission for Refugee Women and Children. Web site: www.womenscommission.org/reports/sl/index.shtml, accessed 25 March 2005.

47 Inter-Agency Network for Education in Emergencies. 2004. *Minimum Standards for Education in Emergencies, Chronic Crises, and Early Reconstruction.* Paris: Inter-Agency Network for Education in Emergencies. Web site: www.ineesite.org/standards/MSEE_report.pdf, accessed 25 March 2005.

48 Sommers, M. 2002. *Children, Education, and War: Reaching Education for All (EFA) Objectives in Countries Affected by Conflict.* Washington, D.C.: The World Bank. Web site: www-wds.worldbank.org/servlet/WDSContentServer/WDSP/IB/2002/10/12/000094946_02091704130527/Rendered/PDF/multi0page.pdf, accessed 25 March 2005.

49 Mazurana and Carlson 2004.

50 UNFPA. 2004d. "Reproductive Health for Communities in Crises." Ch. 10 in: *The State of World Population 2004: The Cairo Consensus at Ten: Population, Reproductive Health and the Global Effort to End Poverty,* by UNFPA. 2004e. New York: UNFPA.

51 New Sudan Centre for Statistics and Evaluation and UNICEF. 2004. "Towards a Baseline: Best Estimates of Social Indicators for Southern Sudan." NSCSE Series Paper. No. 1.

52 United Nations. 1999. *Reproductive Health in Refugee Situations: An Interagency Field Manual.* Geneva: United Nations High Commissioner for Refugees. Web site: www.rhrc.org/resources/general%5Ffieldtools/iafm_menu.htm, accessed 25 March 2005.

53 RHRC resources can be found at the web site of the Reproductive Health Response in Conflict Consortium: www.rhrc.org, last accessed 13 July 2005. Member agencies include the American Refugee Committee, CARE, the Heilbrunn Department of Population and Family Health at Columbia University's Mailman School of Public Health, the International Rescue Committee, JSI Research and Training Institute, Marie Stopes International and the Women's Commission for Refugee Women and Children.

54 UNFPA. 2003. "Iraqi Women Receive UNFPA Emergency Reproductive Health Services and Supplies." *Dispatches.* No. 57.

55 UNFPA. 14 January 2005. "UNFPA Ships Supplies to Ensure Safe Childbirth and Meet Women's Needs in Tsunami-Hit Countries." Press Release. New York: UNFPA. Web site: www.unfpa.org/news/news.cfm?ID=546, accessed 25 March 2005.

56 UNFPA. 2004f. *Into Good Hands: Progress Reports from the Field.* New York: UNFPA. Web site: www.unfpa.org/upload/lib_pub_file/378_filename_hands_en.pdf, accessed 25 March 2005.

57 UNFPA. 3 May 2002. "UN Population Fund Seeks $3.6 Million for Emergency Assistance in Occupied Palestinian Territory: Protecting Pregnant Women a Top Priority." Press Release. New York: UNFPA. Web site: www.unfpa.org/news/news.cfm?ID=80&Language=1, accessed 9 July 2005.

58 United Nations. 1998b. *Report of the Special Rapporteur on Systematic Rape, Sexual Slavery and Slavery-like Practices During Armed Conflict* (E/CN.4/Sub/2/1998/13). New York: United Nations; and Human Rights Watch. 2000a. *Federal Republic of Yugoslavia: Kosovo: Rape as a Weapon of "Ethnic Cleansing",* Web site: www.hrw.org/reports/2000/fry/index.htm#TopOfPage, accessed 12 April 2005.

59 UN Millennium Project 2005d; United Nations. 2005d. *Integration of the Human Rights of Women and the Gender Perspective: Violence Against Women: Intersections of Violence against Women and HIV/AIDS: Report of the Special Rapporteur on Violence against Women, Its Causes and Consequences, Yakin Ertürk* (E/CN.4/2005/72). New York: United Nations; and Adrian-Paul, A. 2004. "HIV/AIDS." *Inclusive Security, Sustainable Peace: A Toolkit for Advocacy and Action.* Washington, D.C., and London: Hunt Alternatives Fund and International Alert. Web site: www.womenwagingpeace.net/content/toolkit/chapters/HIV_AIDS.pdf, accessed 25 March 2005.

60 Human Rights Watch. 2003. *We'll Kill You If You Cry: Sexual Violence in the Sierra Leone Conflict,* p. 3. New York: Human Rights Watch.

61 Adrian-Paul 2004.

62 Human Rights Watch. 2000b. "Tanzania: Violence against Women Refugees." New York: Human Rights Watch. Web site: www.hrw.org/english/docs/2000/09/26/tanzan676.htm, accessed 12 April 2005.

63 UNFPA. 2004g. "Forms of Gender-based Violence and Their Consequences." Interactive Population Center. New York: UNFPA. Web site: www.unfpa.org/intercenter/violence/index.htm, accessed 12 April 2005.

64 Puri, S. n.d. "Challenging Gender-based Violence Across Genders." New York: International Rescue Committee. See web site: www.theirc.org/index.cfm/wwwID/578, accessed 2 March 2005.

65 Reproductive Health Response in Conflict Consortium. 2005. "Gender-based Violence." New York: Reproductive Health Response in Conflict Consortium. Web site: www.rhrc.org/rhr_basics/gbv/, accessed 25 March 2005.

66 UNFPA 2004b.

67 United Nations. 2002. *Investigations into Sexual Exploitation of Refugees by Aid Workers in West Africa: Note by the Secretary-General* (A/57/465). Also see: UN News Centre. 29 April 2005. "UN Probes Allegations of Sex Exploitation by Peacekeepers in Liberia." Web site: www.un.org/apps/news/story.asp?NewsID=14131&Cr=Liberia&Cr1=#, accessed 14 June 2005.

68 United Nations. 2003. *Secretary-General's Bulletin: Special Measures for Protection from Sexual Expoitation and Sexual Abuse* (ST/SGB/2003/13). New York: United Nations.

69 Wax, E. 13 November 2003. "Cycle of War is Spreading AIDS and Fear in Africa." *The Washington Post.*

70 UNAIDS. 2005a. "HIV/AIDS and Uniformed Services." Geneva: UNAIDS. Web site: www.unaids.org/EN/in+focus/hiv_aids_security+and+humanitarian+response/hiv_aids+and+uniformed+services.asp, accessed 25 March 2005.

71 Reproductive Health Response in Conflict Consortium. 2004a. *Guidelines for the Care of Sexually Transmitted Infections in Conflict-Affected Settings.* New York: Reproductive Health in Conflict Consortium; Reproductive Health Response in Conflict Consortium. 2004b. *HIV/AIDS Prevention and Control: A Short Course for Humanitarian Workers: Facilitator's Manual.* New York: Reproductive Health in Conflict Consortium; and United Nations. 2004c. *Guidelines for HIV/AIDS Interventions in Emergency Settings.* New York: Inter-Agency Standing Committee Task Force on HIV/AIDS in Emergency Settings, United Nations.

72 UNFPA. 2001. *Reproductive Health for Communities in Crisis: UNFPA Emergency Response.* New York: UNFPA.

73 UNIFEM. n.d. "Women, War, Peace and HIV/AIDS." New York: UNIFEM Web site: www.womenwarpeace.org/issues/hiv/hiv.htm, last accessed 13 July 2005; UNAIDS. 2005b. "First Quarterly Report 2005." UNAIDS Office on AIDS, Security and Humanitarian Response (SHR). Copenhagen: UNAIDS. Web site: www.unaids.org/html/pub/topics/security/shr-2005quarter1_en_pdf.pdf, accessed 13 July 2005.

74 United Nations. 2003b. *United Nations Population Fund: Report of the Executive Director for 2002: Reports Requested by the Executive Board* (DP/FPA/2003/4 [Part III]). New York: United Nations.

75 UNAIDS. 2004. *On the Front Line: A Review of Policies and Programmes to Address HIV/AIDS Among Peacekeepers and Uniformed Services.* New York: UNAIDS.

76 Women's Commission for Refugee Women and Children. 2005. *Children and Adolescents Project.* New York: Women's Commission for Refugee Women and Children. Web site: www.womenscommission.org/projects/children/index.shtml, accessed 25 March 2005.

77 Nyitambe, N., M. Schilperoord, and R. Ondeko. 2004. "Lessons from a Sexual Reproductive Health Initiative for Tanzanian Adolescents." *Forced Migration Review* 19: 9-10. Web site: www.fmreview.org/FMRpdfs/FMR19/FMR19full.pdf. accessed 25 March 2005.

78 UNFPA 2004c.

79 The Population Council and UNFPA. 2002. *Adolescent and Youth Sexual and Reproductive Health: Charting Directions for a Second Generation of Programming.* A Report on a Workshop of the UNFPA in Collaboration with the Population Council, New York, 1-3 May 2002. New York: The Population Council.

# CHAPTER 9

1 United Nations. 2005a. *World Population Prospects: The 2004 Revision: Highlights* (ESA/P/WP.193). New York: Population Division, Department of Economic and Social Affairs, United Nations.

2 Ad Hoc Working Group for Youth and the MDGs. 2005. *Youth and the Millennium Development Goals: Challenges and Opportunities for Implementation: Final Report of the Ad Hoc Working Group for Youth and the MDGs: April 2005.* Web site: http://tig.phpwebhosting.com/themes/mdg/YouthMDG.pdf, last accessed 27 June 2005.

3 The cost-effectiveness of reproductive health, including family planning, has been established since the early 1990s. The World Bank's 1993 World Health Report on "Investing in Health" identified an "essential health package", based on those services that would provide the most benefits with limited resources. The recommended package included the key components of reproductive health services. In 2001, the Commission on Macroeconomics and Health recognized the importance of reproductive health to economic development, including family planning. See: Singh, S., et al. 2004. *Adding It Up: The Benefits of Investing in Sexual and Reproductive Health Care,* p. 12. New York: The Alan Guttmacher Institute and UNFPA. Expanded access to reproductive health services was identified as a "quick win" by the UN Millennium Project. Quick wins are actions that can reap returns within three or fewer years.

4 In addition to the various regional and global meetings held in commemoration of the ICPD and Beijing Conferences since 2002, other high-level meetings and agreements affirming the links between reproductive health and the MDGs in the course of 2005 include: the World Health Assembly Resolution 57.12, the 38th Session of the UN Commission on Population and Development (Resolution E/CN.9/2005/L.5), and the "Stockholm Call to Action: Investing in Reproductive Health and Rights as a Development Priority" (web site: www.unfpa.org/upload/lib_pub_file/418_filename_stockholm-call-to-action.pdf, last accessed 13 July 2005). See also: United Nations. 2005b. *Draft Submitted by the Chairperson of the Commission for Social Developmenton the Basis of Informal Consultations: Declaration on the Tenth Anniversary of the World Summit for Social Development* (E/CN.5/2005/L.2). New York: United Nations. See also 2005 UN resolutions of the Commission on Population and Development on Reproductive Health and the MDGs, and on HIV/AIDS.

5 UNFPA. 24 February 2005. "Population and Reproductive Health: Key to the Achievement of the MDGs." Statement by Thoraya Ahmed Obaid, Executive Director, UNFPA, to the Canadian International Development Agency. New York: UNFPA.

6 For the complete listing of reproductive health components, see: United Nations. 1995. *Population and Development,* vol. 1: *Programme of Action adopted at the International Conference on Population and Development: Cairo: 5-13 September 1994,* para. 7.6. New York: Department of Economic and Social Information and Policy Analysis, United Nations.

7 UN Millennium Project. 2005a. *Combating AIDS in the Developing World,* p. 89. New York: Working Group on HIV/AIDS, Task Force on HIV/AIDS, Malaria, TB, and Access to Essential Medicines. London and Sterling, Virginia: Earthscan.

8   Singh et al. 2004, p. 18. See also: UN Millennium Project. 2005b. *Investing in Development: A Practical Plan to Achieve the Millennium Development Goals*, Box 5.5, p. 82. Report to the UN Secretary-General. London and Sterling, Virginia: Earthscan.

9   UNFPA. 2004a. *Sexually Transmitted Infections: Breaking the Cycle of Transmission*. New York: UNFPA.

10  Based on pilot projects conduced in Côte d'Ivoire and India. See: UNFPA and the International Planned Parenthood Federation South Asia Regional Office. 2004. *Integrating HIV Voluntary Counselling and Testing Services into Reproductive Health Settings: Stepwise Guidelines for Programme Planners, Managers and Service Providers*. New York and London: UNFPA and International Planned Parenthood Federation.

11  For example, the 2004 "New York Call to Commitment: Linking HIV/AIDS and Sexual and Reproductive Health" (available at: www.unfpa.org/upload/lib_pub_file/321_filename_New%20York%20Call%20to%20Commitment.pdf, last accessed 11 July 2005); the "Glion Call to Action on Family Planning and HIV/AIDS in Women and Children"(available at: www.unfpa.org/upload/lib_pub_file/333_filename_glion_cal_to_action.pdf, last accessed 11 July 2005); and the 2005 UN Commission on Population and Development, Thirty-eighth Session.

12  See, for example: UN Millennium Project 2005b; and UN Millennium Project 2005a, p. 89.

13  UN Millennium Project 2005b; and UN Millennium Project 2005a, p. 7.

14  UN Millennium Project. 2005c. *Who's Got the Power: Transforming Health Systems for Women and Children*. Task Force on Child Health and Maternal Health. London and Sterling, Virginia: Earthscan.

15  Ibid.

16  Studies in Kenya and Zimbabwe found that the introduction of user fees resulted in a 50 and 30 per cent drop, respectively, in the use of maternal health services. Cited in: UN Millennium Project 2005c.

17  Various references to these issues can be found in: UN Millennium Project 2005b, p. 109; and UN Millennium Project 2005c.

18  United Nations. 2003a. *Human Security Now: Protecting and Empowering People*, p. 17. New York: Commission on Human Security, United Nations.

19  UN Millennium Project 2005a, p. 96.

20  UN Millennium Project 2005b, p. 103.

21  Ibid.

22  UNFPA and University of Aberdeen. 2005. *Maternal Mortality Update 2004: Delivering into Good Hands*, p. 23. New York: UNFPA; and UN Millennium Project 2005c.

23  UN Millennium Project 2005a, p. 96.

24  UNFPA and University of Aberdeen 2005, p. 23.

25  As estimated by the Joint Learning Initiative, 2004. Cited in: UN Millennium Project 2005b, p. 101.

26  UN Millennium Project 2005a, p. 96.

27  UN Millennium Project 2005b, pp. 80 and 257.

28  UN Millennium Project 2005c.

29  Freedman, L. P. 2001. "Using Human Rights in Maternal Mortality Programs: From Analysis to Strategy." *International Journal of Gynecology & Obstetrics* 75(1): 51-60.

30  United Nations. 2002. "Draft Guidelines: A Human Rights Approach to Poverty Reduction Strategies." Geneva: Office of the High Commissioner for Human Rights, United Nations. Web site: www.ohchr.org/english/issues/docs/guidelinesfinal-poverty.doc, last accessed 30 June 2005.

31  UN Millennium Project 2005b, p. 118.

32  Whitehead, A. 2003. "Failing Women, Sustaining Poverty: Gender in Poverty Reduction Strategy Papers." Report for the UK Gender and Development Network. London: UK Gender and Development Network and Christian Aid.

33  UNFPA. 2004b. Desk Review of 2003 PRSPs. New York: Population and Development Branch, Technical Support Division, UNFPA.

34  Whitehead 2003. See also: Randriamaro, Z, 2002. "The NEPAD, Gender and the Poverty Trap: The NEPAD and the Challenges of Financing for Development in Africa from a Gender Perspective." Paper presented at the Conference on Africa and the Development Challenges of the New Millenium, Accra, Ghana 23–26 April, 2002. Mowbray, South Africa: Alternative Information and Development Center.

35  The World Bank, 2002. *Gender in the PSRPs: A Stocktaking*. Washington, D.C.: World Bank Poverty Reduction and Economic Management Network, The World Bank. Cited in: Whitehead 2003.

36  Based on PRSPs published in 2003. Cited in: UNFPA. 2005a. *The Case for Investing in Young People as Part of a National Poverty Reduction Strategy*. New York: UNFPA.

37  UNFPA. 2003. "Coverage of Population and Development Themes in Poverty Reduction Strategy Papers." New York: Population and Development Branch, Technical Support Division UNFPA. Cited in: UNFPA 2005a.

38  UNFPA 2004.

39  UN Millennium Project 2005b, p. 118.

40  Ibid., p.54.

41  UN Millennium Project. 2005d. *Taking Action: Achieving Gender Equality and Empowering Women*, p. 149. Task Force on Education and Gender Equality. London and Sterling, Virginia: Earthscan.

42  UN Millennium Project. 2005e. *Investing in Development: A Practical Plan to Achieve the Millennium Development Goals: Overview*. Report to the Secretary-General. London and Sterling, Virginia: Earthscan.

43  UNFPA 2005a, p. 58.

44  UNFPA. 2005b. *Policy Development Supporting Adolescent and Youth Sexual and Reproductive Health: Nine Countries' Experiences and Collaboration with UNFPA*, p. 14. New York: UNFPA.

45  Royal Government of Cambodia. 2004. *Nation Religion King: The Progress Report on Implementation of the Beijing Platform for Action on Women's Issues 1995-2005*. Phnom Penh: Ministry of Women's Affairs, Royal Government of Cambodia.

46  In 2003, total global military expenditures amounted to $956 billion. (See: Stockholm International Peace Research Institute. 2004. *SIPRI Yearbook 2004: Armaments, Disarmament and International Security*. Oxford: Oxford University Press.) A figure of $950 is given in: Deen, T. 10 September 2004. "Battling Poverty or Wars?" IPS News Agency. Web site: www.ipsnews.net/new_nota.asp?idnews=25433, accessed 9 July 2005.

47  According to the UN MDGs Statistical Annex, total official development assistance to all developing countries for 2003 was $69 billion, and $58 billion in 2002. Preliminary data from the Organization for Economic Co-operation and Development released in April 2005 indicates total official development assistance for 2004 at $78.6 billion in current US dollars, which would mark a new high. See: Organization for Economic Co-operation and Development. 11 April 2005. "Official Development Assistance Increases Further: But 2006 Targets Still a Challenge." Paris: Organization for Economic Co-operation and Development. Web site: www.oecd.org/document/3/0,2340,en_2649_201185_34700611_1_1_1,00.html, last accessed 5 July 2005.

48  UN Millennium Project 2005b, p. 250.

49  The International Finance Facility aims to frontload aid funding for the MDGs through the sale of bonds on capital markets. See: Suri, S. 23 May 2005. "Divisions in G-8 May Deepen over Africa." *IPS UN Journal* 13(93); and "Brown and Chirac Propose New Ideas to Finance the Global Fund." Global Fund Observer Newsletter. Web site: www.aidspan.org/gfo/archives/newsletter/GFO-Issue-39.pdf, accessed 7 February 2005.

50  "EU Debate Adds Fuel to Aid." 17 February 2005. *IPS UN Journal* 13(28); and UN Millennium Project 2005b p. 256.

51  Data is for 2003. See: Commission for Africa. 2005. *Our Common Interest: Report of the Commission for Africa*, p. 50. London: Commission for Africa. See also Indicator 15 of: United Nations. 2003b. "Annex: Millennium Development Goals: Targets and Indicators." *Implementation of the United Nations Millennium Declaration: Report of the Secretary-General (A/58/323)*. New York: United Nations.

52  Commission for Africa 2005. The target of allocating 15 per cent of gross domestic product for health was adopted by the Organization of African Unity: "Declaration on HIV/AIDS, Tuberculosis and Other Related Infectious Diseases," para.26. 2001 African Summit on HIV/AIDS, Tuberculosis and Other Related Infectious Diseases, Abuja, Nigeria, 26-27 April 2001.

53  UN Millennium Project 2005e, p. 17.

54  Ibid., Box 1, p. 5.

55  Organization for Economic Co-operation and Development 11 April 2005. See also: Deen 10 September 2004.

56  Bianchi, S. 14 April 2005. "EU Proposes More Aid to Developing Nations: Belgium, France, Finland, Ireland, Spain and the United Kingdom have Set Timetables by or before 2015." *IPS UN Journal* 13(66).

57  The European Union member states pledged to increase spending and established interim targets: 0.51 per cent of gross national income by 2010 for the 15 older EU member states, and 0.17 per cent for the new members. See: Bianchi 14 April 2005.

58  Dugger, C. June 5, 2005. "U.S. Challenged to Increase Aid to Africa." *The New York Times*; and Bianchi, S. 24 May 2005. "EU to IncreaseAid." InterPress Service New Agency. Web site: http://ipsnews.net/new_nota.asp?idnews=28801, accessed 9 July 2005.

59  Reports on developing country expenditures include all funds spent addressing HIV/AIDS, in addition to the set of preventive activities used in estimating the requirements. A large share of the total is comprised of allocations in a small number of very large countries.

60  United Nations. 2005c. *Flow of Financial Resources for Assisting in the Implementation of the Programme of Action of the International Conference on Population and Development (E/CN.9/2005/5)*, p. 16. New York: United Nations

61  Ibid.

62  United Nations 2002, pp. 53 and 60.

63  UNDP. 2003. *Human Development Report 2003: Millennium Development Goals: A Compact among Nations to End Human Poverty*. New York: UNDP.

64  See also the 2000 UN Global Compact, which invites international businesses to join and abide by 10 core guiding principles based on human rights, workers' rights, environmental protection and anti-corruption, in: UN Millennium Project 2005b, p. 142.

65  The World Bank. n.d. "Governance and Anti-corruption." Washington, D.C.: The World Bank. Web site: www.worldbank.org/wbi/governance/, last accessed 27 June 2005.

66  UN Millennium Project 2005b, pp. 99 and 201; and Stapp, K. 7 March 2005. "One Step Forward, Two Steps Back?" *IPS UN Journal* 13(39).

67  UN Millennium Project 2005c.

68  United Nations. 2005d. *Progress Made in the Implementation of the Declaration of Commitment on HIV/AIDS: Report of the Secretary-General (A/59/765)*, para. 41. New York: United Nations.

69  UN Millennium Project 2005a.

70  Sachs, J. D., and J. W. McArthur. 2005. "The Millennium Project: A Plan for Meeting the Millennium Development Goals." *The Lancet* 365(9456): 347-353; and UN Millennium Project 2005b, p. 133.

71  UN Millennium Project 2005b.

72  ILO. 2001. *An ILO Code of Practice on HIV/AIDS and the World of Work*. Geneva: ILO; and "Little Corporate Response Seen in Tackling AIDS Threat." *Population 2005* 7(1): 4.

73  United Nations. 2005e. *In Larger Freedom: Towards Development, Security and Human Rights for All: Report of the Secretary-General (A/59/2005)*, para. 8. New York: United Nations.

74  UN Millennium Project. n.d. "Fast Facts: Faces of Poverty." Web site: www.unmillenniumproject.org/facts/index.htm, accessed 3 June 2005.

# Sources for Quotations

## CHAPTER 1

p. 1: UN Millennium Project. 2005a. *Investing in Development: A Practical Plan to Achieve the Millennium Development Goals: Overview*, Box 1.1 p. 59. Report to the Secretary-General.

## CHAPTER 2

p. 9: Message to the Fifth Asian and Pacific Population Conference, Regional Conference on ICPD+10, Bangkok, 11-17 December 2002.

p. 15: United Nations. 2005a. *Review of the Implementation of the Beijing Platform for Action and the Outcome Documents of the Special Session of the General Assembly Entitled "Women 2000: Gender Equality, Development and Peace for the Twenty-first Century": Report of the Secretary-General* (E/CN.6/2005/2), para. 354.

p. 17: "Declaration on Gender Equality in Africa." Third Ordinary Session, Heads of State and Government of Member States of the African Union, Addis Ababa, Ethiopia, 6-8 July 2004.

## CHAPTER 3

p. 21: United Nations. 28 February 2005. "Empowerment of Women the Most Effective Development Tool" (SG/SM/9738). Press release on address to the 2005 Commission on the Status of Women.

p. 23: United Nations. 2000. *Resolution Adopted by the General Assembly: 55/2: United Nations Millennium Declaration* (A/RES/55.2), para. I.6.

p. 25: United Nations. 1995. *Population and Development*, vol. 1: *Programme of Action adopted at the International Conference on Population and Development: Cairo: 5-13 September 1994*, para. 7.3.

p. 27: "Demographics, HIV/AIDS and Reproductive Health: Implications for the Achievement of the MDGs." Statement delivered at the Overseas Development Institute, London, 2 February 2005.

## CHAPTER 4

p. 33: UN Millennium Project. 2005b. *Investing in Development: A Practical Plan to Achieve the Millennium Development Goals*, Box 5.5, p. 82. Report to the Secretary-General.

p. 34: Statement by Dr. Nafis Sadik, Secretary-General of the International Conference on Population and Development, September 1994.

P. 37: 14th International AIDS Conference, Barcelona, July 2002.

p. 41: UN Millennium Project. 2005c. *Combating AIDS in the Developing World*, p. 54. Working Group on HIV/AIDS, Task Force on HIV/AIDS, Malaria, TB, and Access to Essential Medicines.

## CHAPTER 5

p. 55: UNFPA. 2004. "Too Brief a Child: Voices of Married Adolescents." Video.

## CHAPTER 6

p. 57: United Nations 1995, para. 4.24.

p. 60: Centro de Análisis Sociocultural – Universidad Centroamericana, CEPAL and UNFPA. 2005. "Estudio Masculinidad y factores socioculturales asociados al comportamiento de los hombres frente a la paternidad en Centroamerica: Caso Nicaragua." Draft.

p. 61: The Population Council. 2003. "My Father Didn't Think This Way: Nigerian Boys Contemplate Gender Equality." *Quality/Calidad/Qualite*. No. 14.

## CHAPTER 7

p. 65: United Nations. 2005b. *In Larger Freedom: Towards Development, Security and Human Rights for All: Report of the Secretary-General* (A/59/2005), para. 15.

p. 66: "Uphold My Reproductive Rights: To be Born, To be Safe and To Choose with Dignity." New Delhi: Ministry of Health and Family Welfare, National Human Rights Commission, Government of India, and UNFPA.

p. 67: UNICEF. 2001. *Young People Speaking Out*.

p. 69: Erulkar, A. S., et al. 2004. *The Experience of Adolescence in Rural Amhara Region, Ethiopia*, p. 19. New York and Accra, Ghana: The Population Council, UNICEF, Ministry of Youth Sports and Culture, and UNFPA.

## CHAPTER 8

p. 75: "Women, War and Peace: Mobilising for Peace and Security in the 21st Century." The 2004 Dag Hammarskjold Lecture, Uppsala, Sweden, 22 September, 2004

p. 76: Statement by the United Kingdom on Women, Peace and Security, Open Meeting on Security Council Resolution 1325, 28 October 2004.

p. 81: Rehn, E., and E. Johnson Sirleaf. 2002. *Progress of the World's Women 2002*, vol. 1: *Women War Peace: The Independent Experts' Assessment on the Impact of Armed Conflict on Women and Women's Role in Peacekeeping*, p. 54. New York: UNIFEM.

## CHAPTER 9

p. 85: United Nations 2005b, para. 40.

p. 89: UN Millennium Project 2005b, p. 78.

p. 91: UN Millennium Project. 2005d. *Taking Action: Achieving Gender Equality and Empowering Women*, p. 30. Task Force on Education and Gender Equality.

# Sources for Boxes

## CHAPTER 1

2 UNFPA. 2003. *Achieving the Millennium Development Goals: Population and Reproductive Health as Critical Determinants*. Population and Development Strategies Series. No. 10; UNFPA. 2005. "Reducing Poverty and Achieving the Millennium Development Goals: Arguments for Investing in Reproductive Health and Rights." Stockholm Round Table background document; UN Millennium Project. 2005. *Investing in Development: A Practical Plan to Achieve the Millennium Development Goals*, Box 5.5, p. 82. Report to the UN Secretary-General; The World Bank. 2003a. *Gender Equality and the Millennium Development Goals*; and UN Millennium Project. 2005. *Taking Action: Achieving Gender Equality and Empowering Women*.

## CHAPTER 2

3 United Nations. 2003. *Human Security Now: Protecting and Empowering People*; Middleberg, M. I. 2003. *Promoting Reproductive Security in Developing Countries*. New York: Kluwer Academic/Plenum; and UN Millennium Project. n.d. "Fast Facts: Faces of Poverty." Web site: www.unmillenniumproject.org/facts/index.htm, accessed June 3, 2005.

5 Bruce, J., C. Lloyd, and A. Leonard. 1995. *Families in Focus: New Perspectives on Mothers, Fathers and Children*, pp. 13 and 15. New York: The Population Council; UN Millennium Project. 2005. *Taking Action: Achieving Gender Equality and Empowering Women*, pp. 11, 13,and 89. Task Force on Education and Gender Equality; Diaz-Munoz, A. R., and E. Jelin. 2003. "Major Trends Affecting Families: South America in Perspective." Prepared for United Nations Department of Economic and Social Affairs Division for Social Policy and Development Programme on the Family; UNFPA. n.d. "The Older Years." Web site: www.unfpa.org/intercenter/cycle/older.htm, last accessed 9 May 2005; and The World Bank. 2001. *Engendering Development: Through Gender Equality in Rights, Resources, and Voice*, pp. 25 and 66.

## CHAPTER 3

6 Jonsson, U. 2003. *Human Rights Approach to Development Programming*. Nairobi: UNICEF.

8 Cruz, V. A., and A. E. Badilla. 2005. *VIH/SIDA y Derechos Humanos: de las limitaciones a los desafíos. Análisis comparativo del marco jurídico de los países centroamericanos sobre VIH/SIDA.*, Instituto Interamericano de Derechos Humanos, ONUSIDA, UNFPA, Organización Internacional del Trabajo.

9 Adapted from: UNFPA. 2004. *Culture Matters: Working with Communities and Faith-based Organizations: Case Studies From Country Programmes*.

## CHAPTER 4

12 Starrs, A., and P. Ten Hoope-Bender. 2004. "Dying for Life." Pp. 78-81 in: *Countdown 2015: Sexual and Reproductive Health and Rights for All: Special Report: ICPD at Ten: Where are We Now*, by Countdown 2015. 2004. New York, London, and Washington, D.C.: Family Care International, International Planned Parenthood Federation, and Population Action International; Caro, D. A., S. F. Murray, and P. Putney. 2004. "Evaluation of the Averting Maternal Death and Disability Program." A Grant from the Bill and Melinda Gates Foundation to the Columbia University Mailman School of Public Health." Silver Spring, Maryland: Cultural Practice; Bruce, J., et al. 1995. *Families in Focus: New Perspectives on Mothers, Fathers and Children*. New York: The Population Council; The World Bank. 2001. *Engendering Development: Through Gender Equality in Rights, Resources, and Voice*; WHO, UNICEF and UNFPA. 2004. *Maternal Mortality in 2000: Estimates Developed by WHO, UNICEF and UNFPA*; UNFPA. 2004. *Sexually Transmitted Infections: Breaking the Cycle of Transmission*; Population Services International. 2004. *Giving Families More Room to Breathe: Voluntary Birth Spacing Provides Health, Economic and Social Benefits*. Washington, D.C.: Population Services International; and Rutstein, S. O. 2005. "Effects of Preceding Birth Intervals on Neonatal, Infant and Under-five Years Mortality and Nutritional Status in Developing Countries: Evidence from the Demographic and Health Surveys." *International Journal of Gynecology and Obstetrics* 89(Suppl. 1): S7-S24. The recommended birth spacing interval was being reviewed by the World Health Organization in June 2005 based on recent research.

13 UNAIDS, UNFPA, and UNIFEM. 2004. *Women and HIV/AIDS: Confronting the Crisis*; UNAIDS in: UNFPA. 2002. "Addressing Gender Perspectives in HIV Prevention." *HIV Prevention Now: Programme Briefs*. No. 4; UNAIDS. 2004. "Fact Sheet: Women and AIDS: A Growing Challenge." Geneva: UNAIDS; UNAIDS and WHO. 2004. *AIDS Epidemic Update: December 2004* (UNAIDS/04.45E); Luke, N., and K. Kurtz. 2002. *Cross-generational and Transactional Sexual Relations in Sub-Saharan Africa: Prevalence of Behavior and Implications for Negotiating Safer Sexual Practices*. Washington, D.C.: Population Services International and International Center for Research on Women; A Mother's Promise Campaign. 2003. *A Mother's Promise the World Must Keep: The 10th Anniversary of the Cairo Consensus*. Washington, D.C.: Communications Consortium Media Center; UNAIDS. 2001. *UNAIDS Resource Packet on Gender and AIDS*. Cited in: "Addressing Gender Perspectives in HIV Prevention," by UNFPA. 2002. *HIV Prevention Now: Programme Briefs*. No. 4; UNAIDS. 1999. *Gender and HIV/AIDS: Taking Stock of Research and Programmes* (UNAIDS/99.16E). UNAIDS Best Practice Collection. Key Material; UNIFEM. 2002. "Women's Human Rights: Gender and HIV/AIDS;" Sternberg, S. 23 February 2005. "In India, Sex Trade Fuels HIV's Spread: Women Trapped as Male-dominated Economy Booms." *USA Today*; International Community of Women Living with HIV/AIDS. 2004. *Visibility, Voices and Visions: A Call for Action from HIV Positive Women to Policy Makers*; and UN Millennium Project. 2005. *Combating AIDS in the Developing World*, p. 54. Task Force on HIV/AIDS, Malaria, TB, and Access to Essential Medicines; Commission on Human Rights. 2005, *Integration of the Human Rights of Women and the Gender Perspective: Violence Against Women* (E/CN.4/2005/72), para.33; and Blanc, A. K. et al. 1996. *Negotiating Reproductive Outcomes in Uganda*. Calverton, Maryland: Macro International Inc. and ISAE Makerere University.

THE STATE OF WORLD POPULATION 2005   105

## CHAPTER 5

15 Boender, C. et al 2004. *The 'So What' Report: A Look at Whether Integrating A Gender Focus into Programs Makes a Difference to Outcomes*. Interagency Gender Working Group Task Force Report. Washington, D.C.: Interagency Gender Working Group; Yinger, N. 1998. *Unmet Need for Family Planning: Reflecting Women's Perceptions*, pp. 9, 14 and 17. ICRW Research Report. Washington, D.C.: International Center for Research on Women; Alan Guttmacher Institute. 2003. *In Their Own Right: Addressing the Sexual and Reproductive Health Needs of Men Worldwide*; Zlider, V. M., et al. 2003. "New Survey Findings: The Reproductive Revolution Continues." *Population Reports*. Series M. No 17. Baltimore, Maryland: the INFO Project, Johns Hopkins Bloomberg School of Public Health; and Barnett, B., and J. Stein, 1998. *Women's Voices and Women's Lives: The Impact of Family Planning: A Synthesis of Findings from the Women's Studies Project*, p. 101. Research Triangle Park, North Carolina: Family Health International; and Stanback, J., and K. A. Twum-Baah. 2001. "Why do Family Planning Providers Restrict Access to Services: An Examination in Ghana." *International Family Planning Perspectives* 27(1): 37-41.

## CHAPTER 5

19 Family Care International. 2005. *A Better Future for Rural Girls: Manager's Briefing Kit*.

22 "The Executive Summary of the Lancet Neonatal Survival Series." Web site: www.who.int/child-adolescent-health/New_Publications/NEONATAL/The_Lancet/Executive_Summary.pdf, last accessed 18 July 2005; Countdown 2015. 2004. *Countdown 2015: Sexual and Reproductive Health and Rights for All: Special Report: ICPD at Ten: Where are We Now?* New York, London, and Washington, D.C.: Family Care International, International Planned Parenthood Federation, and Population Action International; United Nations. 2001. *We the Children: End-decade Review of the Follow-up to the World Summit for Children: Report of the Secretary-General* (A/S-27/3); UN Millennium Project. 2005. *Who's Got the Power: Transforming Health Systems for Women and Children*, p. 76. Task Force on Child Health and Maternal Health; and Action Canada for Population and Development. 2004. *Why Invest in Sexual and Reproductive Health and Rights?* Web site: www.acpd.ca/acpd.cfm/en/section//SRResources/articleID/123, last accessed 18 July 2005.

24 Luke, N. 2005. "Confronting the 'Sugar Daddy' Stereotype: Age and Economic Asymmetries and Risky Sexual Behavior in Urban Kenya." *International Family Planning Perspectives* 31(1): 6-14; Luke, N., and K. M. Kurtz, 2002. *Cross-generational and Transactional Sexual Relations in Sub-Saharan Africa: Prevalence of Behavior and Implications for Negotiating Safer Sexual Practices*. Washington, D.C.: Population Services International and International Center for Research on Women; and Fitzgerald, D. W., et al. 2000. "Economic Hardship and Sexually Transmitted Diseases in Haiti's Rural Artibonite Valley." *American Journal of Tropical Medicine and Hygiene* 62(4): 496-501.

## CHAPTER 6

26 Centro de Análisis Sociocultural - Universidad Centroamericana, CEPAL and UNFPA. 2005a. "Masculinidad y factores socioculturales asociados al comportamiento de los hombres frente a la paternidad en Centroamérica." Draft summary; and "Estudio Masculinidad y factores socioculturales asociados al comportamiento de los hombres frente a la paternidad en Centroamerica: Caso Nicaragua." Draft. Emphasis on education in the context of fatherhood and gender equality is also found in: CEPAL. 2002. *Paternidad Responsable en el Istmo centroamericano* (LC/MEX/L.475/Rev.1).

27 Greene, M. E., et al. Forthcoming. "Involving Men in Reproductive Health: Contributions to Development." Occasional paper prepared for the United Nations Millennium Project; Government of Cambodia. 2003. "Policy on Women, the Girl Child, and STI/HIV/AIDS." Phnom Penh: Ministry of Women's and Veterans' Affairs; Baker, G., et al. 2003. "Men's Participation as Fathers in the Latin American and Caribbean Region: A Critical Literature Review with Policy Considerations." Final draft. Document prepared for the World Bank; James, B. 2002. *European, Australian and Canadian Policies to Reconcile Paid Work and Family Life*. Report prepared for the Ministry of Women's Affairs of New Zealand, Wellington, New Zealand; CEPAL. 2002. *Paternidad Responsable en el Istmo Centroamericano*; Socialist Republic of Viet Nam. 2002. "The Comprehensive Poverty Reduction and Growth Strategy." Hanoi; Ministry of Health; Republic of Botswana. 1994. "Botswana Family Planning General Policy Guidelines and Services Standards." Gaborone: Maternal and Child Health/Family Planning, Department of Primary Health Care, Ministry of Health; Deven, F., and P. Moss. 2002. "Leave Arrangements for Parents: Overview and Future Outlook." *Community, Work and Family* 5(3): 237-255; and O'Brien, M. 2004. *Shared Caring: Bringing Fathers into the Frame*. EOC Working Paper Series. No. 18. Manchester, United Kingdom: Equal Opportunities Commission. For Jamaica, see: www.moec.gov.jm/youth/YouthPolicy.pdf, accessed 28 April 2005. For Costa Rica, see: http://ccp.ucr.ac.cr/observa/CRindicadores/naci.htm, accessed 18 September 2004.

## CHAPTER 7

28 United Nations. 1993. *48/104: Declaration on the Elimination of Violence Against Women* (A/RES/48/104); and United Nations. 1996. *The Beijing Declaration and the Platform for Action: Fourth World Conference on Women: Beijing, China: 4-15 September 1995* (DPI/1766/Wom), paras. 114-116.

29 UNFPA. 2001. *Workshop Report: Integrating Socio-Cultural Research into Population and Reproductive Health Programmes*. Kathmandu, Nepal: Country Technical Services Team for South and West Asia, UNFPA; UNFPA, and Department of Women and Child Development, Government of Haryana, India. 2003. *Jagriti: Rural Women Transforming their Lives*. New Delhi: UNFPA; UNFPA. 2004. *China: Sex Ratio: Facts and Figures*. Brochure; UNFPA, Office of the Registrar General and Census Commissioner, and Ministry of Health and Family Welfare, Government of India. 2003. *Missing: Mapping the Adverse Child Sex Ratio in India*. Brochure; UNFPA. 2003. "The Missing Girls of India." *Dispatches*. No. 59; UNFPA. 1999. *Violence Against Girls and Women: A Public Health Priority*; UNICEF. n.d. "China: The Children: Protection." Web site: www.unicef.org/china/children_1142.html, accessed 14 July 2005; UNFPA. n.d. "Population Issues: India: Restoring the Sex Ratio Balance." Web site: www.unfpa.org/culture/case_studies/india_study.htm, accessed 18 June 2005; and UNFPA. 2003. *UNFPA Global Population Policy Update*. Issue 1.

31 The campaign was co-coordinated by UNDP and UNIFEM, in collaboration with the United Nations High Commissioner for Human Rights, the United Nations High Commissioner for Refugees, UNICEF, UNFPA, UNAIDS, and the Economic Commission for Latin America and the Caribbean. See web sites: www.undp.org.rclac/gender and www.paho.org. Symposium 2001: Gender Violence, Health and Rights in the Americas, 4-7 June 2001, was co-sponsored by the Pan American Health Organization/WHO; UNIFEM; UNFPA; UNDP; UNICEF; the Inter-American Commission of Women of the Organization of American States; the Latin American and Caribbean Feminist Network against Domestic and Sexual Violence (ISIS International); the Latin American and Caribbean Women 's Health Network; and the Center for Research in Women 's Health, a WHO collaborating centre in Canada. Web site: www.paho.org/english/hdp/hdw/Symposium2001FinalReport.pdf, last accessed 19 July 2005.

## CHAPTER 8

33 UN Millennium Project. 2005. *Taking Action: Achieving Gender Equality and Empowering Women*. Task Force on Education and Gender Equality; UNIFEM, the World Bank, the Asian Development Bank, UNDP, and the Department for International Development of the United Kingdom. 2004. "A Fair Share for Women: Cambodia Gender Assessment." Phnom Penh; McGrew, L. 2004. *Good Governance from the Ground Up: Women's Roles in Post-Conflict Cambodia*. Washington, D.C.: Hunt Alternatives Fund; and Royal Government of Cambodia. 2004. *Nation Religion King: The Progress Report on Implementation of the Beijing Platform for Action on Women's Issues 1995-2005*. Phnom Penh: Ministry of Women's Affairs.

34 Powley, E., and S. N. Anderlini. 2004. "Democracy and Governance," p. 38. Pp. 36-47 in: *Inclusive Security, Sustainable Peace: A Toolkit for Advocacy and Action*, by International Alert and Women Waging Peace. 2004. Washington, D.C. and London: Hunt Alternatives Fund and International Alert; Inter-Parliamentary Union. 2005. "Women in National Parliaments: World Classification." Situation as of 30 April 2005. Web site: www.ipu.org/wmn-e/classif.htm, accessed 3 July 2005; and Powley, E. 2003. "Strengthening Governance: The Role of Women in Rwanda's Transition." Washington, D.C.: Hunt Alternatives Fund.

## CHAPTER 9

38 Boender, C., et al. 2004. *The 'So What' Report: A Look at Whether Integrating a Gender focus into Programs Makes a Difference to Reproductive Health Outcomes?*

## Monitoring ICPD Goals – Selected Indicators

| | Indicators of Mortality ||| Indicators of Education |||| Reproductive Health Indicators ||||
|---|---|---|---|---|---|---|---|---|---|---|---|
| | Infant mortality Total per 1,000 live births | Life expectancy M/F | Maternal mortality ratio | Primary enrolment (gross) M/F | Proportion reaching grade 5 M/F | Secondary enrolment (gross) M/F | % Illiterate (>15 years) M/F | Births per 1,000 women aged 15-19 | Contraceptive Prevalence Any method | Modern methods | HIV prevalence rate (%) (15-49) M/F |
| **World Total** | 55 | 63.7 / 68.2 | | | | | | 56 | 61 | 54 | |
| **More developed regions (\*)** | 8 | 72.2 / 79.6 | | | | | | 26 | 69 | 55 | |
| **Less developed regions (+)** | 60 | 62.3 / 65.8 | | | | | | 61 | 59 | 54 | |
| **Least developed countries (‡)** | 94 | 50.8 / 52.7 | | | | | | 119 | | | |
| **AFRICA (1)** | 91 | 48.8 / 50.3 | | | | | | 109 | 27 | 20 | |
| **EASTERN AFRICA** | 89 | 46.1 / 47.0 | | | | | | 108 | 22 | 17 | |
| Burundi | 102 | 43.5 / 45.5 | 1,000 | 86 / 69 | 66 / 70 | 13 / 9 | 33 / 48 | 50 | 16 | 10 | 5.2 / 6.8 |
| Eritrea | 61 | 52.8 / 56.6 | 630 | 70 / 57 | 90 / 82 | 34 / 22 | | 93 | 8 | 5 | 2.3 / 3.0 |
| Ethiopia | 95 | 47.1 / 49.0 | 850 | 79 / 61 | 63 / 60 | 28 / 16 | 51 / 66 | 89 | 8 | 6 | 3.8 / 5.0 |
| Kenya | 65 | 49.5 / 47.8 | 1,000 | 95 / 90 | 61 / 57 | 34 / 32 | 22 / 30 | 96 | 39 | 32 | 4.6 / 8.9 |
| Madagascar | 75 | 54.5 / 57.0 | 550 | 122 / 117 | 52 / 53 | 15 / 14 | 24 / 35 | 122 | 27 | 17 | 1.4 / 1.9 |
| Malawi | 107 | 40.6 / 40.1 | 1,800 | 143 / 137 | 50 / 38 | 38 / 29 | 25 / 46 | 157 | 31 | 26 | 12.4 / 16.0 |
| Mauritius (2) | 14 | 69.2 / 76.0 | 24 | 103 / 104 | 98 / 100 | 81 / 81 | 12 / 19 | 32 | 75 | 49 | |
| Mozambique | 96 | 41.3 / 42.3 | 1,000 | 114 / 93 | 53 / 45 | 19 / 13 | 38 / 69 | 102 | 6 | 5 | 10.6 / 13.8 |
| Rwanda | 114 | 42.5 / 45.7 | 1,400 | 122 / 122 | 45 / 48 | 18 / 15 | 30 / 41 | 47 | 13 | 4 | 4.4 / 5.7 |
| Somalia | 120 | 46.3 / 48.7 | 1,100 | | | | | 69 | | | |
| Uganda | 79 | 48.8 / 50.0 | 880 | 142 / 140 | 63 / 64 | 22 / 18 | 21 / 41 | 207 | 23 | 18 | 3.7 / 4.9 |
| United Republic of Tanzania | 104 | 45.9 / 46.6 | 1,500 | 99 / 95 | 86 / 90 | 6 / 5 | 23 / 38 | 108 | 25 | 17 | 7.6 / 9.9 |
| Zambia | 92 | 38.7 / 37.7 | 750 | 85 / 79 | 83 / 78 | 31 / 25 | 24 / 40 | 128 | 34 | 23 | 14.1 / 18.9 |
| Zimbabwe | 61 | 37.9 / 36.6 | 1,100 | 94 / 92 | | 38 / 35 | 6 / 14 | 91 | 54 | 50 | 21.0 / 28.4 |
| **MIDDLE AFRICA (3)** | 113 | 42.9 / 45.0 | | | | | | 184 | 23 | 5 | |
| Angola | 134 | 39.9 / 42.8 | 1,700 | 80 / 69 | | 21 / 17 | 18 / 46 | 141 | 6 | 5 | 3.4 / 4.4 |
| Cameroon | 93 | 45.4 / 46.6 | 730 | 116 / 99 | 64 / 64 | 34 / 29 | 23 / 40 | 112 | 19 | 7 | 6.0 / 7.9 |
| Central African Republic | 96 | 38.7 / 40.2 | 1,100 | 78 / 53 | 24 / 22 | 17 / 7 | 35 / 67 | 124 | 28 | 7 | 11.9 / 15.1 |
| Chad | 114 | 42.9 / 45.1 | 1,100 | 95 / 61 | 67 / 51 | 22 / 7 | 59 / 87 | 192 | 8 | 2 | 4.2 / 5.4 |
| Congo, Democratic Republic of the (4) | 115 | 42.9 / 44.9 | 990 | 52 / 47 | 59 / 50 | 24 / 13 | 20 / 48 | 226 | 31 | 4 | 3.7 / 4.8 |
| Congo, Republic of | 70 | 51.4 / 54.0 | 510 | 83 / 78 | 65 / 67 | 37 / 27 | 11 / 23 | 145 | | | 4.3 / 5.6 |
| Gabon | 54 | 53.4 / 54.5 | 420 | 133 / 132 | 68 / 71 | 49 / 42 | | 105 | 33 | 12 | 7.1 / 9.1 |
| **NORTHERN AFRICA (5)** | 41 | 65.8 / 69.7 | | | | | | 32 | 49 | 43 | |
| Algeria | 34 | 70.3 / 73.0 | 140 | 113 / 105 | 97 / 98 | 77 / 83 | 21 / 40 | 8 | 64 | 50 | 0.1 / <0.1 |
| Egypt | 33 | 68.2 / 72.7 | 84 | 100 / 95 | 96 / 100 | 88 / 82 | 33 / 56 | 42 | 60 | 57 | 0.1 / <0.1 |
| Libyan Arab Jamahiriya | 18 | 72.0 / 76.6 | 97 | 114 / 114 | | 102 / 108 | 9 / 29 | 8 | 45 | 26 | |
| Morocco | 35 | 68.1 / 72.5 | 220 | 115 / 104 | 82 / 80 | 49 / 41 | 37 / 62 | 24 | 50 | 42 | |
| Sudan | 69 | 55.2 / 58.0 | 590 | 65 / 56 | 81 / 88 | 39 / 32 | 31 / 50 | 51 | 10 | 7 | 1.9 / 2.6 |
| Tunisia | 21 | 71.6 / 75.8 | 120 | 113 / 109 | 96 / 97 | 75 / 81 | 17 / 35 | 7 | 63 | 53 | <0.1 / <0.1 |
| **SOUTHERN AFRICA** | 42 | 44.6 / 46.0 | | | | | | 64 | 53 | 51 | |
| Botswana | 47 | 35.5 / 34.9 | 100 | 103 / 103 | 85 / 91 | 71 / 75 | 24 / 19 | 75 | 40 | 39 | 31.7 / 43.1 |
| Lesotho | 63 | 34.6 / 36.2 | 550 | 126 / 127 | 66 / 81 | 30 / 39 | 26 / 10 | 37 | 30 | 30 | 25.4 / 32.4 |
| Namibia | 40 | 47.2 / 47.2 | 300 | 105 / 106 | 92 / 93 | 59 / 66 | 13 / 17 | 52 | 29 | 26 | 18.4 / 24.2 |
| South Africa | 41 | 45.7 / 47.4 | 230 | 108 / 104 | 65 / 64 | 85 / 91 | 16 / 19 | 66 | 56 | 55 | 18.1 / 23.5 |
| Swaziland | 68 | 31.6 / 31.3 | 370 | 102 / 94 | 77 / 69 | 45 / 46 | 20 / 22 | 36 | 28 | 26 | 35.7 / 41.7 |
| **WESTERN AFRICA (6)** | 111 | 46.4 / 47.3 | | | | | | 141 | 13 | 8 | |
| Benin | 101 | 54.0 / 55.6 | 850 | 127 / 92 | 70 / 66 | 38 / 17 | 54 / 77 | 128 | 19 | 7 | 1.7 / 2.1 |
| Burkina Faso | 119 | 47.6 / 49.1 | 1,000 | 53 / 39 | 65 / 68 | 14 / 9 | 82 / 92 | 158 | 14 | 9 | 3.6 / 4.8 |
| Côte d'Ivoire | 116 | 45.4 / 46.9 | 690 | 86 / 69 | 73 / 65 | 30 / 16 | 40 / 62 | 120 | 15 | 7 | 6.0 / 8.1 |
| Gambia | 72 | 55.2 / 58.0 | 540 | 86 / 84 | | 41 / 28 | | 118 | 10 | 9 | 1.0 / 1.3 |

# Monitoring ICPD Goals – Selected Indicators

|  | Indicators of Mortality ||| Indicators of Education |||| Reproductive Health Indicators ||||
|---|---|---|---|---|---|---|---|---|---|---|---|
|  | Infant mortality Total per 1,000 live births | Life expectancy M/F | Maternal mortality ratio | Primary enrolment (gross) M/F | Proportion reaching grade 5 M/F | Secondary enrolment (gross) M/F | % Illiterate (>15 years) M/F | Births per 1,000 women aged 15-19 | Contraceptive Prevalence Any method | Contraceptive Prevalence Modern methods | HIV prevalence rate (%) (15-49) M/F |
| Ghana | 59 | 56.9 / 57.8 | 540 | 87 / 79 | 62 / 65 | 47 / 38 | 37 / 54 | 63 | 25 | 19 | 2.6 / 3.5 |
| Guinea | 101 | 53.7 / 54.2 | 740 | 92 / 71 | 64 / 48 | 33 / 15 |  | 189 | 6 | 4 | 2.7 / 3.7 |
| Guinea-Bissau | 115 | 43.7 / 46.5 | 1,100 | 84 / 56 | 41 / 34 | 23 / 13 |  | 193 | 8 | 4 |  |
| Liberia | 137 | 41.6 / 43.3 | 760 | 122 / 89 |  | 40 / 28 | 28 / 61 | 223 | 6 | 6 | 5.1 / 6.7 |
| Mali | 130 | 47.8 / 49.1 | 1,200 | 66 / 51 | 78 / 71 | 25 / 14 | 73 / 88 | 199 | 8 | 6 | 1.6 / 2.2 |
| Mauritania | 92 | 51.9 / 55.1 | 1,000 | 89 / 87 | 61 / 60 | 25 / 20 | 41 / 57 | 98 | 8 | 5 | 0.6 / 0.7 |
| Niger | 149 | 44.8 / 44.9 | 1,600 | 51 / 36 | 71 / 67 | 8 / 6 | 80 / 91 | 258 | 14 | 4 | 1.0 / 1.4 |
| Nigeria | 111 | 43.6 / 43.9 | 800 | 132 / 107 | 64 / 67 | 40 / 33 | 26 / 41 | 140 | 13 | 8 | 4.6 / 6.2 |
| Senegal | 80 | 55.1 / 57.6 | 690 | 83 / 77 | 83 / 77 | 23 / 16 | 49 / 71 | 81 | 11 | 8 | 0.7 / 0.9 |
| Sierra Leone | 162 | 39.9 / 42.7 | 2,000 | 93 / 65 |  | 31 / 22 | 60 / 80 | 176 | 4 | 4 |  |
| Togo | 90 | 53.2 / 56.8 | 570 | 132 / 110 | 73 / 64 | 51 / 22 | 32 / 62 | 97 | 26 | 9 | 3.6 / 4.7 |
| **ASIA** | **51** | **66.1 / 70.0** |  |  |  |  |  | **43** | **64** | **59** |  |
| **EASTERN ASIA (7)** | 30 | 71.1 / 75.4 |  |  |  |  |  | 5 | 82 | 81 |  |
| China | 33 | 70.3 / 73.9 | 56 | 115 / 115 | 100 / 98 | 71 / 69 | 5 / 14 | 5 | 84 | 83 | 0.2 / 0.1 |
| Democratic People's Republic of Korea | 43 | 60.9 / 66.8 | 67 |  |  |  |  | 2 | 62 | 53 |  |
| Hong Kong SAR, China (8) | 4 | 78.9 / 84.9 |  | 107 / 106 | 100 / 99 | 79 / 81 |  | 5 | 86 | 80 | 0.1 / 0.1 |
| Japan | 3 | 78.7 / 85.8 | 10 [9] | 100 / 101 | 100 / 100 | 102 / 102 |  | 4 | 56 | 51 | <0.1 / <0.1 |
| Mongolia | 55 | 62.9 / 66.9 | 110 | 100 / 102 |  | 78 / 90 | 2 / 3 | 53 | 67 | 54 | <0.1 / <0.1 |
| Republic of Korea | 4 | 73.8 / 81.2 | 20 | 106 / 105 | 100 / 100 | 90 / 91 |  | 4 | 81 | 67 | 0.1 / <0.1 |
| **SOUTH-EASTERN ASIA** | 37 | 65.9 / 70.4 |  |  |  |  |  | 40 | 60 | 51 |  |
| Cambodia | 91 | 53.4 / 60.5 | 450 | 130 / 117 | 60 / 62 | 31 / 20 | 15 / 36 | 47 | 24 | 19 | 3.7 / 1.6 |
| Indonesia | 38 | 65.8 / 69.5 | 230 | 113 / 111 | 88 / 90 | 61 / 60 | 8 / 17 | 54 | 60 | 57 | 0.2 / <0.1 |
| Lao People's Democratic Republic | 84 | 54.3 / 56.8 | 650 | 124 / 108 | 64 / 65 | 50 / 37 | 23 / 39 | 88 | 32 | 29 | 0.1 / <0.1 |
| Malaysia | 10 | 71.4 / 76.0 | 41 | 93 / 93 | 87 / 87 | 67 / 74 | 8 / 15 | 18 | 55 | 30 | 0.7 / 0.1 |
| Myanmar | 71 | 58.1 / 63.9 | 360 | 92 / 92 | 64 / 66 | 40 / 38 | 6 / 14 | 19 | 37 | 33 | 1.6 / 0.7 |
| Philippines | 26 | 68.8 / 73.1 | 200 | 113 / 112 | 72 / 80 | 80 / 88 | 8 / 7 | 36 | 49 | 33 | <0.1 / <0.1 |
| Singapore | 3 | 77.1 / 80.9 | 30 | 106 / 102 | 100 / 100 | 71 / 66 | 3 / 11 | 6 | 62 | 53 | 0.4 / 0.1 |
| Thailand | 18 | 67.3 / 74.3 | 44 | 99 / 95 | 92 / 96 | 77 / 77 | 5 / 10 | 48 | 72 | 70 | 2.0 / 1.1 |
| Viet Nam | 28 | 69.1 / 73.1 | 130 | 105 / 97 | 87 / 87 | 75 / 70 | 6 / 13 | 19 | 79 | 57 | 0.7 / 0.3 |
| **SOUTH CENTRAL ASIA** | 65 | 62.4 / 65.4 |  |  |  |  |  | 72 | 48 | 41 |  |
| Afghanistan | 145 | 46.6 / 47.1 | 1,900 | 120 / 63 |  | 24 / - |  | 123 | 5 | 4 |  |
| Bangladesh | 54 | 62.8 / 64.6 | 380 | 94 / 98 | 49 / 59 | 45 / 50 | 50 / 69 | 120 | 58 | 47 |  |
| Bhutan | 52 | 62.6 / 65.0 | 420 |  | 89 / 93 |  |  | 33 | 19 | 19 |  |
| India | 64 | 62.4 / 65.7 | 540 | 113 / 106 | 60 / 64 | 59 / 47 | 27 / 52 | 72 | 48 | 43 | 1.2 / 0.6 |
| Iran (Islamic Republic of) | 31 | 69.5 / 72.6 | 76 | 93 / 90 | 94 / 94 | 80 / 75 | 17 / 30 | 20 | 73 | 56 | 0.1 / <0.1 |
| Nepal | 60 | 62.0 / 62.9 | 740 | 126 / 112 | 63 / 67 | 50 / 39 | 37 / 65 | 113 | 39 | 35 | 0.1 / <0.1 |
| Pakistan | 75 | 63.6 / 64.0 | 500 | 80 / 57 |  | 26 / 19 | 38 / 65 | 69 | 28 | 20 | 0.2 / <0.1 |
| Sri Lanka | 16 | 72.0 / 77.3 | 92 | 111 / 110 | 98 / 99 | 84 / 89 | 8 / 11 | 19 | 70 | 50 | 0.0 / <0.1 |
| **WESTERN ASIA** | 45 | 66.5 / 70.7 |  |  |  |  |  | 43 | 47 | 28 |  |
| Iraq | 88 | 58.4 / 61.5 | 250 | 120 / 100 | 67 / 63 | 50 / 35 |  | 40 | 14 | 10 |  |
| Israel | 5 | 78.0 / 82.1 | 17 | 112 / 112 | 86 / 85 | 94 / 92 | 2 / 4 | 15 | 68 | 52 |  |
| Jordan | 21 | 70.4 / 73.5 | 41 | 99 / 100 | 97 / 98 | 85 / 87 | 5 / 15 | 26 | 56 | 41 |  |
| Kuwait | 10 | 75.5 / 79.8 | 5 | 93 / 94 |  | 87 / 92 | 15 / 19 | 24 | 50 | 41 |  |
| Lebanon | 21 | 70.3 / 74.7 | 150 | 106 / 102 | 90 / 94 | 76 / 83 |  | 26 | 61 | 37 | 0.2 / 0.0 |
| Occupied Palestinian Territory | 19 | 71.3 / 74.4 | 100 | 99 / 99 |  | 85 / 91 | 4 / 13 | 85 |  |  |  |
| Oman | 15 | 73.2 / 76.2 | 87 | 82 / 80 | 98 / 98 | 82 / 79 | 18 / 35 | 46 | 24 | 18 | 0.2 / 0.1 |

# Monitoring ICPD Goals – Selected Indicators

| | Indicators of Mortality ||| Indicators of Education |||| Reproductive Health Indicators ||||
|---|---|---|---|---|---|---|---|---|---|---|---|
| | Infant mortality Total per 1,000 live births | Life expectancy M/F | Maternal mortality ratio | Primary enrolment (gross) M/F | Proportion reaching grade 5 M/F | Secondary enrolment (gross) M/F | % Illiterate (>15 years) M/F | Births per 1,000 women aged 15-19 | Contraceptive Prevalence Any method | Contraceptive Prevalence Modern methods | HIV prevalence rate (%) (15-49) M/F |
| Saudi Arabia | 21 | 70.5 / 74.4 | 23 | 68 / 65 | 92 / 91 | 70 / 63 | 13 / 31 | 33 | 32 | 29 | |
| Syrian Arab Republic | 17 | 71.9 / 75.6 | 160 | 118 / 112 | 91 / 92 | 50 / 46 | 9 / 26 | 33 | 40 | 28 | <0.1 / <0.1 |
| Turkey (10) | 39 | 66.9 / 71.5 | 70 | 95 / 88 | 98 / 97 | 90 / 67 | 4 / 19 | 41 | 64 | 38 | |
| United Arab Emirates | 8 | 76.8 / 81.4 | 54 | 98 / 95 | 93 / 93 | 78 / 80 | 24 / 19 | 20 | 28 | 24 | |
| Yemen | 64 | 60.2 / 62.9 | 570 | 98 / 68 | 80 / 71 | 65 / 29 | 31 / 72 | 92 | 21 | 10 | |
| **ARAB STATES (11)** | **48** | **65.8 / 69.2** | **252** | **99 / 89** | **87 / 88** | **67 / 60** | **25 / 47** | **42** | **40** | **34** | **0.43 / 0.55** |
| **EUROPE** | **9** | **69.9 / 78.2** | | | | | | **19** | **67** | **49** | |
| **EASTERN EUROPE** | 14 | 62.5 / 73.7 | | | | | | 27 | 61 | 35 | |
| Bulgaria | 13 | 69.3 / 75.9 | 32 | 101 / 99 | 91 / 90 | 100 / 97 | 1 / 2 | 44 | 42 | 26 | |
| Czech Republic | 5 | 72.6 / 79.0 | 9 | 103 / 101 | 97 / 98 | 96 / 98 | | 12 | 72 | 63 | 0.1 / <0.1 |
| Hungary | 8 | 69.1 / 77.2 | 16 | 101 / 100 | 77 / 98 | 106 / 106 | 1 / 1 | 21 | 77 | 68 | |
| Poland | 8 | 70.7 / 78.7 | 13 | 100 / 99 | 89 / 96 | 91 / 87 | | 15 | 49 | 19 | |
| Romania | 17 | 68.2 / 75.3 | 49 | 100 / 98 | | 84 / 85 | 2 / 4 | 34 | 64 | 30 | |
| Slovakia | 7 | 70.5 / 78.3 | 3 | 102 / 100 | | 91 / 92 | 0 / 0 | 20 | 74 | 41 | |
| **NORTHERN EUROPE (12)** | 5 | 75.6 / 80.8 | | | | | | 20 | 79 | 75 | |
| Denmark | 5 | 75.1 / 79.7 | 5 | 104 / 104 | 100 / 100 | 126 / 132 | | 7 | 78 | 72 | 0.3 / 0.1 |
| Estonia | 9 | 66.2 / 77.4 | 63 | 103 / 99 | 98 / 99 | 95 / 98 | 0 / 0 | 24 | 70 | 56 | 1.4 / 0.7 |
| Finland | 4 | 75.5 / 82.0 | 6 | 102 / 102 | 100 / 100 | 122 / 135 | | 10 | 77 | 75 | 0.1 / <0.1 |
| Ireland | 5 | 75.5 / 80.7 | 5 | 106 / 106 | 98 / 100 | 102 / 112 | | 14 | | | 0.2 / 0.1 |
| Latvia | 10 | 66.4 / 77.3 | 42 | 95 / 93 | | 95 / 95 | 0 / 0 | 18 | 48 | 39 | 0.8 / 0.4 |
| Lithuania | 9 | 67.2 / 78.2 | 13 | 99 / 98 | | 103 / 102 | 0 / 0 | 21 | 47 | 31 | 0.1 / 0.0 |
| Norway | 4 | 77.3 / 82.2 | 16 | 101 / 101 | 100 / 99 | 113 / 116 | | 10 | 74 | 69 | 0.1 / 0.0 |
| Sweden | 3 | 78.2 / 82.7 | 2 | 109 / 112 | 100 / 100 | 127 / 151 | | 7 | 78 | 72 | 0.1 / 0.0 |
| United Kingdom | 5 | 76.3 / 80.9 | 13 | 100 / 100 | | 159 / 199 | | 26 | 84 | 81 | 0.2 / 0.0 |
| **SOUTHERN EUROPE (13)** | 7 | 75.5 / 81.9 | | | | | | 12 | 68 | 46 | |
| Albania | 24 | 71.3 / 77.0 | 55 | 105 / 102 | | 81 / 81 | 1 / 2 | 16 | 75 | 8 | |
| Bosnia and Herzegovina | 13 | 71.7 / 77.1 | 31 | | | | 2 / 9 | 23 | 48 | 16 | |
| Croatia | 7 | 71.8 / 78.8 | 8 | 97 / 96 | | 89 / 91 | 1 / 3 | 15 | | | |
| Greece | 6 | 75.8 / 81.1 | 9 | 101 / 101 | 100 / 100 | 98 / 97 | 6 / 12 | 9 | | | 0.3 / 0.1 |
| Italy | 5 | 77.2 / 83.3 | 5 | 102 / 101 | 96 / 97 | 100 / 99 | | 7 | 60 | 39 | 0.7 / 0.3 |
| Macedonia (Former Yugoslav Republic of) | 15 | 71.6 / 76.6 | 23 | 96 / 97 | | 86 / 84 | 2 / 6 | 24 | | | |
| Portugal | 5 | 74.2 / 80.8 | 5 | 118 / 112 | | 108 / 118 | | 19 | 66 | 33 | 0.7 / 0.2 |
| Serbia and Montenegro | 12 | 71.3 / 76.0 | 11 | 98 / 98 | | 88 / 89 | 1 / 6 | 24 | 58 | 33 | 0.3 / 0.1 |
| Slovenia | 5 | 73.0 / 80.3 | 17 | 108 / 107 | | 110 / 109 | 0 / 0 | 6 | 74 | 59 | |
| Spain | 4 | 76.2 / 83.5 | 4 | 109 / 107 | | 114 / 121 | | 10 | 81 | 67 | 1.0 / 0.3 |
| **WESTERN EUROPE (14)** | 4 | 76.1 / 82.3 | | | | | | 9 | 74 | 71 | |
| Austria | 5 | 76.4 / 82.1 | 4 | 103 / 103 | | 102 / 98 | | 13 | 51 | 47 | 0.4 / 0.1 |
| Belgium | 4 | 76.1 / 82.3 | 10 | 106 / 105 | 90 / 92 | 153 / 169 | | 8 | 78 | 74 | 0.3 / 0.1 |
| France | 4 | 76.2 / 83.2 | 17 | 105 / 104 | 98 / 98 | 108 / 110 | | 8 | 75 | 69 | 0.6 / 0.2 |
| Germany | 4 | 76.0 / 81.8 | 8 | 100 / 99 | | 101 / 99 | | 10 | 75 | 72 | 0.2 / 0.0 |
| Netherlands | 4 | 75.9 / 81.3 | 16 | 109 / 107 | 100 / 100 | 123 / 121 | | 5 | 79 | 76 | 0.4 / 0.1 |
| Switzerland | 4 | 77.9 / 83.5 | 7 | 108 / 107 | | 101 / 95 | | 5 | 82 | 78 | 0.5 / 0.2 |
| **LATIN AMERICA & CARIBBEAN** | **24** | **69.0 / 75.5** | | | | | | **78** | **71** | **62** | |
| **CARIBBEAN (15)** | 32 | 65.8 / 70.4 | | | | | | 65 | 62 | 58 | |
| Cuba | 5 | 76.1 / 79.7 | 33 | 100 / 96 | 98 / 98 | 94 / 92 | 3 / 3 | 50 | 73 | 72 | 0.1 / <0.1 |
| Dominican Republic | 32 | 64.6 / 71.6 | 150 | 123 / 126 | 56 / 75 | 53 / 65 | 12 / 13 | 91 | 70 | 66 | 2.5 / 0.9 |

THE STATE OF WORLD POPULATION 2005  109

# Monitoring ICPD Goals – Selected Indicators

| | Indicators of Mortality ||| Indicators of Education |||| Reproductive Health Indicators ||||
|---|---|---|---|---|---|---|---|---|---|---|---|
| | Infant mortality Total per 1,000 live births | Life expectancy M/F | Maternal mortality ratio | Primary enrolment (gross) M/F | Proportion reaching grade 5 M/F | Secondary enrolment (gross) M/F | % Illiterate (>15 years) M/F | Births per 1,000 women aged 15-19 | Contraceptive Prevalence Any method | Contraceptive Prevalence Modern methods | HIV prevalence rate (%) (15-49) M/F |
| Haiti | 59 | 51.7 / 53.1 | 680 | 49 / 46 | | 21 / 20 | 46 / 50 | 61 | 27 | 21 | 4.8 / 6.4 |
| Jamaica | 15 | 69.2 / 72.6 | 87 | 100 / 100 | 88 / 93 | 83 / 85 | 16 / 9 | 78 | 66 | 63 | 1.2 / 1.2 |
| Puerto Rico | 10 | 72.1 / 80.8 | 25 | | | | 6 / 6 | 55 | 78 | 68 | |
| Trinidad and Tobago | 13 | 67.3 / 72.8 | 160 | 101 / 99 | 67 / 76 | 79 / 86 | 1 / 2 | 36 | 38 | 33 | 3.2 / 3.2 |
| **CENTRAL AMERICA** | 22 | 71.6 / 76.7 | | | | | | 77 | 64 | 55 | |
| Costa Rica | 10 | 76.1 / 80.9 | 43 | 109 / 107 | 90 / 93 | 64 / 69 | 4 / 4 | 75 | 80 | | 0.8 / 0.4 |
| El Salvador | 24 | 68.2 / 74.3 | 150 | 116 / 109 | 67 / 71 | 59 / 59 | 18 / 23 | 84 | 67 | | 0.9 / 0.5 |
| Guatemala | 35 | 64.1 / 71.5 | 240 | 110 / 102 | 67 / 64 | 44 / 41 | 25 / 37 | 111 | 43 | 34 | 1.3 / 1.0 |
| Honduras | 30 | 66.4 / 70.5 | 110 | 105 / 107 | | | 20 / 20 | 98 | 62 | 51 | 1.7 / 2.0 |
| Mexico | 19 | 73.1 / 78.0 | 83 | 111 / 110 | 92 / 94 | 76 / 83 | 8 / 11 | 67 | 68 | 60 | 0.3 / 0.2 |
| Nicaragua | 28 | 67.9 / 72.7 | 230 | 109 / 108 | 63 / 67 | 56 / 66 | 23 / 23 | 119 | 69 | 66 | 0.3 / 0.1 |
| Panama | 19 | 72.6 / 77.8 | 160 | 114 / 110 | 89 / 91 | 68 / 73 | 8 / 9 | 86 | 58 | 54 | 1.1 / 0.8 |
| **SOUTH AMERICA (16)** | 24 | 68.5 / 75.6 | | | | | | 80 | 75 | 65 | |
| Argentina | 14 | 71.1 / 78.6 | 82 | 120 / 119 | 91 / 93 | 97 / 103 | 3 / 3 | 59 | | | 1.1 / 0.3 |
| Bolivia | 51 | 62.6 / 66.8 | 420 | 116 / 115 | 85 / 84 | 88 / 85 | 7 / 20 | 81 | 53 | 27 | 0.1 / 0.1 |
| Brazil | 25 | 67.3 / 75.1 | 260 | 151 / 143 | | 105 / 115 | 12 / 11 | 90 | 77 | 70 | 0.8 / 0.5 |
| Chile | 8 | 75.1 / 81.2 | 31 | 99 / 97 | 100 / 98 | 91 / 92 | 4 / 4 | 61 | | | 0.4 / 0.2 |
| Colombia | 24 | 69.8 / 75.8 | 130 | 111 / 110 | 66 / 73 | 67 / 74 | 6 / 5 | 77 | 77 | 64 | 1.0 / 0.5 |
| Ecuador | 23 | 71.7 / 77.6 | 130 | 117 / 117 | 74 / 75 | 59 / 60 | 8 / 10 | 84 | 66 | 50 | 0.4 / 0.2 |
| Paraguay | 36 | 69.1 / 73.7 | 170 | 112 / 108 | 68 / 71 | 64 / 66 | 7 / 10 | 64 | 73 | 61 | 0.7 / 0.3 |
| Peru | 31 | 68.0 / 73.2 | 410 | 119 / 118 | 85 / 83 | 93 / 87 | 7 / 18 | 53 | 69 | 50 | 0.7 / 0.4 |
| Uruguay | 13 | 72.1 / 79.4 | 27 | 110 / 108 | 91 / 95 | 99 / 112 | 3 / 2 | 70 | | | 0.4 / 0.2 |
| Venezuela | 17 | 70.4 / 76.3 | 96 | 105 / 103 | 82 / 87 | 65 / 75 | 7 / 7 | 91 | 49 | 38 | 0.9 / 0.5 |
| **NORTHERN AMERICA (17)** | 7 | 75.2 / 80.5 | | | | | | 47 | 76 | 71 | |
| Canada | 5 | 77.8 / 82.7 | 6 | 101 / 102 | 95 / 99 | 106 / 105 | | 14 | 75 | 73 | 0.5 / 0.2 |
| United States of America | 7 | 74.9 / 80.3 | 17 | 98 / 98 | | 94 / 94 | | 50 | 76 | 71 | 1.0 / 0.3 |
| **OCEANIA** | 27 | 72.4 / 76.7 | | | | | | 29 | 62 | 57 | |
| **AUSTRALIA-NEW ZEALAND** | 5 | 77.9 / 82.9 | | | | | | 17 | 76 | 72 | |
| Australia (18) | 5 | 78.0 / 83.1 | 8 | 104 / 104 | 99 / 100 | 156 / 152 | | 15 | 76 | 72 | 0.2 / <0.1 |
| Melanesia (19) | 59 | 57.9 / 59.6 | | | | | | 54 | | | |
| New Zealand | 5 | 77.2 / 81.6 | 7 | 102 / 101 | 91 / 93 | 109 / 116 | | 24 | 75 | 72 | 0.1 / <0.1 |
| Papua New Guinea | 67 | 55.6 / 56.8 | 300 | 77 / 69 | 52 / 50 | 27 / 21 | 37 / 49 | 58 | 26 | 20 | 0.8 / 0.4 |
| **COUNTRIES WITH ECONOMIES IN TRANSITION OF THE FORMER USSR (20)** |||||||||||||
| Armenia | 30 | 68.2 / 74.9 | 55 | 100 / 97 | | 86 / 88 | 0 / 1 | 30 | 61 | 22 | 0.1 / 0.1 |
| Azerbaijan | 74 | 63.5 / 70.8 | 94 | 94 / 91 | | 84 / 81 | 1 / 2 | 31 | 55 | 12 | |
| Belarus | 15 | 62.8 / 74.3 | 35 | 103 / 101 | | 90 / 92 | 0 / 1 | 27 | 50 | 42 | |
| Georgia | 40 | 66.8 / 74.5 | 32 | 91 / 90 | | 80 / 80 | | 33 | 41 | 20 | 0.3 / 0.1 |
| Kazakhstan | 60 | 58.2 / 69.4 | 210 | 102 / 101 | | 92 / 92 | 0 / 1 | 29 | 66 | 53 | 0.2 / 0.1 |
| Kyrgyzstan | 53 | 63.1 / 71.5 | 110 | 102 / 100 | | 92 / 92 | 1 / 2 | 33 | 60 | 49 | 0.1 / <0.1 |
| Republic of Moldova | 24 | 64.9 / 72.1 | 36 | 86 / 86 | | 72 / 75 | 3 / 5 | 31 | 62 | 43 | |
| Russian Federation | 16 | 58.9 / 72.0 | 67 | 118 / 118 | | 91 / 96 | 0 / 1 | 29 | 73 | 53 | 1.5 / 0.8 |
| Tajikistan | 87 | 61.3 / 66.7 | 100 | 114 / 108 | | 94 / 78 | 0 / 1 | 30 | 34 | 27 | |
| Turkmenistan | 77 | 58.6 / 67.1 | 31 | | | | 1 / 2 | 17 | 62 | 53 | |
| Ukraine | 15 | 60.4 / 72.5 | 35 | 93 / 93 | | 97 / 96 | 0 / 1 | 29 | 68 | 38 | 1.8 / 0.9 |
| Uzbekistan | 57 | 63.6 / 70.1 | 24 | 103 / 102 | | 97 / 94 | 0 / 1 | 36 | 68 | 63 | 0.1 / 0.1 |

# Demographic, Social and Economic Indicators

| | Total population (millions) (2005) | Projected population (millions) (2050) | Ave. pop. growth rate (%) (2005) | % urban (2003) | Urban growth rate (2000-2005) | Population/ ha arable & perm. crop land | Total fertility rate (2005) | % births with skilled attendants | GNI per capita PPP$ (2003) | Expenditures/ primary student (% of GDP per capita) | Health expenditures, public (% of GDP) | External population assistance (US$,000) | Under-5 mortality M/F | Per capita energy consumption | Access to improved drinking water sources |
|---|---|---|---|---|---|---|---|---|---|---|---|---|---|---|---|
| **World Total** | 6,464.7 | 9,075.9 | 1.2 | 48 | 2.1 | | 2.60 | 62 | 8,180 | | | (4,686,000) | 83 / 81 | 1,699 | 83 |
| **More developed regions (*)** | 1,211.3 | 1,236.2 | 0.3 | 75 | 0.5 | | 1.57 | | | | | | 10 / 9 | | |
| **Less developed regions (+)** | 5,253.5 | 7,839.7 | 1.4 | 42 | 2.8 | | 2.82 | | | | | | 91 / 89 | | |
| **Least developed countries (‡)** | 759.4 | 1,735.4 | 2.4 | 27 | 4.3 | | 4.86 | 32 | 1,330 | | | | 160 / 149 | 297 | 58 |
| **AFRICA (1)** | 905.9 | 1,937.0 | 2.1 | 39 | 3.6 | | 4.83 | | | | | 1,195,052[21] | 160 / 148 | | |
| **EASTERN AFRICA** | 287.7 | 678.7 | 2.4 | 26 | 4.3 | | 5.41 | | | | | | 159 / 144 | | |
| Burundi | 7.5 | 25.8 | 3.4 | 10 | 6.5 | 4.4 | 6.80 | 25 | 620 | 12.5 | 0.6 | 2,960 | 191 / 169 | | 79 |
| Eritrea | 4.4 | 11.2 | 3.7 | 20 | 5.8 | 6.1 | 5.29 | 28 | 1,110 | 11.8 | 3.2 | 8,183 | 91 / 84 | | 57 |
| Ethiopia | 77.4 | 170.2 | 2.4 | 16 | 4.1 | 5.3 | 5.65 | 6 | 710 | | 2.6 | 68,629 | 172 / 157 | 297 | 22 |
| Kenya | 34.3 | 83.1 | 2.4 | 39 | 4.4 | 4.6 | 4.98 | 41 | 1,020 | | 2.2 | 70,577 | 120 / 105 | 489 | 62 |
| Madagascar | 18.6 | 43.5 | 2.7 | 27 | 3.6 | 3.5 | 5.15 | 46 | 800 | 8.2 | 1.2 | 16,043 | 130 / 119 | | 45 |
| Malawi | 12.9 | 29.5 | 2.2 | 16 | 4.6 | 3.7 | 5.89 | 61 | 600 | | 4.0 | 68,418 | 181 / 171 | | 67 |
| Mauritius (2) | 1.2 | 1.5 | 0.9 | 43 | 1.5 | 1.2 | 1.96 | 99 | 11,260 | 9.0 | 2.2 | 139 | 19 / 15 | | 100 |
| Mozambique | 19.8 | 37.6 | 1.9 | 36 | 5.1 | 3.2 | 5.31 | 48 | 1,070 | | 4.1 | 68,671 | 180 / 164 | 436 | 42 |
| Rwanda | 9.0 | 18.2 | 2.3 | 18 | 11.6 | 5.4 | 5.45 | 31 | 1,290 | 6.9 | 3.1 | 24,016 | 202 / 178 | | 73 |
| Somalia | 8.2 | 21.3 | 3.1 | 35 | 5.7 | 6.2 | 6.24 | 34 | | | 1.2 | 3,240 | 204 / 194 | | 29 |
| Uganda | 28.8 | 126.9 | 3.5 | 12 | 3.9 | 2.7 | 7.10 | 39 | 1,440 | | 2.1 | 61,945 | 140 / 127 | | 56 |
| United Republic of Tanzania | 38.3 | 66.8 | 1.9 | 35 | 4.9 | 5.5 | 4.74 | 36 | 610 | | 2.7 | 64,268 | 170 / 155 | 408 | 73 |
| Zambia | 11.7 | 22.8 | 1.7 | 36 | 1.9 | 1.4 | 5.42 | 43 | 850 | 7.1 | 3.1 | 80,514 | 175 / 159 | 639 | 55 |
| Zimbabwe | 13.0 | 15.8 | 0.6 | 35 | 1.8 | 2.4 | 3.37 | 73 | | | 16.2 | 4.4 | 44,253 | 122 / 108 | 751 | 83 |
| **MIDDLE AFRICA (3)** | 109.6 | 303.3 | 2.7 | 37 | 4.1 | | 6.18 | | | | | | 209 / 187 | | |
| Angola | 15.9 | 43.5 | 2.8 | 36 | 5.4 | 2.8 | 6.59 | 45 | 1,890 | | 2.1 | 18,807 | 252 / 223 | 672 | 50 |
| Cameroon | 16.3 | 26.9 | 1.7 | 51 | 3.4 | 1.1 | 4.36 | 60 | 1,980 | 8.5 | 1.2 | 8,391 | 167 / 152 | 417 | 63 |
| Central African Republic | 4.0 | 6.7 | 1.4 | 43 | 2.5 | 1.3 | 4.77 | 44 | 1,080 | | 1.6 | 5,371 | 188 / 155 | | 75 |
| Chad | 9.7 | 31.5 | 3.0 | 25 | 4.6 | 1.7 | 6.65 | 16 | 1,100 | 9.7 | 2.7 | 4,202 | 210 / 187 | | 34 |
| Congo, Democratic Republic of the (4) | 57.5 | 177.3 | 2.9 | 32 | 4.4 | 4.1 | 6.70 | 61 | 640 | | 1.1 | 22,886 | 215 / 193 | 299 | 46 |
| Congo, Republic of | 4.0 | 13.7 | 3.0 | 54 | 3.4 | 5.9 | 6.29 | | 710 | 8.1 | 1.5 | 2,184 | 116 / 93 | 252 | 46 |
| Gabon | 1.4 | 2.3 | 1.6 | 84 | 2.7 | 0.9 | 3.78 | 86 | 5,700 | 4.7 | 1.8 | 758 | 96 / 87 | 1,209 | 87 |
| **NORTHERN AFRICA (5)** | 190.9 | 311.9 | 1.7 | 50 | 2.7 | | 3.04 | | | | | 63,743[22] | 61 / 51 | | |
| Algeria | 32.9 | 49.5 | 1.5 | 59 | 2.6 | 0.9 | 2.46 | 92 | 5,940 | 11.1 | 3.2 | 1,379 | 38 / 35 | 985 | 87 |
| Egypt | 74.0 | 125.9 | 1.9 | 42 | 2.1 | 7.4 | 3.14 | 69 | 3,940 | | 1.8 | 33,417 | 43 / 35 | 789 | 98 |
| Libyan Arab Jamahiriya | 5.9 | 9.6 | 1.9 | 86 | 2.3 | 0.1 | 2.88 | 94 | | 3.0 | 1.6 | | 20 / 20 | 3,433 | 72 |
| Morocco | 31.5 | 46.4 | 1.5 | 58 | 2.8 | 1.1 | 2.67 | 40 | 3,950 | 18.9 | 1.5 | 9,123 | 49 / 34 | 363 | 80 |
| Sudan | 36.2 | 66.7 | 2.0 | 39 | 4.6 | 1.2 | 4.20 | 86 | 1,880 | | 1.0 | 11,875 | 120 / 106 | 483 | 69 |
| Tunisia | 10.1 | 12.9 | 1.1 | 64 | 1.6 | 0.5 | 1.93 | 90 | 6,840 | 15.8 | 2.9 | 1,474 | 25 / 22 | 846 | 82 |
| **SOUTHERN AFRICA** | 54.1 | 56.0 | 0.4 | 54 | 1.5 | | 2.81 | | | | | | 82 / 74 | | |
| Botswana | 1.8 | 1.7 | -0.1 | 52 | 1.8 | 2.1 | 3.06 | 94 | 7,960 | 6.1 | 3.7 | 21,193 | 107 / 96 | | 95 |
| Lesotho | 1.8 | 1.6 | -0.1 | 18 | 0.9 | 2.1 | 3.46 | 60 | 3,120 | 23.8 | 5.3 | 4,802 | 125 / 111 | | 76 |
| Namibia | 2.0 | 3.1 | 1.2 | 32 | 3.0 | 1.1 | 3.71 | 78 | 6,620 | 21.0 | 4.7 | 12,092 | 78 / 71 | 599 | 80 |
| South Africa | 47.4 | 48.7 | 0.5 | 57 | 1.4 | 0.4 | 2.72 | 84 | 10,270 | 14.3 | 3.5 | 96,542 | 77 / 69 | 2,502 | 87 |
| Swaziland | 1.0 | 1.0 | -0.1 | 24 | 1.4 | 1.8 | 3.72 | 70 | 4,850 | 11.2 | 3.6 | 7,069 | 148 / 130 | | 52 |
| **WESTERN AFRICA (6)** | 263.6 | 587.0 | 2.3 | 42 | 4.2 | | 5.59 | | | | | | 192 / 184 | | |
| Benin | 8.4 | 22.1 | 3.1 | 45 | 4.4 | 1.2 | 5.64 | 66 | 1,110 | 9.7 | 2.1 | 14,760 | 156 / 152 | 341 | 68 |
| Burkina Faso | 13.2 | 39.1 | 3.0 | 18 | 5.0 | 2.6 | 6.51 | 31 | 1,180 | | 2.0 | 15,072 | 196 / 185 | | 51 |
| Côte d'Ivoire | 18.2 | 34.0 | 1.7 | 45 | 2.6 | 1.1 | 4.76 | 63 | 1,390 | 14.6 | 1.4 | 20,375 | 196 / 177 | 397 | 84 |
| Gambia | 1.5 | 3.1 | 2.6 | 26 | 2.6 | 4.3 | 4.46 | 55 | 1,820 | 11.9 | 3.3 | 1,634 | 126 / 114 | | 82 |

# Demographic, Social and Economic Indicators

| | Total population (millions) (2005) | Projected population (millions) (2050) | Ave. pop. growth rate (%) (2005) | % urban (2003) | Urban growth rate (2000-2005) | Population/ ha arable & perm. crop land | Total fertility rate (2005) | % births with skilled attendants | GNI per capita PPP$ (2003) | Expenditures/ primary student (% of GDP per capita) | Health expenditures, public (% of GDP) | External population assistance (US$,000) | Under-5 mortality M/F | Per capita energy consumption | Access to improved drinking water sources |
|---|---|---|---|---|---|---|---|---|---|---|---|---|---|---|---|
| Ghana | 22.1 | 40.6 | 2.0 | 45 | 3.2 | 1.8 | 4.11 | 44 | 2,190 | | 2.3 | 34,123 | 98 / 94 | 411 | 79 |
| Guinea | 9.4 | 23.0 | 2.2 | 35 | 3.8 | 4.5 | 5.71 | 35 | 2,100 | 9.2 | 0.9 | 12,807 | 155 / 158 | | 51 |
| Guinea-Bissau | 1.6 | 5.3 | 3.0 | 34 | 5.4 | 2.2 | 7.08 | 35 | 660 | | 3.0 | 1,506 | 214 / 191 | | 59 |
| Liberia | 3.3 | 10.7 | 2.1 | 47 | 5.3 | 3.6 | 6.79 | 51 | | | 1.4 | 2,675 | 225 / 207 | | 62 |
| Mali | 13.5 | 42.0 | 2.9 | 32 | 5.2 | 2.1 | 6.75 | 41 | 960 | 15.2 | 2.3 | 25,070 | 216 / 210 | | 48 |
| Mauritania | 3.1 | 7.5 | 2.9 | 62 | 5.1 | 2.9 | 5.62 | 57 | 2,010 | 14.0 | 2.9 | 3,978 | 155 / 142 | | 56 |
| Niger | 14.0 | 50.2 | 3.3 | 22 | 6.1 | 2.2 | 7.71 | 16 | 820 | 15.5 | 2.0 | 6,175 | 253 / 258 | | 46 |
| Nigeria | 131.5 | 258.1 | 2.2 | 47 | 4.4 | 1.2 | 5.58 | 35 | 900 | | 1.2 | 81,796 | 199 / 191 | 718 | 60 |
| Senegal | 11.7 | 23.1 | 2.3 | 50 | 3.9 | 2.9 | 4.75 | 58 | 1,660 | 13.6 | 2.3 | 26,130 | 130 / 124 | 319 | 72 |
| Sierra Leone | 5.5 | 13.8 | 3.1 | 39 | 5.6 | 4.9 | 6.49 | 42 | 530 | 16.8 | 1.7 | 6,803 | 297 / 271 | | 57 |
| Togo | 6.1 | 13.5 | 2.6 | 35 | 4.0 | 1.1 | 5.08 | 49 | 1,500 | 5.7 | 5.1 | 6,365 | 141 / 124 | 324 | 51 |
| **ASIA** | **3,905.4** | **5,217.2** | **1.2** | **39** | **2.7** | | **2.41** | | | | | **609,901** | **68 / 71** | | |
| **EASTERN ASIA (7)** | **1,524.4** | **1,586.7** | **0.6** | **43** | **2.6** | | **1.68** | | | | | | **31 / 41** | | |
| China | 1,315.8 | 1,392.3 | 0.6 | 39 | 3.2 | 5.5 | 1.72 | 97 | 4,990 | | 2.0 | 32,141 | 33 / 44 | 960 | 77 |
| Democratic People's Republic of Korea | 22.5 | 24.2 | 0.5 | 61 | 1.0 | 2.4 | 1.97 | 97 | | | 3.5 | 2,550 | 59 / 52 | 869 | 100 |
| Hong Kong SAR, China (8) | 7.0 | 9.2 | 1.1 | 100 | 1.1 | | 0.95 | | 28,810 | 13.5 | | | 5 / 4 | 2,413 | |
| Japan | 128.1 | 112.2 | 0.1 | 65 | 0.3 | 0.9 | 1.35 | 100 | 28,620 | 21.5 | 6.5 | (128,068) [23] | 5 / 4 | 4,058 | 100 |
| Mongolia | 2.6 | 3.6 | 1.2 | 57 | 1.4 | 0.5 | 2.33 | 99 | 1,800 | 38.3 | 4.6 | 3,881 | 81 / 77 | | 62 |
| Republic of Korea | 47.8 | 44.6 | 0.4 | 80 | 0.9 | 2.0 | 1.22 | 100 | 17,930 | 16.6 | 2.6 | | 5 / 5 | 4,272 | 92 |
| **SOUTH-EASTERN ASIA** | **555.8** | **752.3** | **1.3** | **42** | **3.3** | | **2.42** | | | | | | **54 / 43** | | |
| Cambodia | 14.1 | 26.0 | 2.0 | 19 | 5.5 | 2.5 | 3.93 | 32 | 2,060 | 5.9 | 2.1 | 36,969 | 138 / 127 | | 34 |
| Indonesia | 222.8 | 284.6 | 1.2 | 46 | 3.9 | 2.8 | 2.28 | 68 | 3,210 | 3.7 | 1.2 | 48,084 | 53 / 42 | 737 | 78 |
| Lao People's Democratic Republic | 5.9 | 11.6 | 2.2 | 21 | 4.6 | 4.2 | 4.55 | 19 | 1,730 | 7.9 | 1.5 | 3,351 | 136 / 130 | | 43 |
| Malaysia | 25.3 | 38.9 | 1.8 | 64 | 3.0 | 0.5 | 2.78 | 97 | 8,940 | 17.0 | 2.0 | 700 | 14 / 11 | 2,129 | 95 |
| Myanmar | 50.5 | 63.7 | 1.0 | 29 | 3.1 | 3.2 | 2.27 | 56 | | | 0.4 | 14,340 | 114 / 96 | 258 | 80 |
| Philippines | 83.1 | 127.1 | 1.7 | 61 | 3.1 | 2.8 | 3.03 | 60 | 4,640 | 11.6 | 1.1 | 36,120 | 36 / 25 | 525 | 85 |
| Singapore | 4.3 | 5.2 | 1.3 | 100 | 1.7 | 3.0 | 1.33 | 100 | 24,180 | | 1.3 | 1 | 4 / 4 | 6,078 | |
| Thailand | 64.2 | 74.6 | 0.8 | 32 | 1.9 | 1.5 | 1.90 | 99 | 7,450 | 16.5 | 3.1 | 16,109 | 28 / 18 | 1,353 | 85 |
| Viet Nam | 84.2 | 116.7 | 1.3 | 26 | 3.2 | 6.0 | 2.23 | 85 | 2,490 | | 1.5 | 21,441 | 40 / 30 | 530 | 73 |
| **SOUTH CENTRAL ASIA** | **1,610.9** | **2,495.0** | **1.6** | **30** | **2.5** | | **3.04** | | | | | | **92 / 97** | | |
| Afghanistan | 29.9 | 97.3 | 4.1 | 23 | 6.0 | 1.9 | 7.27 | 14 | | | 3.1 | 21,652 | 242 / 247 | | 13 |
| Bangladesh | 141.8 | 242.9 | 1.8 | 24 | 3.5 | 9.2 | 3.10 | 14 | 1,870 | 8.9 | 0.8 | 85,760 | 72 / 72 | 155 | 75 |
| Bhutan | 2.2 | 4.4 | 2.2 | 9 | 6.3 | 12.4 | 4.12 | 24 | | | 4.1 | 870 | 78 / 75 | | 62 |
| India | 1,103.4 | 1,592.7 | 1.5 | 28 | 2.3 | 3.3 | 2.92 | 43 | 2,880 | 12.4 | 1.3 | 99,471 | 90 / 95 | 513 | 86 |
| Iran (Islamic Republic of) | 69.5 | 101.9 | 1.1 | 67 | 2.3 | 1.0 | 2.08 | 90 | 7,190 | 11.3 | 2.9 | 2,472 | 36 / 35 | 2,044 | 93 |
| Nepal | 27.1 | 51.2 | 2.0 | 15 | 5.2 | 6.9 | 3.50 | 11 | 1,420 | 12.0 | 1.4 | 26,421 | 78 / 83 | 353 | 84 |
| Pakistan | 157.9 | 304.7 | 2.1 | 34 | 3.4 | 3.4 | 4.00 | 23 | 2,060 | | 1.1 | 57,075 | 102 / 112 | 454 | 90 |
| Sri Lanka | 20.7 | 23.6 | 0.8 | 21 | 0.7 | 4.5 | 1.92 | 97 | 3,730 | | 1.8 | 15,862 | 22 / 14 | 430 | 78 |
| **WESTERN ASIA** | **214.3** | **383.2** | **2.0** | **65** | **2.4** | | **3.23** | | | | | **67,968** [22] | **60 / 52** | | |
| Iraq | 28.8 | 63.7 | 2.6 | 67 | 2.4 | 0.4 | 4.54 | 72 | | | 0.3 | 14,330 | 119 / 110 | 1,199 | 81 |
| Israel | 6.7 | 10.4 | 1.8 | 92 | 2.1 | 0.4 | 2.76 | 99 | 19,200 | 21.7 | 6.0 | 3 | 6 / 6 | 3,191 | 100 |
| Jordan | 5.7 | 10.2 | 2.4 | 79 | 2.8 | 1.4 | 3.33 | 100 | 4,290 | 15.0 | 4.3 | 27,202 | 25 / 23 | 1,036 | 91 |
| Kuwait | 2.7 | 5.3 | 3.1 | 96 | 3.5 | 1.7 | 2.32 | 98 | | | 16.1 | 2.9 | 12 / 12 | 9,503 | |
| Lebanon | 3.6 | 4.7 | 1.0 | 88 | 1.9 | 0.4 | 2.26 | 89 | 4,840 | | 5.4 | 3.5 | 1,261 | 29 / 19 | 1,209 | 100 |
| Occupied Palestinian Territory | 3.7 | 10.1 | 3.2 | 71 | 4.1 | 1.6 | 5.28 | 97 | | | | 12,613 | 25 / 20 | | 94 |
| Oman | 2.6 | 5.0 | 1.6 | 78 | 3.6 | 12.0 | 3.50 | 95 | | 17.7 | 2.8 | 162 | 17 / 16 | 4,265 | 79 |

## Demographic, Social and Economic Indicators

|  | Total population (millions) (2005) | Projected population (millions) (2050) | Ave. pop. growth rate (%) (2005) | % urban (2003) | Urban growth rate (2000-2005) | Population/ ha arable & perm. crop land | Total fertility rate (2005) | % births with skilled attendants | GNI per capita PPP$ (2003) | Expenditures/ primary student (% of GDP per capita) | Health expenditures, public (% of GDP) | External population assistance (US$,000) | Under-5 mortality M/F | Per capita energy consumption | Access to improved drinking water sources |
|---|---|---|---|---|---|---|---|---|---|---|---|---|---|---|---|
| Saudi Arabia | 24.6 | 49.5 | 2.5 | 88 | 3.4 | 0.5 | 3.84 | 91 | | 32.6 | 3.3 | | 28 / 20 | 5,775 | |
| Syrian Arab Republic | 19.0 | 35.9 | 2.4 | 50 | 2.5 | 0.9 | 3.28 | 76 | 3,430 | 13.8 | 2.3 | 3,550 | 22 / 17 | 1,063 | 79 |
| Turkey (10) | 73.2 | 101.2 | 1.3 | 66 | 2.2 | 0.7 | 2.39 | 81 | 6,690 | 11.6 | 4.3 | 1,008 | 51 / 40 | 1,083 | 93 |
| United Arab Emirates | 4.5 | 9.1 | 4.4 | 85 | 2.1 | 0.5 | 2.45 | 96 | | | 6.9 | 2.3 | 4 | 10 / 9 | 9,609 | |
| Yemen | 21.0 | 59.5 | 3.1 | 26 | 4.8 | 5.6 | 5.93 | 22 | 820 | | 1.0 | 7,816 | 91 / 83 | 221 | 69 |
| **ARAB STATES (11)** | **321.1** | **598.5** | **2.1** | **55** | **2.9** | **1.5** | **3.59** | **70** | **2,768** | **21.2** | **2.7** | **135,890** | **61 / 54** | **1,244** | **74** |
| **EUROPE** | **728.4** | **653.3** | **0.0** | **73** | **0.1** | | **1.42** | | | | | | **12 / 10** | | |
| **EASTERN EUROPE** | **297.3** | **223.5** | **-0.5** | **68** | **-0.4** | | **1.29** | | | | | **114,546** [22, 24] | **21 / 16** | | |
| Bulgaria | 7.7 | 5.1 | -0.7 | 70 | -0.3 | 0.1 | 1.23 | | 7,610 | 16.9 | 4.4 | 1,646 | 17 / 14 | 2,417 | 100 |
| Czech Republic | 10.2 | 8.5 | -0.1 | 74 | 0.0 | 0.2 | 1.19 | 99 | 15,650 | 11.8 | 6.4 | 38 | 6 / 6 | 4,090 | |
| Hungary | 10.1 | 8.3 | -0.3 | 65 | 0.1 | 0.2 | 1.29 | | 13,780 | 20.3 | 5.5 | 100 | 11 / 9 | 2,505 | 99 |
| Poland | 38.5 | 31.9 | -0.1 | 62 | 0.0 | 0.5 | 1.25 | 99 | 11,450 | 34.4 | 4.4 | 343 | 11 / 9 | 2,333 | |
| Romania | 21.7 | 16.8 | -0.4 | 55 | -0.2 | 0.3 | 1.26 | 98 | 7,140 | | 4.2 | 10,501 | 24 / 18 | 1,696 | 57 |
| Slovakia | 5.4 | 4.6 | 0.0 | 57 | 0.5 | 0.3 | 1.19 | | 13,420 | 11.4 | 5.3 | 47 | 10 / 9 | 3,448 | 100 |
| **NORTHERN EUROPE (12)** | **95.8** | **105.6** | **0.3** | **83** | **0.4** | | **1.66** | | | | | | **7 / 6** | | |
| Denmark | 5.4 | 5.9 | 0.3 | 85 | 0.3 | 0.1 | 1.76 | 100 | 31,210 | 24.4 | 7.3 | (59,527) | 6 / 6 | 3,675 | 100 |
| Estonia | 1.3 | 1.1 | -0.4 | 69 | -1.0 | 0.2 | 1.40 | | 12,480 | 20.1 | 3.9 | 1,077 | 14 / 9 | 3,324 | |
| Finland | 5.2 | 5.3 | 0.2 | 61 | 0.1 | 0.1 | 1.72 | 100 | 27,100 | 17.8 | 5.5 | (23,697) | 5 / 4 | 6,852 | 100 |
| Ireland | 4.1 | 5.8 | 1.5 | 60 | 1.5 | 0.3 | 1.94 | 100 | 30,450 | 12.0 | 5.5 | (26,786) | 7 / 7 | 3,894 | |
| Latvia | 2.3 | 1.7 | -0.5 | 66 | -1.2 | 0.1 | 1.27 | 100 | 10,130 | 22.0 | 3.3 | 113 | 14 / 12 | 1,825 | |
| Lithuania | 3.4 | 2.6 | -0.4 | 67 | -0.7 | 0.2 | 1.27 | | 11,090 | | 4.3 | 163 | 13 / 9 | 2,476 | |
| Norway | 4.6 | 5.4 | 0.5 | 79 | 1.6 | 0.2 | 1.79 | 100 | 37,300 | 27.1 | 8.0 | (91,648) | 5 / 4 | 5,843 | 100 |
| Sweden | 9.0 | 10.1 | 0.3 | 83 | 0.1 | 0.1 | 1.68 | 100 | 26,620 | 22.5 | 7.8 | (80,029) | 4 / 4 | 5,718 | 100 |
| United Kingdom | 59.7 | 67.1 | 0.3 | 89 | 0.4 | 0.2 | 1.66 | 99 | 27,650 | 15.1 | 6.4 | (589,650) | 7 / 6 | 3,824 | |
| **SOUTHERN EUROPE (13)** | **149.4** | **138.7** | **0.3** | **66** | **0.3** | | **1.37** | | | | | | **9 / 8** | | |
| Albania | 3.1 | 3.5 | 0.5 | 44 | 2.1 | 2.1 | 2.23 | 94 | 4,700 | | 2.4 | 8,261 | 34 / 30 | 617 | 97 |
| Bosnia and Herzegovina | 3.9 | 3.2 | 0.2 | 44 | 2.2 | 0.2 | 1.31 | 100 | 6,320 | | 4.6 | 3,307 | 16 / 13 | 1,052 | 98 |
| Croatia | 4.6 | 3.7 | 0.1 | 59 | 0.5 | 0.2 | 1.35 | 100 | 10,710 | 48.7 | 5.9 | 1,312 | 8 / 7 | 1,852 | |
| Greece | 11.1 | 10.7 | 0.2 | 61 | 0.6 | 0.4 | 1.25 | | 19,920 | 14.5 | 5.0 | (9,293) | 8 / 7 | 2,637 | |
| Italy | 58.1 | 50.9 | 0.1 | 67 | 0.0 | 0.3 | 1.33 | | 26,760 | 24.7 | 6.4 | (27,068) | 7 / 6 | 2,994 | |
| Macedonia (Former Yugoslav Republic of) | 2.0 | 1.9 | 0.2 | 60 | 0.6 | 0.4 | 1.49 | 98 | 6,720 | | 5.8 | 1,074 | 18 / 16 | | |
| Portugal | 10.5 | 10.7 | 0.5 | 55 | 1.1 | 0.5 | 1.47 | 100 | 17,980 | 23.3 | 6.6 | (1,119) | 7 / 7 | 2,546 | |
| Serbia and Montenegro | 10.5 | 9.4 | -0.1 | 52 | 0.2 | 0.5 | 1.62 | 99 | | 38.3 | 5.1 | 1,401 | 16 / 13 | 1,981 | 93 |
| Slovenia | 2.0 | 1.6 | 0.0 | 51 | -0.1 | 0.2 | 1.21 | 100 | 19,240 | | 6.2 | 2 | 7 / 7 | 3,486 | |
| Spain | 43.1 | 42.5 | 0.8 | 77 | 0.3 | 0.1 | 1.31 | | 22,020 | 18.9 | 5.4 | (29,949) | 6 / 5 | 3,215 | |
| **WESTERN EUROPE (14)** | **185.9** | **185.5** | **0.2** | **81** | **0.5** | | **1.56** | | | | | | **6 / 5** | | |
| Austria | 8.2 | 8.1 | 0.2 | 66 | 0.0 | 0.3 | 1.40 | 100 | 29,610 | 23.8 | 5.4 | (2,727) | 6 / 5 | 3,774 | 100 |
| Belgium | 10.4 | 10.3 | 0.2 | 97 | 0.2 | 0.2 | 1.66 | 100 | 28,930 | 18.7 | 6.5 | (26,400) | 6 / 6 | 5,505 | |
| France | 60.5 | 63.1 | 0.4 | 76 | 0.7 | 0.1 | 1.86 | 99 | 27,460 | 17.8 | 7.4 | (56,559) | 6 / 5 | 4,470 | |
| Germany | 82.7 | 78.8 | 0.0 | 88 | 0.3 | 0.2 | 1.33 | 100 | 27,460 | 16.9 | 8.6 | (132,088) [25] | 5 / 5 | 4,198 | 100 |
| Netherlands | 16.3 | 17.1 | 0.4 | 66 | 1.3 | 0.5 | 1.72 | 100 | 28,600 | 16.6 | 5.8 | (275,434) | 7 / 6 | 4,827 | 100 |
| Switzerland | 7.3 | 7.3 | 0.2 | 68 | -0.1 | 1.0 | 1.41 | | 32,030 | 23.2 | 6.5 | (31,522) | 6 / 5 | 3,723 | 100 |
| **LATIN AMERICA & CARIBBEAN** | **561.3** | **782.9** | **1.4** | **77** | **1.9** | | **2.47** | | | | | **221,948** | **36 / 29** | | |
| **CARIBBEAN (15)** | **39.1** | **46.4** | **0.8** | **64** | **1.3** | | **2.42** | | | | | | **57 / 48** | | |
| Cuba | 11.3 | 9.7 | 0.2 | 76 | 0.5 | 0.5 | 1.62 | 100 | | 32.3 | 6.5 | 5,988 | 7 / 6 | 1,262 | 91 |
| Dominican Republic | 8.9 | 12.7 | 1.4 | 59 | 2.1 | 0.9 | 2.64 | 99 | 6,210 | 8.9 | 2.2 | 8,524 | 52 / 42 | 948 | 93 |

THE STATE OF WORLD POPULATION 2005   113

# Demographic, Social and Economic Indicators

| | Total population (millions) (2005) | Projected population (millions) (2050) | Ave. pop. growth rate (%) (2005) | % urban (2003) | Urban growth rate (2000-2005) | Population/ ha arable & perm. crop land | Total fertility rate (2005) | % births with skilled attendants | GNI per capita PPP$ (2003) | Expenditures/ primary student (% of GDP per capita) | Health expenditures, public (% of GDP) | External population assistance (US$,000) | Under-5 mortality M/F | Per capita energy consumption | Access to improved drinking water sources |
|---|---|---|---|---|---|---|---|---|---|---|---|---|---|---|---|
| Haiti | 8.5 | 13.0 | 1.4 | 38 | 3.0 | 4.6 | 3.79 | 24 | 1,630 | | 3.0 | 39,388 | 113 / 98 | 251 | 71 |
| Jamaica | 2.7 | 2.6 | 0.4 | 52 | 1.0 | 1.8 | 2.38 | 95 | 3,790 | 15.1 | 3.4 | 4,677 | 21 / 19 | 1,493 | 93 |
| Puerto Rico | 4.0 | 4.4 | 0.6 | 97 | 1.1 | 1.2 | 1.89 | | | | | 36 | 13 / 10 | | |
| Trinidad and Tobago | 1.3 | 1.2 | 0.3 | 75 | 0.9 | 0.9 | 1.61 | 96 | 9,450 | 16.1 | 1.4 | 849 | 21 / 16 | 7,121 | 91 |
| **CENTRAL AMERICA** | 147.0 | 209.6 | 1.5 | 69 | 2.0 | | 2.55 | | | | | | 31 / 25 | | |
| Costa Rica | 4.3 | 6.4 | 1.7 | 61 | 2.8 | 1.6 | 2.19 | 98 | 9,040 | 16.2 | 6.1 | 660 | 13 / 10 | 904 | 97 |
| El Salvador | 6.9 | 10.8 | 1.7 | 60 | 2.1 | 2.2 | 2.78 | 69 | 4,890 | 10.0 | 3.6 | 7,626 | 35 / 29 | 670 | 82 |
| Guatemala | 12.6 | 25.6 | 2.4 | 46 | 3.4 | 3.1 | 4.38 | 41 | 4,060 | 6.7 | 2.3 | 19,757 | 53 / 41 | 616 | 95 |
| Honduras | 7.2 | 12.8 | 2.2 | 46 | 3.3 | 1.6 | 3.52 | 56 | 2,580 | | 3.2 | 11,635 | 51 / 41 | 504 | 90 |
| Mexico | 107.0 | 139.0 | 1.2 | 76 | 1.8 | 0.8 | 2.27 | 86 | 8,950 | 13.8 | 2.7 | 15,646 | 25 / 20 | 1,560 | 91 |
| Nicaragua | 5.5 | 9.4 | 2.0 | 57 | 3.1 | 0.5 | 3.12 | 67 | 2,400 | 8.9 | 3.9 | 15,823 | 42 / 33 | 544 | 81 |
| Panama | 3.2 | 5.1 | 1.7 | 57 | 2.4 | 1.0 | 2.63 | 90 | 6,310 | 10.4 | 6.4 | 594 | 29 / 22 | 1,028 | 91 |
| **SOUTH AMERICA (16)** | 375.2 | 526.9 | 1.4 | 81 | 2.0 | | 2.44 | | | | | | 36 / 28 | | |
| Argentina | 38.7 | 51.4 | 1.0 | 90 | 1.4 | 0.1 | 2.30 | 99 | 10,920 | 12.4 | 4.5 | 3,478 | 18 / 14 | 1,543 | |
| Bolivia | 9.2 | 14.9 | 1.9 | 63 | 2.7 | 1.2 | 3.73 | 65 | 2,450 | 15.5 | 4.2 | 11,248 | 71 / 62 | 499 | 85 |
| Brazil | 186.4 | 253.1 | 1.3 | 83 | 2.0 | 0.4 | 2.30 | 88 | 7,480 | 11.3 | 3.6 | 11,489 | 37 / 28 | 1,093 | 89 |
| Chile | 16.3 | 20.7 | 1.1 | 87 | 1.6 | 1.0 | 1.97 | 100 | 9,810 | 15.8 | 2.6 | 4,162 | 10 / 8 | 1,585 | 95 |
| Colombia | 45.6 | 65.7 | 1.5 | 77 | 2.2 | 2.2 | 2.54 | 86 | 6,520 | 15.9 | 6.7 | 1,692 | 33 / 28 | 625 | 92 |
| Ecuador | 13.2 | 19.2 | 1.4 | 62 | 2.3 | 1.1 | 2.70 | 69 | 3,440 | 3.0 | 1.7 | 3,492 | 32 / 24 | 706 | 86 |
| Paraguay | 6.2 | 12.1 | 2.3 | 57 | 3.5 | 0.7 | 3.71 | 71 | 4,740 | 13.0 | 3.2 | 4,167 | 48 / 38 | 709 | 83 |
| Peru | 28.0 | 42.6 | 1.5 | 74 | 2.0 | 1.8 | 2.76 | 59 | 5,090 | 7.0 | 2.2 | 18,839 | 54 / 44 | 450 | 81 |
| Uruguay | 3.5 | 4.0 | 0.7 | 93 | 0.9 | 0.3 | 2.26 | 100 | 7,980 | 11.0 | 2.9 | 288 | 17 / 12 | 747 | 98 |
| Venezuela | 26.7 | 42.0 | 1.7 | 88 | 2.1 | 0.7 | 2.64 | 94 | 4,740 | | 2.3 | 1,312 | 30 / 26 | 2,141 | 83 |
| **NORTHERN AMERICA (17)** | 330.6 | 438.0 | 0.9 | 80 | 1.4 | | 1.98 | | | | | | 8 / 8 | | |
| Canada | 32.3 | 42.8 | 0.9 | 80 | 1.2 | 0.0 | 1.49 | 98 | 29,740 | | 6.7 | (56,626) | 6 / 6 | 7,973 | 100 |
| United States of America | 298.2 | 395.0 | 0.9 | 80 | 1.4 | 0.0 | 2.04 | 99 | 37,500 | 21.2 | 6.6 | (1,807,643) | 8 / 8 | 7,943 | 100 |
| **OCEANIA** | **33.1** | **47.6** | **1.2** | **73** | **1.4** | | **2.27** | | | | | | **36 / 38** | | |
| **AUSTRALIA-NEW ZEALAND** | 24.2 | 32.7 | 1.0 | 91 | 1.3 | | 1.78 | | | | | | 6 / 6 | | |
| Australia (18) | 20.2 | 27.9 | 1.1 | 92 | 1.4 | 0.0 | 1.75 | 100 | 28,290 | 16.6 | 6.5 | (38,966) | 6 / 6 | 5,732 | 100 |
| Melanesia (19) | 7.7 | 13.2 | 1.9 | 20 | 2.5 | | 3.69 | | | | | | 78 / 85 | | |
| New Zealand | 4.0 | 4.8 | 0.9 | 86 | 0.8 | 0.1 | 1.96 | 100 | 21,120 | 18.9 | 6.6 | (5,917) | 7 / 6 | 4,573 | |
| Papua New Guinea | 5.9 | 10.6 | 2.0 | 13 | 2.3 | 4.9 | 3.85 | 53 | 2,240 | 12.4 | 3.8 | 11,287 | 88 / 98 | | 39 |
| **COUNTRIES WITH ECONOMIES IN TRANSITION OF THE FORMER USSR (20)** | | | | | | | | | | | | | | | |
| Armenia | 3.0 | 2.5 | -0.3 | 64 | -0.8 | 0.7 | 1.34 | 97 | 3,770 | 9.6 | 1.3 | 2,445 | 37 / 32 | 632 | 92 |
| Azerbaijan | 8.4 | 9.6 | 0.7 | 50 | 0.6 | 1.1 | 1.85 | 84 | 3,380 | 7.3 | 0.8 | 994 | 92 / 84 | 1,435 | 77 |
| Belarus | 9.8 | 7.0 | -0.6 | 71 | 0.1 | 0.2 | 1.23 | 100 | 6,010 | | 4.7 | 144 | 20 / 14 | 2,496 | 100 |
| Georgia | 4.5 | 3.0 | -0.9 | 52 | -1.4 | 0.9 | 1.44 | 96 | 2,540 | | 1.0 | 3,554 | 46 / 38 | 494 | 76 |
| Kazakhstan | 14.8 | 13.1 | -0.2 | 56 | -0.3 | 0.1 | 1.90 | 99 | 6,170 | 8.1 | 1.9 | 5,265 | 89 / 61 | 3,123 | 86 |
| Kyrgyzstan | 5.3 | 6.7 | 1.2 | 34 | 1.0 | 0.9 | 2.59 | 98 | 1,660 | 6.1 | 2.2 | 3,395 | 70 / 58 | 507 | 76 |
| Republic of Moldova | 4.2 | 3.3 | -0.3 | 46 | 0.1 | 0.4 | 1.22 | 99 | 1,750 | 18.1 | 4.1 | 7,187 | 32 / 27 | 703 | 92 |
| Russian Federation | 143.2 | 111.8 | -0.5 | 73 | -0.6 | 0.1 | 1.37 | 99 | 8,920 | | 3.5 | 16,969 | 24 / 19 | 4,288 | 96 |
| Tajikistan | 6.5 | 10.4 | 1.3 | 25 | -0.4 | 1.9 | 3.58 | 71 | 1,040 | 6.8 | 0.9 | 3,253 | 119 / 107 | 518 | 58 |
| Turkmenistan | 4.8 | 6.8 | 1.4 | 45 | 2.0 | 0.8 | 2.63 | 97 | 5,840 | | 3.0 | 1,322 | 107 / 87 | 3,465 | 71 |
| Ukraine | 46.5 | 26.4 | -1.1 | 67 | -0.7 | 0.2 | 1.13 | 100 | 5,410 | 11.9 | 3.3 | 14,181 | 20 / 15 | 2,684 | 98 |
| Uzbekistan | 26.6 | 38.7 | 1.4 | 37 | 1.0 | 1.4 | 2.61 | 96 | 1,720 | | 2.5 | 8,388 | 74 / 62 | 2,047 | 89 |

## Selected Indicators for Less Populous Countries/Territories

| Monitoring ICPD Goals – Selected Indicators | Infant mortality Total per 1,000 live births | Life expectancy M/F | Maternal mortality ratio | Primary enrolment (gross) M/F | Secondary enrolment (gross) M/F | Births per 1,000 women aged 15-19 | Contraceptive Prevalence Any method | Contraceptive Prevalence Modern methods | HIV prevalence rate (%) (15-49) M/F |
|---|---|---|---|---|---|---|---|---|---|
| Bahamas | 13 | 67.6 / 74.0 | 60 | 92 / 93 | 90 / 93 | 60 | 62 | 60 | 3.0 / 3.0 |
| Bahrain | 13 | 73.4 / 76.2 | 28 | 97 / 97 | 93 / 99 | 18 | 62 | 31 | 0.1 / 0.2 |
| Barbados | 10 | 72.1 / 78.8 | 95 | 109 / 108 | 105 / 107 | 43 | 55 | 53 | 2.0 / 1.0 |
| Belize | 30 | 69.5 / 74.3 | 140 | 123 / 121 | 76 / 80 | 82 | 47 | 42 | 3.0 / 1.8 |
| Brunei Darussalam | 6 | 74.6 / 79.3 | 37 | 106 / 106 | 88 / 92 | 29 | | | <0.1 / <0.1 |
| Cape Verde | 27 | 67.5 / 73.7 | 150 | 124 / 118 | 67 / 73 | 89 | 53 | 46 | |
| Comoros | 53 | 61.9 / 66.3 | 480 | 98 / 81 | 34 / 28 | 54 | 26 | 19 | |
| Cyprus | 6 | 76.3 / 81.3 | 47 | 97 / 98 | 98 / 99 | 9 | | | |
| Djibouti | 88 | 52.1 / 54.4 | 730 | 48 / 37 | 29 / 20 | 53 | | | 0.3 / 0.3 |
| Equatorial Guinea | 98 | 42.1 / 42.9 | 880 | 132 / 120 | 38 / 22 | 187 | | | |
| Fiji | 21 | 66.1 / 70.5 | 75 | 109 / 109 | 78 / 83 | 36 | 41 | 35 | 0.2 / <0.1 |
| French Polynesia | 8 | 71.2 / 76.3 | 20 | | | 39 | | | |
| Guadeloupe | 7 | 75.4 / 82.1 | 5 | | | 19 | 44 | 31 | |
| Guam | 9 | 72.8 / 77.5 | 12 | | | 67 | | | |
| Guyana | 46 | 61.0 / 67.1 | 170 | 126 / 123 | 87 / 89 | 62 | 37 | 36 | 2.2 / 2.8 |
| Iceland | 3 | 79.1 / 82.9 | 0 | 100 / 99 | 110 / 119 | 17 | | | 0.2 / 0.2 |
| Luxembourg | 5 | 75.5 / 81.8 | 28 | 99 / 99 | 93 / 99 | 9 | | | |
| Maldives | 38 | 67.8 / 67.1 | 110 | 119 / 117 | 62 / 71 | 62 | 42 | 33 | |
| Malta | 7 | 76.2 / 81.0 | 21 | 105 / 104 | 95 / 95 | 16 | | | |
| Martinique | 7 | 75.9 / 81.9 | 4 | | | 31 | 51 | 38 | |
| Micronesia (26) | 27 | 69.2 / 73.6 | | | | 47 | | | |
| Netherlands Antilles | 12 | 73.3 / 79.5 | 20 | 104 / 104 | 67 / 75 | 26 | | | |
| New Caledonia | 6 | 73.1 / 78.3 | 10 | | | 30 | | | |
| Polynesia (27) | 18 | 69.9 / 75.1 | | | | 33 | | | |
| Qatar | 11 | 71.6 / 76.5 | 7 | 107 / 104 | 92 / 96 | 19 | 43 | 32 | |
| Réunion | 7 | 71.7 / 79.9 | 41 | | | 36 | 67 | 62 | |
| Samoa | 24 | 67.8 / 74.2 | 130 | 107 / 104 | 73 / 80 | 32 | | | |
| Solomon Islands | 33 | 62.1 / 63.6 | 130 | 92 / 79 | 17 / 11 | 46 | | | |
| Suriname | 24 | 66.4 / 72.9 | 110 | 127 / 125 | 63 / 85 | 43 | 42 | 41 | 2.2 / 1.1 |
| Timor-Leste, Democratic Republic of | 87 | 55.4 / 57.6 | 660 | | | 175 | 10 | 9 | |
| Vanuatu | 31 | 67.5 / 71.2 | 130 | 113 / 113 | 27 / 29 | 48 | | | |

## Selected Indicators for Less Populous Countries/Territories

| Demographic, Social and Economic Indicators | Total population (thousands) (2005) | Projected population (thousands) (2050) | % urban (2003) | Urban growth rate (2000-2005) | Population/ ha arable & perm. crop land | Total fertility rate (2005) | % births with skilled attendants | GNI per capita PPP$ (2003) | Under-5 mortality M/F |
|---|---|---|---|---|---|---|---|---|---|
| Bahamas | 323 | 466 | 89.5 | 1.5 | 0.8 | 2.25 | 99 | | 17 / 13 |
| Bahrain | 727 | 1,155 | 90.0 | 2.3 | 1.2 | 2.37 | 98 | | 16 / 16 |
| Barbados | 270 | 255 | 51.7 | 1.5 | 0.6 | 1.50 | 91 | 15,060 | 12 / 10 |
| Belize | 270 | 442 | 48.3 | 2.3 | 0.7 | 3.01 | 83 | | 41 / 39 |
| Brunei Darussalam | 374 | 681 | 76.2 | 3.2 | 0.2 | 2.40 | 99 | | 8 / 6 |
| Cape Verde | 507 | 1,002 | 55.9 | 3.5 | 2.2 | 3.57 | 89 | 5,440 | 42 / 22 |
| Comoros | 798 | 1,781 | 35.0 | 4.6 | 4.1 | 4.59 | 62 | 1,760 | 78 / 61 |
| Cyprus | 835 | 1,174 | 69.2 | 1.0 | 0.6 | 1.62 | 100 | 19,530 | 8 / 6 |
| Djibouti | 793 | 1,547 | 83.7 | 2.1 | | 4.80 | 61 | 2,200 | 141 / 124 |
| Equatorial Guinea | 504 | 1,146 | 48.1 | 4.7 | 1.5 | 5.89 | 65 | | 184 / 167 |
| Fiji | 848 | 934 | 51.7 | 2.5 | 1.1 | 2.81 | 100 | 5,410 | 27 / 25 |
| French Polynesia | 257 | 360 | 52.1 | 1.2 | | 2.32 | | | 11 / 11 |
| Guadeloupe | 448 | 474 | 99.7 | 0.9 | 0.5 | 2.02 | | | 10 / 8 |
| Guam | 170 | 254 | 93.7 | 1.7 | | 2.81 | | | 12 / 9 |
| Guyana | 751 | 488 | 37.6 | 1.4 | 0.3 | 2.20 | 86 | 3,950 | 73 / 54 |
| Iceland | 295 | 370 | 92.8 | 0.9 | 3.1 | 1.95 | | 30,140 | 4 / 4 |
| Luxembourg | 465 | 721 | 91.9 | 1.6 | 0.1 | 1.74 | 100 | 54,430 | 7 / 6 |
| Maldives | 329 | 682 | 28.8 | 4.5 | 6.5 | 4.06 | 70 | | 41 / 56 |
| Malta | 402 | 428 | 91.7 | 0.7 | 0.6 | 1.50 | 98 | | 8 / 8 |
| Martinique | 396 | 350 | 95.7 | 0.8 | 0.7 | 1.94 | | | 9 / 9 |
| Micronesia (26) | 556 | 849 | 69.1 | 2.6 | | 3.31 | | | 37 / 30 |
| Netherlands Antilles | 183 | 203 | 69.7 | 1.1 | 0.1 | 2.08 | | | 17 / 11 |
| New Caledonia | 237 | 382 | 61.2 | 2.2 | | 2.37 | | | 9 / 9 |
| Polynesia (27) | 656 | 763 | 43.6 | 1.7 | | 3.10 | | | 23 / 21 |
| Qatar | 813 | 1,330 | 92.0 | 1.7 | 0.3 | 2.91 | 98 | | 14 / 12 |
| Réunion | 785 | 1,092 | 91.5 | 2.0 | 0.6 | 2.47 | | | 11 / 9 |
| Samoa | 185 | 157 | 22.3 | 1.3 | | 4.17 | 100 | 5,700 | 30 / 27 |
| Solomon Islands | 478 | 921 | 16.5 | 4.5 | 4.5 | 4.06 | 85 | 1,630 | 58 / 52 |
| Suriname | 449 | 429 | 76.1 | 1.6 | 1.2 | 2.52 | 85 | | 35 / 23 |
| Timor-Leste, Democratic Republic of | 947 | 3,265 | 7.6 | 4.8 | 4.4 | 7.48 | 24 | | 128 / 120 |
| Vanuatu | 211 | 375 | 22.8 | 4.1 | | 3.92 | 89 | 2,880 | 43 / 33 |

# Notes for Indicators

*The designations employed in this publication do not imply the expression of any opinion on the part of the United Nations Population Fund concerning the legal status of any country, territory or area or of its authorities, or concerning the delimitation of its frontiers or boundaries.*

*Data for small countries or areas, generally those with population of 200,000 or less in 1990, are not given in this table separately. They have been included in their regional population figures.*

(\*) More-developed regions comprise North America, Japan, Europe and Australia-New Zealand.

(+) Less-developed regions comprise all regions of Africa, Latin America and Caribbean, Asia (excluding Japan), and Melanesia, Micronesia and Polynesia.

(‡) Least-developed countries according to standard United Nations designation.

(1) Including British Indian Ocean Territory and Seychelles.

(2) Including Agalesa, Rodrigues and St. Brandon.

(3) Including Sao Tome and Principe.

(4) Formerly Zaire.

(5) Including Western Sahara.

(6) Including St. Helena, Ascension and Tristan da Cunha.

(7) Including Macau.

(8) On 1 July 1997, Hong Kong became a Special Administrative Region (SAR) of China.

(9) This entry is included in the more developed regions aggregate but not in the estimate for the geographical region.

(10) Turkey is included in Western Asia for geographical reasons. Other classifications include this country in Europe.

(11) Comprising Algeria, Bahrain, Comoros, Djibouti, Egypt, Iraq, Jordan, Kuwait, Lebanon, Libyan Arab Jamahiriya, Mauritania, Morocco, Occupied Palestinian Territory, Oman, Qatar, Saudi Arabia, Somalia, Sudan, Syria, Tunisia, United Arab Emirates and Yemen. Regional aggregation for demographic indicators provided by the UN Population Division. Aggregations for other indicators are weighted averages based on countries with available data.

(12) Including Channel Islands, Faeroe Islands and Isle of Man.

(13) Including Andorra, Gibraltar, Holy See and San Marino.

(14) Including Leichtenstein and Monaco.

(15) Including Anguilla, Antigua and Barbuda, Aruba, British Virgin Islands, Cayman Islands, Dominica, Grenada, Montserrat, Netherlands Antilles, Saint Kitts and Nevis, Saint Lucia, Saint Vincent and the Grenadines, Turks and Caicos Islands, and United States Virgin Islands.

(16) Including Falkland Islands (Malvinas) and French Guiana.

(17) Including Bermuda, Greenland, and St. Pierre and Miquelon.

(18) Including Christmas Island, Cocos (Keeling) Islands and Norfolk Island.

(19) Including New Caledonia and Vanuatu.

(20) The successor States of the former USSR are grouped under existing regions. Eastern Europe includes Belarus, Republic of Moldova, Russian Federation and Ukraine. Western Asia includes Armenia, Azerbaijan and Georgia. South Central Asia includes Kazakhstan, Kyrgyzstan, Tajikistan, Turkmenistan and Uzbekistan. Regional total, excluding subregion reported separately below.

(21) Regional total, excluding subregion reported separately below.

(22) These subregions are included in the UNFPA Arab States and Europe region.

(23) Estimates based on previous years' reports. Updated data are expected.

(24) Total for Eastern Europe includes some South European Balkan States and Northern European Baltic States.

(25) More recent reports suggest this figure might have been higher. Future publications will reflect the evaluation of this information.

(26) Comprising Federated States of Micronesia, Guam, Kiribati, Marshall Islands, Nauru, Northern Mariana Islands, and Pacific Islands (Palau).

(27) Comprising American Samoa, Cook Islands, Johnston Island, Pitcairn, Samoa, Tokelau, Tonga, Midway Islands, Tuvalu, and Wallis and Futuna Islands.

# Technical Notes

The statistical tables in this year's *The State of World Population* report once again give special attention to indicators that can help track progress in meeting the quantitative and qualitative goals of the International Conference on Population and Development (ICPD) and the Millennium Development Goals (MDGs) in the areas of mortality reduction, access to education, access to reproductive health services including family planning, and HIV/AIDS prevalence among young people. The sources for the indicators and their rationale for selection follow, by category.

## Monitoring ICPD Goals

### INDICATORS OF MORTALITY

**Infant mortality, male and female life expectancy at birth.** Source: Spreadsheets provided by United Nations Population Division. These indicators are measures of mortality levels, respectively, in the first year of life (which is most sensitive to development levels) and over the entire lifespan. Data for 2000-2005 and 2005-2010 were averaged to arrive at 2005 point estimates.

**Maternal mortality ratio.** Source: WHO, UNICEF, and UNFPA. 2003. *Maternal Mortality in 2000: Estimates Developed by WHO, UNICEF, and UNFPA*. Geneva: WHO. This indicator presents the number of deaths to women per 100,000 live births which result from conditions related to pregnancy, delivery and related complications. Precision is difficult, though relative magnitudes are informative. Estimates below 50 are not rounded; those 50-100 are rounded to the nearest 5; 100-1,000, to the nearest 10; and above 1,000, to the nearest 100. Several of the estimates differ from official government figures. The estimates are based on reported figures wherever possible, using approaches to improve the comparability of information from different sources. See the source for details on the origin of particular national estimates. Estimates and methodologies are reviewed regularly by WHO, UNICEF, UNFPA, academic institutions and other agencies and are revised where necessary, as part of the ongoing process of improving maternal mortality data. Because of changes in methods, prior estimates for 1995 levels may not be strictly comparable with these estimates.

### INDICATORS OF EDUCATION

**Male and female gross primary enrolment ratios, male and female gross secondary enrolment ratios.** Source: Spreadsheet provided by the UNESCO Institute for Statistics, April 2005. Population data is based on: United Nations Population Division. 2003. *World Population Prospects: The 2002 Revision*. New York: United Nations. Gross enrolment ratios indicate the number of students enrolled in a level in the education system per 100 individuals in the appropriate age group. They do not correct for individuals who are older than the level-appropriate age due to late starts, interrupted schooling or grade repetition. Data are for 2002, or for 2001 if later date not available.

**Male and female adult illiteracy.** Source: See gross enrolment ratios above for source; data adjusted to illiteracy, from literacy. Illiteracy definitions are subject to variation in different countries; three widely accepted definitions are in use. Insofar as possible, data refer to the proportion who cannot, with understanding, both read and write a short simple statement on everyday life. Adult illiteracy (rates for persons above 15 years of age) reflects both recent levels of educational enrolment and past educational attainment. The above education indicators have been updated using estimates from: United Nations Population Division. 2003. *World Population Prospects: The 2002 Revision*. New York: United Nations. Data are for the most recent year estimates available for the 2000-2004 period.

**Proportion reaching grade 5 of primary education.** Source: See gross enrolment ratios above for source. Data are most recent within the school years beginning in 1999, 2000, 2001 or 2002.

### INDICATORS OF REPRODUCTIVE HEALTH

**Births per 1,000 women aged 15-19.** Source: Spreadsheet provided by the United Nations Population Division. This is an indicator of the burden of fertility on young women. Since it is an annual level summed over all women in the age cohort, it does not reflect fully the level of fertility for women during their youth. Since it indicates the annual average number of births per woman per year, one could multiply it by five to approximate the number of births to 1,000 young women during their late teen years. The measure does not indicate the full dimensions of teen pregnancy as only live births are included in the numerator. Stillbirths and spontaneous or induced abortions are not reflected. Data for 2000-2005 and 2005-2010 were averaged to arrive at 2005 point estimates.

**Contraceptive prevalence.** Source: Spreadsheet provided by the United Nations Population Division using "World Contraceptive Use 2005: Database maintained by the Population Division of the United Nations Department of Economic and Social Affairs". These data are derived from sample survey reports and estimate the proportion of married women (including women in consensual unions) currently using, respectively, any method or modern methods of contraception. Modern or clinic and supply methods include male and female sterilization, IUD, the pill, injectables, hormonal implants, condoms and female barrier methods. These numbers are roughly but not completely comparable across countries due to variation in the timing of the surveys and in the details of the questions. All country and regional data refer to women aged 15-49. The most recent survey data available are cited, ranging from 1980-2002.

**HIV prevalence rate, M/F, 15-49.** Source: UNAIDS. 2004. "Estimated Adult (15-49) HIV Prevalence among Men and Women in 2003." Spreadsheet. Geneva: UNAIDS. These data derive from surveillance system reports and model estimates. Data provided for men and women aged 15-49 are point estimates for each country. The reference year is 2003. Male-female differences reflect physiological and social vulnerability to the illness and are affected by age differences between sexual partners.

### Demographic, Social and Economic Indicators

**Total population 2005, projected population 2050, average annual population growth rate for 2005.** Source: Spreadsheet provided by the United Nations Population Division. These indicators present the size, projected future size and current period annual growth of national populations. Data for 2000-2005 and 2005-2010 were averaged to arrive at 2005 point estimates

**Per cent urban, urban growth rates.** Source: United Nations Population Division. 2004. *World Urbanization Prospects: The 2003 Revision*. New York: United Nations, available on CD-ROM (POP/DP/WUP/Rev.2003); and United Nations Population Division. 2004. *World Urbanization Prospects: The 2003 Revision: Data Tables and Highlights* (ESA/P/WP.190). New York: United Nations. These indicators reflect the proportion of the national population living in urban areas and the growth rate in urban areas projected.

**Agricultural population per hectare of arable and permanent crop land.** Source: Data provided by Food and Agriculture Organization, Statistics Division, using agricultural population data based on the total populations from United Nations Population Division. 2003. *World Population Prospects: The 2002 Revision*. New York: United Nations. This indicator relates the size of the agricultural population to the land suitable for agricultural production. It is responsive to changes in both the structure of national economies (proportions of the workforce in agriculture) and in technologies for land development. High values can be related to stress on land productivity and to fragmentation of land holdings. However, the measure is also sensitive to differing development levels and land use policies. Data refer to the year 2002.

**Total fertility rate (2005).** Source: Spreadsheet provided by the United Nations Population Division. The measure indicates the number of children a woman would have during her reproductive years if she bore children at the rate estimated for different age groups in the specified time period.

Countries may reach the projected level at different points within the period. Data for 2000-2005 and 2005-2010 were averaged to arrive at 2005 point estimates.

**Births with skilled attendants.** Source: UNICEF. 2004. *The State of World's Children 2005: Childhood Under Threat*. New York: UNICEF. This indicator is based on national reports of the proportion of births attended by "skilled health personnel or skilled attendant: doctors (specialist or non-specialist) and/or persons with midwifery skills who can diagnose and manage obstetrical complications as well as normal deliveries". Data for more developed countries reflect their higher levels of skilled delivery attendance. Because of assumptions of full coverage, data (and coverage) deficits of marginalized populations and the impacts of chance and transport delays may not be fully reflected in official statistics. Data estimates are the most recent available after 1995.

**Gross national income per capita.** Source: Most recent (2003) figures from: The World Bank. *World Development Indicators Online*. Web site: http://devdata.worldbank.org/dataonline/ (by subscription). This indicator (formerly referred to as gross national product [GNP] per capita) measures the total output of goods and services for final use produced by residents and non-residents, regardless of allocation to domestic and foreign claims, in relation to the size of the population. As such, it is an indicator of the economic productivity of a nation. It differs from gross domestic product (GDP) by further adjusting for income received from abroad for labour and capital by residents, for similar payments to non-residents, and by incorporating various technical adjustments including those related to exchange rate changes over time. This measure also takes into account the differing purchasing power of currencies by including purchasing power parity (PPP) adjustments of "real GNP". Some PPP figures are based on regression models; others are extrapolated from the latest International Comparison Programme benchmark estimates. See original source for details.

**Central government expenditures on education and health.** Source: Most recent data point in last seven years from: The World Bank. *World Development Indicators Online*. Web site: http://devdata.worldbank.org/dataonline/ (by subscription). These indicators reflect the priority afforded to education and health sectors by a country through the government expenditures dedicated to them. They are not sensitive to differences in allocations within sectors, e.g., primary education or health services in relation to other levels, which vary considerably. Direct comparability is complicated by the different administrative and budgetary responsibilities allocated to central governments in relation to local governments, and to the varying roles of the private and public sectors. Reported estimates are presented as shares of GDP per capita (for education) or total GDP (for health). Great caution is also advised about cross-country comparisons because of varying costs of inputs in different settings and sectors.

**External assistance for population.** Source: UNFPA. Forthcoming. *Financial Resource Flows for Population Activities in 2003*. New York: UNFPA. This figure provides the amount of external assistance expended in 2003 for population activities in each country. External funds are disbursed through multilateral and bilateral assistance agencies and by non-governmental organizations. Donor countries are indicated by their contributions being placed in parentheses. Regional totals include both country-level projects and regional activities (not otherwise reported in the table). Data for 2003 are provisional.

**Under-5 mortality.** Source: Spreadsheet provided by the United Nations Population Division. This indicator relates to the incidence of mortality to infants and young children. It reflects, therefore, the impact of diseases and other causes of death on infants, toddlers and young children. More standard demographic measures are infant mortality and mortality rates for 1 to 4 years of age, which reflect differing causes of and frequency of mortality in these ages. The measure is more sensitive than infant mortality to the burden of childhood diseases, including those preventable by improved nutrition and by immunization programmes. Under-5 mortality is here expressed as deaths to children under the age of 5 per 1,000 live births in a given year. Data for 2000-2005 and 2005-2010 were averaged to arrive at 2005 point estimates.

**Per capita energy consumption.** Source: The World Bank. *World Development Indicators Online*. Web site: http://devdata.worldbank.org/dataonline/ (by subscription). This indicator reflects annual consumption of commercial primary energy (coal, lignite, petroleum, natural gas and hydro, nuclear and geothermal electricity) in kilograms of oil equivalent per capita. It reflects the level of industrial development, the structure of the economy and patterns of consumption. Changes over time can reflect changes in the level and balance of various economic activities and changes in the efficiency of energy use (including decreases or increases in wasteful consumption). Data estimates are for 2002.

**Access to improved drinking water sources.** Source: UNICEF. 2005. *The State of the World's Children 2005: Childhood Under Threat*. New York: UNICEF. This indicator reports the percentage of the population with access to an *improved source* of drinking water providing an *adequate amount of safe water* located within a *convenient distance* from the user's dwelling. The italicized words use country-level definitions. The indicator is related to exposure to health risks, including those resulting from improper sanitation. Data are estimates for the year 2002.

## Editorial Team

*The State of World Population 2005*

**Coordinator/Author/Researcher:** María José Alcalá
**Editor:** Janet Jensen
**Production Manager:** Patricia Leidl
**Editorial Assistant:** Phyllis Brachman
**Research Assistant/Intern:** Zeina Boumechal
**Editorial and Administrative Associate:** Mirey Chaljub

**Contributors:**
Delawit Amelga-Aklilu, Lori Ashford, Margaret Bald, Stan Bernstein, Ann Blanc, Camille Conaway, Margaret Greene, Karen Hardee, Don Hinrichsen, Gloria Jacobs, Toshiko Kaneda, Patricia Leidl, Alex Marshall, Karen Newman, Joanne Omang, Erin Sines and Martha Wood.

**Acknowledgements:**
The contributions of the following are gratefully acknowledged for inputs provided and information shared on national and regional initiatives featured in this report: partner organizations and UN agencies working on gender equality and reproductive health issues; various UNFPA colleagues from Country Offices and Headquarters; Gender Advisors of the Country Support Technical Teams; and the Geneva Office. Special appreciation to Lindsay Edouard, Ann Erb-Leoncavallo and Stafford Mousky.

## Photo captions and credits

**Front cover**
© Mark Edwards/Still Pictures
*Young girls celebrate during an Imaraguen festival on a small west-coast village in Mauritania.*

**Chapter 1**
© Mikkel Ostergaard/Panos Pictures
*A girl balances on flimsy bridge over a polluted and flooded alley in one of Phnom Penh's slums.*

© Caroline Penn/Panos Pictures
*Muslim girls chatting on a doorstep in Cape Town's Malay Quarter.*

**Chapter 2**
© Jacob Silberberg/Panos Pictures
*Three girls watch as their teacher points to a chalk board in a school classroom in the village of Koutagba, South Benin.*

**Chapter 3**
© Chris de Bode/Panos Pictures
*An old woman prays for peace in the Oromo Camp for internally displaced people in Uganda. For 19 years the Lord's Resistance Army has terrorized the people living in the Northern provinces.*

© Gary Knight/VII
*A woman begs in the streets of Srinigar, Kashmir where civil war has devastated the local economy.*

**Chapter 4**
© Alex Webb/Magnum Photos
*Pregnant woman stands in the doorway of a house in Abidjan, Côte D'Ivoire.*

**Chapter 5**
© Tim Dirven/Panos Pictures
*Young Afghan mother and malnourished child wait at a nutrition centre run by Medecins Sans Frontieres.*

**Chapter 6**
© David Alan Haviv/VII
*Man proudly displays his baby boy to onlookers in a village on Chacahua Island, Mexico.*

**Chapter 7**
© Marie Dorigny/UNFPA
*Villager covers face in the town of Tigray, Ethiopia.*

© Wayne Leidenfrost/Province
*500 pairs of shoes are displayed on the steps of the Vancouver Art Gallery in Vancouver, Canada, to commemorate women who died at the hands of men and to raise awareness of violence against women.*

**Chapter 8**
© James Nachtwey/VII
*An internally displaced woman cares for her ailing son at the city hospital in Mornei, West Darfur.*

© Jacob Silberberg/Panos Pictures
*Separated from her family as they fled the fighting in Monrovia, Liberia, a little girl stares at the Red Cross insignia ICRC headquarters in Bushrod Island.*

**Chapter 9**
© Maria Soderberg/Panos Pictures
*A woman pulls off her Burqa in Kandahar, Afghanistan.*

**United Nations Population Fund**
220 East 42nd Street, 23rd Fl.
New York, NY 10017 U.S.A.
www.unfpa.org